LET'S TALK SEX

Q & A
on Sex and Relationships

Preface by Michael Castleman

by Isadora Alman

The Crossing Press
Freedom, Ca 95019

This book is dedicated to the cherished memories
of loved ones who have passed through my life
leaving echoes of many more giggles than tears.

Library of Congress Cataloging-in-Publication Data

Alman, Isadora
　　　Let's Talk Sex: Q & A on sex and relationships/ Isadora Alman.
　　　　　p.　　　cm.
　　　Includes index.
　　　ISBN 0-89594-633-5 (cloth).　　—ISBN 0-89594-632-7 (pbk.)
　　　1. Sex.　　2. Interpersonal relations.　　3. Sex (Psychology)
I. Title.
HQ21 .A4525　　1993
306.7—dc20　　　　　　　　　　　　　　93-5279
　　　　　　　　　　　　　　　　　　　CIP

Contents

Homage to "Isadorable"

By Michael Castleman

Every week, when my local alternative newspaper, the *San Francisco Bay Guardian,* appears, I first turn to "Ask Isadora," the sex-and-relationship advice column by the author of this volume. Isadora is a fountain of sexual wisdom. I've written about sexuality myself for over a decade, and answer sex questions for a certain national magazine, but when *I* have a question, I often call Isadora.

No other intimate advice columnist celebrates human diversity as enthusiastically. Isadora often reassures anxious correspondents, "Yes, you're in the minority, but it doesn't mean you're weird."

No other columnist is as well-informed. Who but Isadora would remind a recent transexual to fill out the special form that gets her a replacement driver's license with her new gender?

No other columnist defies the sexual party line as gleefully. When men express concern about penis size, the "correct" response is that size doesn't matter. In most cases, Isadora would agree, but she also recognizes that some people have a real size preference, and happily refers those interested in stallions to one organization, The Hung Jury, and those who prefer ponies to another, the Small Club.

No other columnist is as witty, supportive, and nonjudgmental. Readers may enjoy Isadora most when she fields questions about the wilder side of sex: What's the best way to preserve semen so it can be used later as salad dressing? Personally, I think she's at her best when discussing the eternal mysteries of loving relationships: How can I meet someone? How can I ask for something new? How can we both get what we want when what we want seems so different?

Finally, no other intimate advice columnist publishes as much reader feedback. Isadora is a humble advisor, an avid student as well as a wise teacher. Her work transcends the advice genre to become an intellectual salon for those with a special interest in sex.

I've visited several cities where "Ask Isadora" is syndicated. People always want to know: Who is she? Is she real? I can testify that Isadora is 100 percent geniune. Her real name is Isadora Alman. She's a sweet, surprisingly conservative woman whose cozy San

Francisco Victorian home is filled with family photos, antiques, and original art (no nudes, as far as I know.) She's a Mom. She's a wonderful conversationalist. She loves to introduce her friends to each other. She's *zoftig* and proud of it. She serves beer and wine, but drinks mineral water. In her personal life, she's not obsessed with sex, yet in her own charming way, she's sexy and "Isadorable." Isadora is really Everywoman with a special twinkle in her eye...and just maybe a little vibrator in her purse.

P.S. If you're ever in San Francisco, New York, Philadelphia, or the other cities whose alternative weeklies carry "Ask Isadora," the papers usually appear every Thursday. Pick one up and join the thousands like me who rip through them to get "Ask Isadora" hot— very hot—off the press.

Michael Castleman is the author of Sexual Solutions: For Men and the Women Who Love Them. *(Touchstone, 1980, 1989)*

Introduction

You may notice, as you give the pages of this book a preliminary riffle, that many of the questions are variations of "What's the right way to...?" and "Is what I feel, think or do normal?" Given the lack of accurate sex information in our sex saturated society, is it any wonder why? Yet these letters were all from readers in the alternative papers for which I write in San Francisco, New York, Philadelphia and other cities. The demographics for readers of major city alternative paper always show a higher than average educational level, with a large proportion of readers having schooling beyond college. Of anybody, these educated people are the most likely to know how to seek information and find answers. Although sex is everywhere from toothpaste ads to health statistic reports, unfortunately for us all, honest information about human sexual behavior just is not.

In search of information about what other people really do in bed (or the back seats of cars, maybe even actually in Macy's window) some of us ask our partners about the behaviors of our own sex, and hear that "none of the other women I've been with took as long as you do" or "every man I've known took longer." Not trusting such reports, often wisely, maybe we'll choose to believe our own eyes. Inspection of popular commercial erotica shows a great many men (perhaps everyone but your partner or you?) who are built like bulls and ejaculate like fire hoses, and a preponderance of women who smile in delight when semen is rubbed in their faces. (Are you the only one who finds this unhygienic, to say the least?)

Even the popular "scientific" research is suspect. Just compare the statistics from reader polls in *Redbook, Psychology Today,* and *Playboy,* for example, on the numbers of people having extramarital affairs. The figures will differ because their populations and polling methods do.

In my own research, both professional and personal, for accurate information on what people actually do to get it on or get it off I diligently attend conferences and read publications of organizations such as the Society for the Scientific Study of Sex, The American Association of Sex Educators, Counselors, and Therapists, and the and the Sex Information and Education Council of the United States. Most of what I read in the professional literature is, would you believe it, excruciatingly dull. Even the facts about who is doing what to whom don't seem to translate realistically into something enjoyable you or I might like to do this very evening.

When some new sexual wrinkle does hold potential popular appeal, you'll hear about it almost immediately in the major daily press. There are dozens of neophyte reporters combing the professional literature for just such nits to pick. Since I do the same, you might save yourself some trouble by becoming a regular reader of my weekly column in a publication near you. (What a good idea!)

Better yet, become active. I don't mean sexually active (although, please, be my guest), or not only that, but politically active. Some of my most important sex information was gained through "interactive field research." I hope the same is true for yours. But the doing of it isn't it all. Having gained what wisdom you now possess, spread the good word. Be a sexual guerrilla! Redefine some labels. Look at "kinky," for instance, as meaning "something sexual I haven't tried...yet" and "promiscuous" as "having more sexual partners than I've had...so far." Become a peacemaker in the Battle of the Sexes, a warrior in the fight against homophobia, heterophobia, biphobia or "other than me" phobias. Do what you personally can to attain rights for all consenting adults to consent, or refuse, adult behaviors about which they have some accurate information. Be its source. When you talk about intimate topics to a child, a friend, a lover, *tell the truth* as you personally know it to be.

The solution to a major percentage of personal predicaments, maybe even to a great many global ones, can be distilled in four words: more communication, more lubrication.

How to find what you're looking for

Some time ago *FRISKO* magazine, in an article about me, did a subject enumeration on one year's worth of my columns as they appeared in the *San Francisco Bay Guardian*.

Topic	Frequency of Column Mention
Relationships and commitments	23
Orgasm difficulties	17
Penis size	9
AIDS	8

This book contains two years of columns and, if cross-referenced, many more topics than those listed here. I would like you, Reader, to easily find what you're looking for (sure, even if it's Perpetual Euphoria or "to live happily ever after"). I hope also that you will read beyond the topics of immediate personal interest and at least note the other questions and answers between these covers, even if you're convinced they would never apply to you. And, if that isn't sufficient agenda, I would like to broaden your knowledge of sociology and sexology — that is, what people do in their eagerness to connect with each other. I would also like to entertain you in equal measure during the process. The manner in which my editors and I have outlined this collection takes all of these factors into account.

You may, for instance, be surprised that I have listed ejaculation concerns in a section that is separate from Men's Orgasms. Don't they automatically come together so to speak? In fact, not necessarily, and I wish to make that point again by separating them lexicographically. Or you may be looking for something about giving oral sex to a woman under Sexual Orientation if you're a woman or under the Old In and Out if you think it's an absolutely essential part of any sexual interaction. Meanwhile I have placed all such queries under Techniques because who's doing it or under what circumstances, at least to me, seem secondary to the general topic of Oral Sex. Also, as an example, where you stand on the

Nature/Nurture controversy might create differences with something listed under Bodies which you think should be located elsewhere. My apologies if organizational differences get in the way of your enjoyment of this book.

If you don't find a particular topic where you think it should be, keep on reading. Since you undoubtedly are not the only person interested in that subject, it's bound to pop up somewhere else. Happy hunting. Read and enjoy and afterward please remember to pass along anything you have learned.

♂ ▲ ♀ ◀ ♂ ◀ ♀ ◀ ♂ ▼ ♀ ▲ ♂ ▶ ♀ ▼ ♂ ▲ ♀

A Rose by
Any Other Name:
Terminology

♂ ▲ ♀ ◀ ♂ ◀ ♀ ◀ ♂ ▼ ♀ ▲ ♂ ▶ ♀ ▼ ♂ ▲ ♀

Q About the term "homophobia": My understanding is that a phobia is a fear of something. Most persons I know who do not approve of the gay lifestyle, myself included, have no fear of gays, do not engage in gay-bashing, and do not run the other way, cross the street, or leave the room when meeting an openly gay person. Just as I prefer not to socialize with the southern rednecks I met in the military twenty years ago, I now would not choose to socialize with gays. Does that mean I have "redneck phobia"?

A Nope, just garden variety bigotry. Fortunately it is curable, usually by one-to-one contact with a likable human person of the category you condemn.

Q I read about cross-dresser groups in previous columns of yours. I'm really confused. As a dame who wears steel-toed boots for work, am I cross-dressing? Shouldn't I be wearing 4" spike heels on the tug barges? And, pray tell, what the devil is a "transgenderist?"

A A transgenderist is one of those newly coined exquisitely politically correct words (like "special-abled" and "persons of size") which, I believe, is intended to cover all those who do not fall unequivocally into the stereotypes of biological, psychological, and social sex roles. As for your confusion, any female who in this day and age refers to herself as a dame, to my way of thinking, *is* confused.

Q Could you please pretend I'm from another planet, or just from a very small Midwestern town (which I am), and be as detailed and explicit as possible in discussing what exactly is a bidet used for and when? I guess it's a washing facility of some kind. Does one use soap? A washcloth? Hands? Does one sit on it front to back or the other way? Afterward, is there a special towel or something? Do a lot of people use these all the time? How can I qualify for yuppiedom if I don't have this knowledge?

A You don't have to be a Midwesterner to be unfamiliar with this most sensible of fixtures, only an American. Why this is so in a culture that spends millions annually on such exotica as strawberry-scented douches I'll never fathom! The apprentice plumber who installed mine thought it was a toilet for square-asses! A bidet is a bathroom fixture that greatly resembles the bottom portion of a toilet without the wooden seat. On the rim, near, where the water pipes enter the wall, there are faucets for hot and cold water and a stopper lever like those found in the sink. The bowl, which is squarer and shallower than a commode, has a drinking fountain-type bubbler.

A user sits facing the wall, the reverse of the seating arrangement for the other major bathroom fixture. Adjusting the water to a comfortable temperature, the user either closes the stopper and allows the bowl to fill, thus being able to dunk buttocks and labia or scrotum, or, without filling the bowl, adjusts the height and force of the fountain and positions her/himself so the spray is aimed at the appropriate nether part. Using washcloth and/or soap is optional.

Bidets can also be used to rinse your feet, store cut flowers, and chill champagne. A towel can be kept handy or the user can dry off with toilet tissue. Bidets are great for menstruating women and for both sexes to soothe hemorrhoids, or to generally freshen up after evacuation, sex, or a hard day at the office. They are wonderful relationship insurance as well: My lover has assured me he wouldn't consider leaving me for anyone who doesn't have one in her home.

Q What is the definition of "frottage"? I came across it in some AIDS prevention material aimed at a gay audience. I made a cursory look in a couple of dictionaries and then I realized I could ask Isadora.

A The word is in my dictionary. The first meaning given is rubbing, polishing. A later meaning is "masturbation by rubbing against another person." When the activity is consensual, it is a form of safe sex for people of all persuasions. When it is not, it is what is experienced by any user of metropolitan transportation at rush hour.

Q I'm new to the business world. Do most women prefer being called Ms. do you think, or only single ones?

A If it's used only with single women it defeats the whole purpose of the title since we already have "Miss." Ms. is an equivalent of Mr., a designation that indicates the gender of the person but not her/his marital status. I, for one, don't see why the gender of someone we are doing business with is any more important than marital status. I like title oriented addresses: Captain or Director or Editor. When in doubt, address a letter to such a designation and, if dealing with an individual known to you, ask her preference.

Q I overheard a conversation of two female coworkers about a third. They described her, giggling, as a WFW. The giggles lead me to suspect a sexual allusion. Do you know the term?

A My understanding is that it literally means "well-fucked woman," but is applied broadly to any woman who appears by glowing good looks, or gentled demeanor, to be having a satisfying sex life.

Q What is the female equivalent of "phallic" (e.g. phallic symbol)?

A Vaginal, I suppose, as in "a broom could be considered a phallic symbol since it's long and hard, and the dust pan a vaginal one because it is a receptive space" even though the root of the word phallus is Greek and that of vagina, Latin. The word clitoris is of Greek origin but other than a green pea or a marble, I can't think of a whole lot of clitoral symbols (except a phallus).

The person who asked about the female equivalent of "phallic" might like to know that Paul Krassner's magazine *The Realist* used to reproduce "yonic" symbols found in advertising.

I have always believed that the antonym of *phallic* was the Sanskrit *yonic*. Although why it would be *phallic* rather than *lingamic* I don't know...except it sounds better that way. (What did enlightened ancient Greek women say instead of "down there," anyway?)

Q Although communicating in English is an acquired habit of mine, I have noticed a definite shift in the semantics of the verb "date." It has all but replicated the unfortunate history of the French *baiser,* which when used as a noun still means kiss, but heaven forbid that one should use it as a verb in mixed company. Has the word "date" lost its innocence, or only me? Is the time not too far away when someone can offer as an insult the suggestion to "go get dated?"

A Prostitutes and other sellers of sexual services have adopted the word as a gentle euphemism — "Hey, buddy, want a date?" — because to say outright what, in fact, they are offering is asking to be charged with soliciting. For us laymen, however, to ask for a date does not imply that sex is agreed upon, only (usually) that it is hoped for.

Q What's a 12-Stepper? I've seen it in the relationship ads as a self-description and as both a wanted and a decidedly unwanted quality/habit/avocation. You have used the phrase in some columns but I got no clue from the context.

A A 12-Stepper is one who follows a specific method of getting rid of an unwanted behavior or set of them with a system taken from the addiction model of Alcoholics Anonymous. The 12 steps include a searching inventory of one's behavior to date, making whatever amends are possible, and seeking help in changing one's ways in the future — not at all unlike what religious Jews do on the Day of Atonement or Catholics at Confession.

Q Twelve-Step programs seem to be springing up everywhere these days. I think I've heard of everything but 12-Step Programs Addicts Anonymous, and I bet there are more than a fair share of those. What other ones do you know of? Are there any to do with sex?

A "In Recovery" is a catalog of books, tapes, and other resources (P.O. Box 973, Larkspur, CA 94939) for those kicking bad habits. It lists Alcoholics Anonymous, AlAnon, AlaTeen and other family groups, and 12-Step groups focusing on narcotics, cocaine, codependents, debtors, emotions, gamblers, incest survivors, overeaters, prostitutes, molesters, batterers, and yes, sex & love addicts. *Recovering*, a Northern California freebie newspaper (333 Valencia #250, San Francisco, CA 94103) lists chapters for Marijuana users, Workaholics, smokers, and Arts Anonymous (for those whose issue is creative avoidance), as well more than a dozen computer bulletin boards that feature these topics. More groups form even as we speak. To find support in the 12 Step format for any given issue, you can contact a national Self-Help Group Information line (800-222-5465).

Q This may be a profoundly stupid question, but I am profoundly curious. I don't want to ask anyone I know or anyone to know I'm asking. What exactly is a sex surrogate? Is this some type of therapist who will have sex with you if you need it desperately and don't have a lover? I'm serious. I really don't know.

A It's okay not to know something and very wise to ask when you realize you don't. It doesn't imply anything about you other than you know enough to try to correct your ignorance. Next, I must editorialize again to tell you nobody ever *needs* sex, although a person may convince himself (usually) or herself that's the case.

Now I'll answer your question: A sexual surrogate is a hands-on therapist who works with clients who have sexual problems such as ejaculatory control, fear and inexperience, or adjusting to a new physical condition. The therapy includes relaxation techniques, communication skills, learning how to touch, and optionally but not necessarily, sex acts up to and including sexual intercourse. The surrogate usually requires the client to see a verbal psychotherapist for support in dealing with the emotions these physical learning sessions might arouse, and most will take new clients only by referral from such therapists. There is no licensing for this profession, although reputable surrogates belong to a self-monitoring and policy-setting organization known as IPSA, the International Professional Surrogates Association.

Q A local weekly newspaper recently solicited personal ads from the gay community and I know of at least two instances where the word "uncut" was not published. "Full figured," "big bottomed," ethnic preferences, and other similar qualifications are examples of what has been published. If hairy armpits and HIV status can be noted and sought, is looking for a man whose genitals have not faced the knife all that bad? If you feel stating my uncut preference is unreasonable, would you suggest an alternative word to get by the word police?

A How about "genitally intact"? I don't see what's wrong with the word "uncut" either, but then here I am, a writer about matters sexual, still gasping inwardly when I see the word "fuck" in print. I think you just happened to hit some ad taker's shock button, or ran up against Editorial Policy set by someone higher up according to her/his comfort level. I suspect that sometimes these seemingly irrational rules are set up to test client creativity.

Q To your knowledge, has a dildo ever been referred to as a "Steely Dan"?

A Not to my knowledge, no. Neither has the band Steely Dan been referred to as a bunch of dildos. But then, while I do get around, I don't get to hear everything.

Q I have been fascinated recently with various "no sex" erotic service ads that appear in adult tabloids offering prostate massage by attractive young women. Am I safe to assume that I am expected to masturbate myself while receiving this digital prostate massage? I am too embarrassed to ask.

A When an ad says "no sex" that may mean only no intercourse. It could also mean no genital contact (which is against the law), or it could mean "What we want to do in this ad is minimize the chance of being busted so come on in and once we assure ourselves you're not a cop we'll negotiate." I asked a sex worker of my acquaintance what might be expected under such circumstances and her reply was "I wouldn't be putting my fingers up there unless I wanted the guy to have a good time," so my guess is that you are correct in your assumption. I would ask, but if you are too embarrassed to say "Do you mind if I...?" you could just go ahead and do it, hoping the masseuse won't gasp "What are you doing?," or you could relax and allow her to do you her way and see what happens.

Q What are Kegel exercises and where can I find out more?

A They are exercises designed to strengthen the pubococcygeus muscle, the pelvic area's major sphincter, sometimes called "the love muscle." If you can stop the flow of your urine midstream, you've located it. Man or woman, if one practices contracting this muscle in rhythmic patterns developed by gynecologist Arnold Kegel, intercourse can be made more enjoyable by giving each partner more voluntary genital control. Browse in the Sexuality section of a library or bookstore and check the index of any sexuality textbook you pick up. Many describe the specific exercises.

Q I am a 26-year-old virgin who decided to learn as much as I could about sexual relations of any kind — heterosexual, homosexual, bestiality, pedophilia, necrophilia, urophilia, etc. I haven't participated, just grabbed selected literature, watched movies, and went to strip shows. Inexperience is no excuse for ignorance and you can learn a lot from watching and reading, especially columns like yours. The trouble is I hear some sexual terms — slang, profanity, colloquialisms—that baffle me. Since these are transitory in nature it's difficult to learn what they mean. In a back column of yours a man used the term "rimming." What does that mean? What books are there that would be devoted to defining such terms?*

A There are dictionaries of sexual slang available, even subsets of gay slang and black ghetto slang, but as you say, they tend to be quickly dated. Virgins are not the only ones who miss many allusions. Keep your eyes and ears open, make wild guesses like the rest of us do, or simply and sweetly ask outright. Rimming, by the way, means tonguing of the anus; not, obviously, one's own.

Q My produce clerk coworkers and I field a lot of questions. The one we seem unable to answer is the term for someone who is into sex with fruits and vegetables. P.S. We tell people to use only organics and with condoms. Roughage is roughage.

A I want to be around when some innocent shopper asks you guys what to do with a rutabaga. As to what you would call folks who do, I say "creative," you might say "merchandise abusers."

---

* Confidential to the reader who wanted the personal sex ad deciphered: This guy was into heavy duty penis stimulation (the rings and tattoos should give you a clue), and can expand his urethra to accommodate entrance by another penis. He was searching for someone experienced in this practice. If you happened to be a devotee of such activities, the various terms would be familiar to you. Since they are not, he wasn't looking for you.

♀◀♂◀♀▲♂▼♀▲♂►♀▼♂

Bodies:
Mine, Yours,
Hers, and His

♀◀♂◀♀▲♂▼♀▲♂►♀▼♂

Q I am a 35-year-old gay male in good health with a strong sexual drive. How strong? I can do what most men were doing only in their adolescence, namely have two or three orgasms. Great! you may be thinking, but here's the problem: I must maintain a high level of sexual activity, solo or partnered, or I experience physical discomfort of the stress-related type. My main "symptom" is extreme sensitivity in my nipples. The only relief I get from this is through ejaculation. Fine, but how often can I orchestrate this? It seems like my body demands something of me that I cannot always deliver — a consistent avenue of sexual release regardless of my mood. I had a hormonal workup which showed no abnormalities, save for a high-normal level of estrogen. Could this be a hormonal aberration that wasn't caught by tests because it gyrates so much?

A I wouldn't think so. No body needs sex. No body needs coffee, tomato juice, or Gatorade either, but people who use these regularly might be uncomfortable and unhappy if only tea, grapefruit juice, or buttermilk were available. There are other means of reducing stress than wanking, honest — physical means such as athletic workouts or warm baths, and psychological ones such as meditations or affirmations. Explore some of these next time your nipples bother you and see if you can't broaden your repertoire, thereby saving sex for when you really want exactly those sensations.

Q I'm a college-educated man in my mid-twenties with a keen intelligence and a quick wit. I also happen to have a large penis. I think my body is of more interest to the women I've been with than my brain is, and I feel demeaned. What can I do to feel more valued for what I value in myself?

A Why is this an either/or? Enjoy! In my book — and I'm sure there are others who will agree — a fine mind and a big dick are an unbeatable combination.

I usually find your column amusing, informative and sensitive, but your answer to the well-endowed young man missed the mark. I doubt you would have answered a young woman who was bright, witty, and had large breasts with a reply of "Why complain?" Feelings of objectification are not reserved for women. This young man wants to share who he is, rather than just what he has between his legs. How about the suggestion that he spend more time establishing a rapport and finding out if his lady friends are even interested in the real person. Big dicks are wonderful, but I can understand how a man might begin to feel like a walking dildo if women only saw that and not who it belongs to.

A You're right. I am hung...by my own glib tongue.

I think you really goofed with "a fine mind and a big dick are an unbeatable combination." This promotes the myth that Bigger is Better and implies that a man with a fine mind and an average-sized penis (and there are many such good men) does not "have what it takes." I am a sexual health educator and according to my misinformed clients, there is just one size and that's "too small."

I've spent many hours patiently convincing my male clients that what they have peniswise is just fine, and carefully explaining why bigger may not be better, may be OK but not necessarily superior as far as women are concerned. I once knew a man with a big dick who thought it was so great that he didn't need to bother using his hands, arms, mouth, or loving words. What a disappointment! I think there should be a law against using men with big dicks in porn films. They too perpetuate the myth and do a lot of harm. I hope other women will write to you about their satisfying lovers who please them with their average or smaller penises.

A It was a misleadingly insensitive response and you're absolutely right. While, as you say, penis size is of little or no importance to many women, politically incorrect as it may be, I must point out that for some it is.

Regarding the "unbeatable combination of a fine mind and a big dick": Can't you imagine that some women actually prefer a smaller dick? I personally find slightly smaller than average most satisfying. I like a dick I can take down my throat to its root without gagging, one that can thrust uninhibited with all its power while my legs are entwined around its owner's neck without causing me sharp pangs of pain as it slams against my tipped uterus. I hate having to tell a big-dicked man to be careful; that's no fun. And I don't much like a dick so thick I'm sore for three days after. A very small dick doesn't fill me up, but I'm sure there are women smaller than I and that women like best a dick that fits best. Different strokes for different folks. Why even mention a particular preference?

A Because preferences exist. You certainly know what you want. In saying so, explicitly, in print, you may cause some specific dick owner some discomfiture, but many men with average or small penises will be delighted to hear from a woman with your predilections, and women who share your judgments will feel their preferences validated. That's what sex education is about.

Regarding the "You've Got What It Takes" column: Men often judge women on the basis of physical attributes. Penthouse and Playboy always mention the measurements of their centerfolds. Not all women are, want, or need to be 36"-24"-36," not all men have 10" penises — yet we all can enjoy playful, healthy, sexual relationships. As we should all know, the biggest (and best!) sex organ is between the ears. We've all got what it takes.

A Ain't Nature grand?

I'm writing to give you my feedback on your answer to the guy who wants women to like him for himself and not (only) his big cock. I see the problem from a different perspective: if a person feels he/she is being related to as a sexual object by others, it's because this person is, in fact, presenting himself as such. No matter how nice, intelligent, caring, etc. you are, if your main focus and persona are sexual — even unconsciously — then you'll get that back. I think this man needs to look inside very deeply to see what kind of image he's giving, how this has served him in the past, and what he can do to change it now that it's no longer serving him. Usually this pattern evolves over years and takes a long time to evolve into something more honest, but I'm here to say it can be done!

A Good for you!

Q It took weeks of convincing before my lover would let me go down on her while she was lying on top of me. (Maybe this is called "going *up*"?) Her reluctance had to do with exposing her rectum to me, even though she enjoyed an occasional rimming when we were side by side. No matter how I rhapsodized about the splendid view, she held on to her judgment that the panorama was repulsive. Well, she now enjoys the position, saying she likes the feeling of being sprawled across my torso. Now she has asked me to reciprocate and, much to my chagrin, I find I am terminally resistant to the idea of her staring up at my own backside. What is wrong here? Why do I see her own bottom as a glorious altar but my own as the city dump? I'm wondering if this might be a new twist in the proverbial male double standard.

A You're looking for logic about emotions and it just doesn't work that way. Your lover had body issues and she got over them; you have them, too, and you haven't...yet. Double standards are not the prerogative of traditional males. Most of us really believe that certain behaviors, thoughts, and feelings are all right for us and not for them, or the other way around, "for you, okay, but not for me." If you want to delve further into "how come" you are as you are, that is the province of psychoanalysis. My own predilection, both as a therapist and as a columnist, is solution oriented. So suppose she promises to close her eyes when she goes "up" on you, or, better yet, wears a blindfold?

Q As an avid listener of your past radio program and a regular reader of your weekly column, I appreciate your friendly and sensible advice. I hope to receive from you a reference that will help me with the following problem — my perception of women. I agree with all my rational being with the idea that a woman's external appearance is not extremely important, that to be attractive a woman does not have to resemble "Penthouse" models, and that the important thing is the whole human being, the personality, intelligence, etc...and I am attracted to intelligent, feminist "real" women.

The problem is that I'm also attracted to women I'd prefer not to be attracted to — bimbos in high heels and miniskirts without an ounce of intelligence, semi-naked prostitutes on a street corner. Often, these latter types, whom I don't respect, are much more sexually attractive than the former. I'd like to create some sort of harmony between my rational and sexual selves and I would appreciate any reference books, groups, discussions, that will help me obtain this goal.

A I see you creating in yourself opposing and warring camps, the animal vs. the intellect, the devil vs. the angel, a division beloved of fundamentalist Hell pushers — "You're with us or agin' us." The fact is we are all creatures of myriad inconsistencies, believing The Golden Rule and in Me First simultaneously, or espousing vegetarianism for the most part while occasionally craving barbecue. Accept your politically correct sentiments and your "incorrect" ones. Women who dress in what our society says is a sexy manner — current commercial norm being young and slim in short skirts and high heels — are designing themselves to elicit exactly the response they do in you.

Acknowledge that you are a creature programmed by both your hormones and your culture, and then decide how you will behave based on your convictions, as well as your gonads. You might play Henry Higgins to some uneducated dolly, shaping her into a worthy companion, but it's probably easier to summon the sexpot that lurks in the heart of Everywomen, no matter how correct her exterior.

I appreciate your advice to the man (?) who grappled with his attraction to "bimbos" and prostitutes, yet I was disturbed by a part of his letter you did not address. It appalls me that a man who seems concerned with being politically "correct" could so blithely buy all that virgin/whore crap. I am an ex-prostitute. It's been a few years since I stood on a street corner semi-naked, but I was as worthy of respect then as I am now. If this guy is so anxious to create harmony between his "rational and sexual self," perhaps he should start by showing some respect to the women who *do* turn him on.

A You're right. Point well taken.

Q I am a 25-year-old gay male who loves body building, perhaps too much. It seems I can't bring myself to orgasm and ejaculation without the strong flexing of my developed muscles, particularly the chest and arms. I've practiced solo and in partnered sex (safely) to bring myself to climax without focusing on my bulging biceps and pulsing pectorals, but I always find my mind wandering back to the visual and physical pleasure that only my pumped-up body gives me. In short, no sex without flex.

I've already seen two therapists about this situation. One suggests meditating on a nonphysical image while masturbating as a starting place; the other thinks I don't have a problem. What do you think? Do other people have this limitation or is it perfectly normal to have a hyperawareness of one's anatomy during sex? Could it be that I'm simply "into" muscles the way some people are "into" outdoor sex or sex with costumes? Am I making this more important than it needs to be? Though I choose to have big muscles, I'm feeling limited by having to have sex in only one way — fully flexed.

A Regardless of whether a specific behavior is typical or common (more exact terms than "normal"), if you liked what was going on and you were able to find partner(s) who didn't object, for whom would it be a problem? No matter how many therapists vote on the issue, by stating you feel limited you have defined the situation as a problem for you.

James D. Weinrich, Ph.D. in his sensible and fascinating book, *Sexual Landscapes: Why We Are What We Are, Why We Love Whom We Love* (Chas. Scribner's Sons, 1987, $19.95), describes the difference between something one is "partial" to, like your example of outdoor sex, and a paraphilia: "a particular sexual turn-on in which something not inherently sexual is added to the process of sexual arousal and then becomes an essential or extremely important component of sexual arousal. For example, a shoe fetishist is only profoundly aroused when a person wears particular kinds of sexy shoes. Sometimes he is only aroused by the shoes and can dispense with the partner."

Now, whether a well-muscled male body could be classified as "not inherently sexual" to a gay body builder is a matter of debate. Still, I think the issue is that you feel your sexual expression is being limited. That's sufficient reason to seek some assistance in broadening your erotic requirements.

Q I spent a lovely day with a lovely lady recently who has been a widow for 10 years. When we went to bed that evening after lengthy foreplay, she was unable to have intercourse. When I attempted penetration, it was too painful for her. She said that because of her long abstinence, her muscles had tightened up. Is there any cure for this short of surgery?

A I sincerely doubt surgery is at issue. All those guys who return to baseball camp after a winter off have the same problem as your lady friend. Her body is out of condition for this particular sport. Gentle reintroduction to it will get her back into playing shape. Frequent introduction of fingers, yours or hers, will help reacquaint her body with penetration. If that's uncomfortable, suggest a visit to a gynecologist for a check up. In the meantime, don't push for intercourse. Do a lot of what you call foreplay (and I call love play since it needn't be *before* anything else.) Your patience will be rewarded, I'm sure.

Q I am 53 years old, have had a very active sex life, and am very passionate when making love. Within the past four months, a new wrinkle has developed that is casting a shadow on an otherwise satisfactory sexual relationship. Bluntly, on occasion when I am very aroused during lovemaking, I involuntarily defecate a small amount of feces. This has happened about three times and my partner and I have become inhibited due to nervousness that it might happen again. If you have any advice to give on solving this embarrassing problem I would be very grateful.

A One immediate and simple solution is to make sure your rectum (the pouch directly behind the anal sphincter) is emptied before you have sex. Be aware of your eating patterns and/or take a local enema or rectal douche beforehand. I also strongly suggest being checked out by your health care provider or a consulting proctologist. Such a sudden change in body response ought to be evaluated.

Q I am a 35-year-old woman. My problem is that I have very large labia minora, which extend about an inch beyond my body. I once consulted a gynecologist who, upon first seeing me, asked if I'd been in an accident. I also saw a surgeon who agreed to perform cosmetic surgery after making it plain he thought it was silly, since I had a "pretty face." I didn't go through with it because I underestimated the cost.

Now I have the money and I want to try again and what I'd like to know is how rare or common is this? Are the pictures in men's magazines fairly representative, or do the women who choose to display themselves have not only culturally ideal figures but culturally ideal genitals too? How important is female genital appearance to men? Are there any surgeons in my area who perform this kind of surgery, and is anything known about any reduction in sensation resulting from surgery?

A As you have discovered, the medical profession is not without its share of insensitive clods. Those who are aware of the power of words often refer to inner and outer vaginal lips rather than major and minor since, as in your case, the "minor" lips of many women are the larger. And, as you have also discovered, there is a cultural "norm" for genitals. This does not mean that those which differ are ugly. There are always some who find these deviations from the average particularly attractive just because of their distinction.

You might consider spending your accumulated operation money on therapy geared toward self-acceptance, that being far less painful and more likely to increase sensation rather than risk its loss. But for information, seek out a surgical consultation if you want. Look for someone who specializes in gynecological surgery, seeking such a referral through a women's services clinic, from various women friends, a teaching hospital, or a care provider whom you already know and trust.

I'd like to respond to the woman who was self-conscious about her large labia minora and encourage her not to have cosmetic surgery. She needs a supportive man who will take a special interest in her most wonderful intimate part and tell her how pretty her pussy is. It must be a lovely sight in full bloom! In my 39 years as a practicing heterosexual male, I've discovered that gently sucking is a most enjoyable part of cunnilingus, but it's not always easy to keep those wet inner lips in my mouth. Her extra large labia would make the loving just that much more delightful.

I must respond to that letter from the most fortunate and unfortunate with the especially luscious labia. Please don't let her maim herself sensually, visually, psychically, or otherwise. I am a 37-year-old male with the good fortune of being intimate with scores of vaginas. Visually I've loved them all, though each is as different from another as faces. I've found extended labia to be most erotic.

From this male's point of view, as long as the woman can enjoy oral sex and motorcycle rides, where's the problem?

Q I have heard it is possible to have plastic surgery to decircumcise the penis, in other words, to replace the lost foreskin. Is this true? If so, where can I find more information on the subject?

A NO-CIRC (National Organization of Circumcision Information Resource Center) is, as its acronym implies, a group lobbying against the common practice of infant circumcision. They can recommend physicians who perform such operations and can also suggest nonsurgical techniques of resensitizing the circumcised glans. SASE to them at P.O. Box 2512, San Anselmo, CA 94960.

Q I think I found out the hard way what the foreskin is for. From masturbation and rough handling by lovers, the head of my penis has developed a callous-like texture in parts. Even after applying much Vaseline and abstaining from stimulation for several weeks, when I do have partnered sex or masturbate using plenty of lubricant and not touching the glans, it still seems that the very act of ejaculating irritates it. Any suggestions, or am I forever to suffer the results of "too much man's hands glans"?

A A callous from rough handling is only one of several possibilities. An allergy to your lubricant is another. Undoubtedly there are many more possible causes of your discomfort — most of them avoidable. Were it my penis, I would get it as quickly as possible into the knowledgeable hands of a urologist.

Q I am no spring chicken and neither is my new husband. (I guess you could tell that by my using that phrase.) This is a second marriage for both of us. I've noticed that my new husband wakes up every morning with an erection. Can I expect this to continue or is this part of our honeymoon phase?

A Expect? No. Hope? Sure. If a man is ever going to get a spontaneous erection, the middle of the night and early morning is the most likely time. That phenomenon could continue on until the most ancient of old age. However, nothing is certain, particularly erections, so get it while the getting is good.

Re: the question on a new bride's husband waking up with erections: The phenomenon is known as the "Dread Morning Piss Hard" and is quite common, if not actually ubiquitous. It results from a full bladder and resultant pressures on the urethra.

A Whether this common — but by no means ubiquitous (alas!) — phenomenon is caused by a full bladder, a residue of erotic dreaming, or is occasioned by a daily early-morning rise in testosterone levels, it can be a cause of rejoicing as opposed to dread. Enjoy!

Q Once again, that awful issue of vaginal odor. My last three lovers have been one time only because I just can't stand the smell. So far as I know, they're clean, but the smell of the last one reminded me of — forgive me — a raunchy urinal. Since I think I'd be sexually unattractive if I don't go down on a woman, I've reluctantly taken myself out of circulation. I've read your past columns where you've good-naturedly said it's an issue one can learn to deal with, but I can't. I wish I were like some of your male readers who love the smell, but I find it extremely off-putting. Is there anything you can recommend?

A First, resolve to do in bed what you are willing to do to please your partner and/or yourself and to refrain from doing what does not without any apology. That's a matter of accepting who and how you are and setting limits. On the other hand, there are ways to lessen or do away with the smell you find objectionable. Lovingly wash your prospective partner's genitals with a warm wet cloth or bathe together beforehand, caress her genitals with a (nonalcoholic) sweet-smelling or -tasting lubricant, use a latex dental dam, dab cologne or Vicks VapoRub on your own upper lip, or only go down on women during hay fever season when your nose might be stopped up.

Lighten up on this, it's no reason to become a hermit. Some women not only don't require oral sex, they don't like it, so get rid of the notion that oral sex is mandatory. In some states it's against the law, so for a really drastic solution you could move.

Q My lover and I are very sexually active. Often we make love two or three times a day. Recently, however, his penis has literally been rubbed raw during intercourse. Part of the problem is that pubic hair grows on the shaft which gets pulled during intercourse. Can you recommend any safe way to remove this hair? Also, is it normal for the skin of the penis to get rubbed and irritated like that?

A If you chose a finger on your hand at random, and several times a day wet it and rubbed it vigorously for several minutes, I would bet it would be sore and irritated in a matter of days. The skin on the shaft of a penis is more sensitive than any finger. If you are using a commercial lubricant, there is also the possibility that he is sensitive to something in it. If you use a condom, the same applies. If you don't regularly use condoms, it's even possible that he has a sensitivity to your body secretions. Experiment with these possibilities. I'm not sure removing the hair on the shaft is the first option to exercise, but if you want to try, use either a safety razor or any depilatory designed for "sensitive skin." Electrolysis (yes, there!) is the only permanent method of removing unwanted hair. To find someone who works on that particular area, I'd check the ads in the gay press.

Q I'm not sure I'm having normal erections. When I say normal, I'm referring to erect penises that I've seen in a condom brochure and in the only porno movie I've ever watched. My fully erect penis doesn't seem to "rise" as much as ones I've seen.

About three years ago I talked about this with my doctor. He examined my flaccid penis and said that everything looked fine. He also said that a larger penis might not rise as much as a smaller one. I don't know if he was just trying to make me feel better or what, because I know my penis is not as large as the ones I saw in the porno movie.

I decided to talk to my doctor's partner, a woman, for a second opinion. She started by telling me that there is no perfect size or angle of erection, and then asked me if I wanted her to examine me. I said yes. As soon as she gave me the instruction to remove my pants, my head started pounding and I felt myself perspiring. Watching her pull my underwear down to my mid thighs and handle me made me get an erection. She tried to ease the tension by talking about my now semi-erect penis. "It seems to be reacting normally," she said. She was being extremely professional I thought at the time, yet she was turning me on. A string of precum came out of my penis and that was it. She didn't know what to say and stopped touching me. I was extremely embarrassed, pulled up my underwear and put on my pants. I said thanks for talking with me and rushed out of the room.

After that experience, I've been afraid to see another doctor, man or woman, because I fear I'll just remember my last experience and get another erection. I'm thinking that perhaps I have a lack of blood flowing to the end of my penis. Could this be the case? Will I have to live and make love with a three-quarter erection for the rest of my life? Was my doctor's partner acting professionally during the examination I have described?

A I've reprinted this much of your even longer letter because you've raised two very important issues. First, your erection. What you've described (and drawn in a diagram, which is an excellent idea for future consultation) is well within the range of normal erections. Just as being 6'6" tall is *atypical* but not *abnormal*, so is a full erection that points downward rather than straight ahead or upward. There is a possibility of restricted blood flow, but in that case your erection would remain semi-flaccid rather than hard, a fact you didn't mention. A consultation with a urologist, just to reassure yourself, would not be out of order. Bring in a drawing or Polaroid picture of your erect penis and tell the person examining you — whether male or female — that the last time you were examined you felt embarrassed by the resulting erection. Having said it may relieve some of your own fear and tension, will prepare the doctor, and will undoubtedly elicit reassurances on her/his part that such an occurrence would not be the first time.

The female doctor who examined you when you were 19 should have been prepared for your reaction and had a colleague in the room, as many male doctors have done for years when examining a female patient. Other than a possible lack of foresight, she appears to have behaved correctly. And, by the way, few men have penises that look like the ones seen in porno films, just like very few men have chests like Stallone's.

I enjoy your column. It's the first thing I turn to in the paper. I just have a comment about your response to the man who got turned on during his medical exam. You said that the female doctor "should have had a colleague in the room, as many male doctors have for years when examining a female patient." The bottom (no pun intended) line reason male doctors have someone in the room is to prevent any accusation — or possibility — of sexual abuse, not to decrease the chance of the female patient getting turned on. The sexual power dynamic between a male in a power position and a female in a nonpower position is different than the sexual power dynamic in the reverse situation (although there is some similarity in terms of sexual vulnerability).

A I agree that a witness is generally more for the doctor's protection from accusations of impropriety than for the patient's comfort. (Why would exposing one's private parts to two strangers be any less embarrassing?) I did infer a suggestion of abuse in that reader's question of whether the doctor behaved professionally. As to who is more or less at a disadvantage with whom, I'd judge it to be a matter of personal perception, rather than power politics.

Q How come after I spend the night with somebody all my body functions smell like them?

A I'd be inclined to suspect that the person's scent is not in your excretory systems, but on your skin and in your nose, pervading your sense of smell. There are said to be some men who grow mustaches in order to prolong that very condition.

Q I don't know whether it was in your column or elsewhere that I read about a woman who had a minor operation because her clitoris was hooded. I'm wondering whether mine might be because I don't really feel any pleasurable sensations from sheer intercourse. I know that a lot of women don't, but lately it's bothered me. Maybe the idea that I might have a hooded clitoris is just a wish that it could all be solved easily, but how does one know? Is it a common phenomenon? Is there a place to be checked for it? Is it an operation you'd recommend or not?

A All clitorises are hooded, some more tightly than others. There are operations that "loosen" the covering or cut some away and might be occasionally warranted, but rarely. If you are in a position where your clitoris can be stimulated by the thrusting of intercourse (a rare enough situation), it would generally be felt through the clitoral hood, too. I don't recommend surgery of any sort lightly, and particularly in an area where there are so many sensitive nerve endings. Ask your gynecologist, if you have one, or a doctor at a women's clinic if you don't, to examine you and state her/his opinion. There are simpler ways to learn to become orgasmic during intercourse if that's an important goal for you than dubiously successful surgical intervention.

Q The other evening some friends and I were discussing a curiosity for which none of us had an answer. Since I brought the subject up, I was elected to write to you. We all felt that you would answer honestly and not think us too crude. Here goes: why do some men come more than others? That is, in our experience, some men come in buckets while others just barely dribble. Is it that state of arousal or the size of the testicles (some of our theories)?

A Like (but not exactly like) the buildup of ear wax or navel lint, some bodies simply produce more copiously than others...of whatever. Since come (ejaculate) is the product of the secretions of several glands — seminal vesicles, prostate, Cowper's, and the testes themselves — there are many possible variations. How recently a man has ejaculated will also affect the quantity he produces.

Q You recently wrote something about varying quantities of semen production. Doesn't age have something to do with it? My own volume seems to have declined over the years. Comment?

A Age brings with it several factors that would cause a change in perceived ejaculate quantity. Liquid expelled under great pressure (the Vesuvius-like spurts of some young men) will appear more copious. Events of one's youth often seem to have been bigger and better than what is now available. And, of course, the various producers of what goes into ejaculate (seminal vesicles, Cowper's gland, the testes and the prostate) lower their production as they age.

Q My boyfriend has a very long penis. When we make love it feels like he penetrates through my cervix into my uterus. It took me a while to learn to open up, but now he fits inside me completely without discomfort. I've never experienced such deep penetration before.

We've learned to make love slowly this way, but we do have great sex. I'm curious if this is a common experience for women. Is it normal or common for a man to actually penetrate into a uterus? Is there any danger to my body from this?

A My guess would be that your boyfriend's penis is not actually penetrating your uterus, but is really slipping behind the cervix, an area still within the vagina. The typical cervix does not open easily. That's what pre-childbirth labor is, the gradual dilation of the cervix enough to allow an infant's passage out of the body. Even with months of preparation for the event, and the assistance of uterine contractions and gravity, it is often a very long and painful process. So even though you use deep relaxation and slow movement, it would be extremely rare for the cervix to open and allow penetration without pain.

If it does, however, a normally inaccessible body cavity open to the outside does put you at much greater risk of infection. I recommend a gynecological exam to assess the state of your cervix. Maybe it is atypically elastic and/or you have extraordinary capabilities of relaxation. Nothing is impossible.

Q I wonder if you could explain this. When I go pee-pee it feels really good, almost like orgasm. Does this just happen to good little girls who have little curls right in the middle of their foreheads, or are the (ugh) boys having an extra tingle when they tinkle, too?

A I often tell people who have pain from some "natural" body function to seek medical advice. To those who have pleasure from some natural body function, I say something like "Enjoy! If it isn't broken, don't fix it." I don't really know if what you experience is available to both boys and girls, just girls, or — because you're verrrry special — just to you and you alone.

In reference to the lady with the near orgasm when she peed, as a male I can tell you that I have as close to zero sensation as is possible to imagine. On the other hand, I remember a day when I was living back East and I had a girlfriend who wanted to practice her penmanship in the snow. Now that was a sensation! I recall reading about a paper describing scientists observing 18- to 24-month-old girls and boys peeing. The main observation was that girl babies are far more likely to giggle or laugh when they pee than boys are.

A What a fascinating observation...and what an odd way to earn a living.

✍ There was a letter I read in your column about a woman who experienced some sexual sensation during urinating. I thought it was funny enough that I had to write. It happens that just a few weeks ago, while having a casual conversation about sexual matters with eight of my buddies, they all admitted to having had some type of sexual or pleasurable sensation while urinating, some frequently and some not so frequently. This usually occurred when the penis was in a sensitive but flaccid state, semi-erect. So I guess it's a common thing for most people to experience at some time.

A This is what you guys talked about during Superbowl season? Wow, I'm impressed!

Q To douche or not to douche? The question has come up in my life again recently. It seems the older the man, the more demand to douche. My latest partner, mid-sixties, says the last few times we made love his penis burned a little afterward and what kind of douche was I using. I told him I'm a natural woman, to which he responded "Would you consider using a douche?" I said no. He is the type of man who jumps in the shower right after sex. I no longer have my menses and am not crazy about douching. What do you think? Are you for or against?

A I don't think it unreasonable for a man whose penis burns when he enters you to ask you to remedy the situation if you can. Some people like to keep pleasure and pain distinctly separate events. He may be reacting to your natural juices, which sound like they could be too acidic for him. If so, a warm water rinse before intercourse would be a considerate act on your part. He could also wear a condom. In general, a thorough cleansing of a woman's outer genitals, which includes retracting the clitoral hood, is more than sufficient for most cleanliness buffs. A washing of the inner genitals, a vaginal enema, if you will, which is what a douche is, is generally unnecessary in healthy females. Introducing chemicals and artificial scents, such as those marketed in commercial douching preparations, is absurd.

Q I'm a 23-year-old woman with a wonderful girlfriend and a really irritating problem. When I get sexually excited I tend to become very, very overlubricated. My lover and I have been together for several years, and the closer and more comfortable I feel with her in bed, the worse the problem gets. She's been game about it, but it has definitely put a damper (sorry!) on extended foreplay, which we both enjoy a lot. I've tried to mentally distance myself during sex, but that's no fun at all, and it doesn't work anyway. Is there any dietary, psychological, or (last and least) medical approach I can take to this?

A How about a terry cloth approach? There are women who ejaculate copious quantities of fluid upon climax, there are people of both sexes who are incontinent when highly aroused, and then there are many people who quite regularly wet the area wherein they are sexual. For most people, hot and juicy are synonymous. You are making a major trauma over what is, at worst, an inconvenience, and what would be for many women an absolute blessing. Certain substances, when ingested, are known to dry up mucous membranes — alcohol, marijuana, antihistamines. If any of these are part of your life in any case, you might experiment; if not, I sure wouldn't use them instead of a handy towel.

I read with interest your reply to the 23-year-old woman who lubricated lavishly. You recommended "the terry cloth approach." How about searching for cervicitis in this woman? That pathology is known to cause copious discharge. Also, if she and her lover engage in oral-genital sex, how about investigating the flora and fauna of her lover's teeth and throat? Furthermore, foreign bodies cause hypersecretion. Does the woman wear an IUD? I have gynecological training; that is why I know about these things.

Q I am a 31-year-old sexually active male. I've noticed over the years that the frequency of my erections has declined, and the recovery period between erections has increased. I understand this to be normal. I am concerned about the intensity of my erections when I do get them. They just don't seem to be as hard or as firm as in The Good Old Days. Is this normal, too? Could it have something to do with arteriosclerosis, reduced blood flow, etc.?

A Yes, it is normal for firmness to decrease and yes, it could also be due to narrowing of the arteries. If you are worried (since you are quite young to have these concerns), by all means see a urologist with your questions.

Q Do you ever hear of any complaints from women who after about one hour's worth of sexual activity find that the vagina has expanded or stretched to the point of being too big, causing a loss of friction and inhibiting further arousal for the male? Sometimes I'm afraid I'm too wet and the penis is sliding in and out without feeling any sensation. I'd like to know how to prevent my vaginal walls from becoming "too excited," or know about what I can do to "tighten up my act."

A If they are enjoying the proceedings, I seldom hear from women complaining about anything after an hour's worth of sexual activity. I often say that communication is the best lubrication, but it can also work in reverse. There's a person in charge of your vaginal walls, and presumably one in charge of the penis going in and out. If you feel too wet, interrupt the activities for a moment by saying you want to towel dry, and then do; one can be kept handy at bedside. If you're afraid your partner isn't enjoying intercourse, ask "Shall we stop a moment while I dry off?" or discuss your fears at another time outside of bed. Some people really enjoy that slippery swollen feeling of lots and lots of lubrication.

In response to the woman who wants to know how to "tighten up her act": I, too, enjoy long sessions of sex. The vagina stretches and after a while the old in and out does get rather senseless, as she suspects. My solution is to (1) spend interludes with the tip of my penis just inside the labia, making small strokes at maximum sensitivity locations while the vagina tightens up; and (2) take breaks and switch to oral enjoyment. What the woman can do, besides suggesting these techniques to her partner, is Kegel exercises to strengthen muscle tone in the genital area. A caution, however: Excessive stroking with low lubrication can cause friction burns on the penis! One more reason to use a well-fitted condom.

Q So what's the deal with these penis pumps? I saw excerpts from a "how-to" video and the guy didn't seem adversely affected; quite the opposite, actually. Still, three main questions arise: Does the pump result in permanent enlargement, or merely temporary? Is it simply an exercise or is it also enjoyable? Is there any possibility of damage — bruises, torn ligaments, busted capillaries?

A The video in question is Stryker Tool Company's "How To Enlarge Your Penis" (around $30 wherever such things are sold.) The device he demonstrates has been around in various forms for some time, from a masturbation device called a Vacu-jack to a prescription-only potency aid called the ErecAid System. Porn actor Jeff Stryker's development was not effected through using a pump, alas. Erections produced by the device are temporary. (That's what's meant by "enlarging the penis" here — from flaccid to erect.) Suction devices like the one he demonstrates are pleasurable for some, painful for others, and boring for a certain percentage more. They do have to be used with care since, yes, it is possible to cause injury through such vigorous suction.

Q I ride a bicycle regularly for exercise, transportation, and enjoyment. My problem is that my clitoris gets rather smashed by the pressure of the seat and so it loses sensitivity, which it regains after not riding for about a month. I am a slim person, so it is not my crushing weight causing this. I don't want to stop riding because I love it. What do you suggest?

A Such repeated numbing pressure puts you at risk of permanent nerve damage, so try different bicycle seats. As a last resort, try some sort of protective padding, even a men's sports cup.

In response to the woman who commuted by bicycle and found her clitoris was being squashed, mashed genitals are common among bike riders whose seats are improperly adjusted. Women often find relief by tilting the seat slightly forward, men by tilting it slightly back. This is a simple adjustment one can perform at home, but a bike shop could do it and also make sure the bike fit properly. A gel saddle may also help. The woman should also check seat height and frame height. If the seat is so high she has to rock to pedal, this puts too much pressure on her genitals. Bicycling is energy-efficient, environmentally safe, and fun. I hope all your readers try this libido-enhancing form of exercise!

Q I always knew my ears were an erogenous zone, but until recently, no one I knew stimulated them long enough to discover their full potential to give me a multiple orgasm. What a great way to have safe sex! You might want to put out the word on this for people who think their ears might be extra-sensitive.

A While you're experimenting, see what happens with nipples, another often highly responsive unisex part.

Q This may seem like a dumb question, but why do women almost never think about a penis, or if it is mentioned why do they get embarrassed or grossed out?

A Your experience does not match mine or the people I talk to. Many women think about penises — in general or, more usually, one or more in particular. If they seem, or are, embarrassed or grossed out when caught at it...well, under other circumstances they might not be. My guess is that you are generalizing about women from a very small and possible inaccurate reporting sample.

Q As a sexually liberated 45-year-old woman, I've had many experiences in the last 10 years of being single. This last year I encountered two men who were not circumcised. It was a real problem. I didn't know what felt good or how to have oral sex. Both men complained afterward of irritation at the tip of the head from using a condom. They said it didn't allow the head to go in and out of the foreskin. Please tell me how to deal with this and give me some reading references on the subject, so I'll be ready to enjoy the next time.

A I don't know of anything that treats specifically with uncut penises, but you had a much better learning "instrument" right at hand. What feels good, how to touch, fondle, care for, and feed any particular penis, is best learned by asking its owner. Any man can provide more slippery friction and less chafing by putting a dab of lubricant onto the head of the bare penis or into the condom before rolling it on. If the condom doesn't have a reservoir tip, leave a little extra dangling at the end. Some lubricants feel so sensually slippery and "woman-like" that a man could forget he's wearing latex.

Q Why do females vary in genital tastes?

A Because females vary in what they put in or on their bodies. If you're asking why different women have different preferences about genitals — which is also "genital taste" — I'd say because females vary in that, too.

Q Why do so many people wear cologne or perfume when the true aphrodisiac is a natural-smelling armpit? A whiff of clean sweat and I swoon. I can understand deodorants on the job, but for lovemaking? Am I an animal?

A Undoubtedly, and though those in the billion dollar cosmetic and "health aid" industry would have you think otherwise, you have a lot of company. Be sure to let those closest to you in on your preferences. If they don't share them, however, be respectful. Perhaps a compromise of one armpit for you and one for him/her?

Q Why do men wake up with erections? How frequently does this happen?

A There are several possible reasons — the need to urinate; arousal from dreams; arousal from rubbing against covers, pajamas, or partner; a natural early morning rise in hormone levels; habit, and associations. Most men who are capable of erections will wake up with at least a partial one most mornings.

Q I find myself impotent about half the time I'm with a new partner. Usually the relationship doesn't last long enough for me to find out if it would correct itself, but in one or two cases it did. I am 59, and I went to a psychiatrist/hypnotist who made a tape for me that I played repeatedly with no benefit. I have deduced that the problem is most likely to occur with very passive partners. Is it better for me to advise a new partner beforehand that this might happen, or should I hope for the best and only explain if it recurs?

A Since what you describe is classic performance anxiety, only you know what will help in reducing your anxiety. If disclosure in advance takes some of the worry away, by all means do. I might suggest that you either avoid very passive partners or else postpone sex until you are much more comfortable with your partner.

Q Some years ago there was an item in the newspaper saying that hypothetically a man could be pregnant. Then several months ago you mentioned in your column, that it was one of the issues for the future discussed at a sexologists convention. As far as I know, no legitimate announcement has been made about a man giving birth, tabloids excepted. Is anyone exploring this? Has any research been done and published?

A I have read of a woman without a uterus carrying to term a pregnancy which had attached itself to her bowel. This came over the UPI wire service some time ago; I have no idea whether to give it any more weight than the tabloids. But if carrying a fertilized ovum to term is possible under such cases, a bowel is a bowel. I suppose a male might also carry such a pregnancy if implanted and supervised with hormone therapy. I've not come across anything on the subject in the professional literature I've read, but that's a small sample of what is available. You can access whatever research has been done in any good university library. The annual meeting of The Society for the Scientific Study of Sex, which I have reported upon in the past, is coming up. If I hear anything more on the subject, I'll let you know.

Q There is an old Irish legend about the hero Diarmuid who had a "love spot" on his forehead. Any women who glimpsed this spot would instantly fall in love with him. I have discovered what is for me the equivalent of the love spot — a chin cleft, with chin dimples coming a close second. It doesn't matter what other physical attributes a man has, if his chin is dented I cream in my jeans. I am embarrassed to admit that all during the sixties, although I abhorred his politics, I wanted to get it on with LBJ. Luckily, I had Bobby Kennedy to distract me.

I am aware that this is just another form of "cleavage," a misplaced bust or fanny, but an examination of stars of stage, screen, and recording studio indicates the appeal of the cloven chin — witness Michael Jackson who gave himself one. Is this a fetish? How common is it? What percentage of the population is born with a chin cleft or dimple? And since there seem to be porn magazines and special-interest groups for such specialties as foot fanciers, big bosom fans, uncircumcised penis appreciators, and cross-dressing cravers, are there places I can satisfy *my* craving?

A I have no idea how many people either share your preference or are able to trigger it; statistics have never been my forte. Since you mention wanting to get it on with cleft chin owners, rather than confining your attentions exclusively above the neck, I'd say what you have is a partiality, rather than a fetish, defined by Webster as "an object or a part of the body which arouses libidinal interest often to the exclusion of genital impulses."

In any case, turn-ons are often culturally determined (bones through noses, protruding buttocks) and follow fads (tiny breasts, big breasts, hairy chests or bare). Obviously our culture has offered some support for yours — I doubt if Kirk Douglas made it solely on his acting talent. Consider yourself lucky to be able to indulge your fancies in any public place where people-watching is practiced. Some folks' preference is only visible after long courtships or under very special circumstances. My own odd partiality is for "ruined" skin on men, like the deeply pockmarked face of the late Richard Burton. Want others of your predilection? Put it out there, in print or word of mouth, and there will soon be a whole bunch of you sitting around together, jawing.

Q I just read a back issue of *The Guardian* where you wrote about a social club for guys with large penises and for their admirers. Ever the optimist, I'm going to ask what is probably a very foolish question. Is there, by any chance under the sun, something like that for guys with small ones?

A I believe optimism should be rewarded and I'm delighted to be able to do so. From a 1990 San Francisco Sex Information Newsletter: "The Small Club is for the small person and those wishing to meet us. The club includes guys with small genital equipment and/or short stature, those who do not care about size, as well as those who prefer 'small anything.' The club spans the ages from 19 through guys in their 70s. Members are gay, bisexual, and married. Membership in The Small Club costs $25 per year. For an application blank and further information send SASE to Small, ETC., P.O. Box 294, Bayside, NY 11361." I get the impression that this is a man-to-man organization. Is that what you're looking for? In any case, check it out.

Q I have a problem I am sure other females have experienced, too. As I was growing up, I was often embarrassed by certain exercises that caused my vagina to "swallow"' and then "regurgitate" air, resulting in an embarrassing sound. Now I am 24 and have two children, and the problem seems to be worse. Now, in my favorite sexual positions or when I put a lot of energy into sex, this horrible noise is a constant. I also feel as if there is an air buffer between me and my partner, and my enjoyment ceases. My partner tries to encourage me to finish, but I am too distracted and disappointed. This is the time in my life when I should be at my sexual peak, but instead I feel inadequate and over the hill. Is there a way to reduce this disturbance or put an end to the vaginal air-sucking? I want to enjoy a normal sex life again.

A There are really two issues here and the situation is more likely to improve if you treat them as separate challenges. One is that you swallow and expel air, creating a noise. I really don't know what to suggest about that, other than to interrupt sexual proceedings now and again to expel the air trapped inside, thereby removing the "buffer." Have you asked your gynecologist? There may be some physical solutions of exercise or diet that affect the phenomenon. If any readers know of any, I'm sure I'll hear.

The second issue is that you allow this to spoil your sexual pleasure, and changing your attitude is entirely within your control. While you are exploring ways to eliminate the occurrence, *also* work on accepting it as inevitable. Find it funny, rather than terrible, part of what makes you the woman you are and sex with you a unique experience. Play loud music when you make love, speak about interruptions as "burping baby." Given a list of all the things that can go wrong with the human body which could negatively affect one's sex life, vaginal farting really is way down there.

Comment: In six years of writing this column I am constantly surprised by what piques responses or causes controversy. Topics I address with great trepidation provoke nary a post card and then something like this comes along. There is a belief in the media biz that one letter from a listener, viewer or reader expresses the views of at least 99 others who did not take the trouble to write so that every piece of mail, unless from an obvious crack pot, is taken quite seriously. I take every piece of mail I get quite seriously too, even those from, shall we call them, eccentrics. Apparently a great many people have a great deal to say about vaginas that make noise. No, having a talking one will be unlikely to qualify you for appearance on Letterman's stupid pet tricks segment. If vaginas, audible or otherwise, are not of interest to you, I do apologize. For those myriad others who wrote and who didn't, here is a sampling of letters on that topic.

"Vaginal farting" is not "way down there" on the list of problems that could interfere with happy lovemaking if it happens to you. Managing to laugh it off and go on is something I can only rarely do with a very comfortable partner, and only if my self-esteem happens to be in an especially strong state. It is pretty disturbing to have this happen when, for example, your partner's face is in the vicinity. I've had men recoil in shock. It's a definite turn-off for both. I don't have solutions, but I have been looking for what causes it in the hope of preventing it. One cause is a certain effect of making the outer vagina flare open and therefore taking in air. The other cause is if the man inserts his finger and somehow pulls it open. I hope to see more information on this as it is very disconcerting and makes me sometimes unable to relax for fear of it happening.

I didn't think much about the letter from the woman concerned about vaginal farting until last night when my husband and I were making love. I realized that the sound which I have always found incredibly erotic — that sucking noise giving audible expression to that perfect combination of lust, liquid, and emotion — is what she thinks of as farting. One of us is clearly misguided. One woman's meat is...

I liked your response to the woman complaining about her horrible noise. Please let her know that there are people, I for one, who appreciate the noise and, more importantly, the feel a vagina gives when this noise is present. Also, adding to "burping baby," I remember the singer Millie Jackson has a record where she refers to this noise. She says "It's talkin' to ya, Daddy." That letter writer may enjoy that reference. So don't get distracted, get with it!

The woman who complained about persistent vaginal farting during sex is not alone. Not only do I emit loud obnoxious sounds from my nether regions just as things begin to heat up, I also seem to be formed just perfectly for creating chest and stomach farts with my husband! Yes, sex can be very noisy, but it is not the end of the world. The first time it happened to us I was ready to crawl under the bed and my (then) fiancé said, "Can you do that again?" After giggling over it for some time we decided that we just fit so well together that we can trap air. So body farts indicate a good fit. If she is really bothered by it, she could try pausing momentarily, pressing down hard on her abdomen to expel any remaining air, and/or changing positions. But most of all, it has less to do with her biological design than the way she and her mate fit together, so don't sweat it.

Air-sucking pussies are a gas, pun intended. After our first child was born this phenomenon began to happen to my wife, probably as a result of the vaginal changes due to childbirth. With us it happens most often in the doggie position, but it can also be induced by forming a tight seal, lip-to-lip as it were, and blowing air into the vagina. Gentle, firm pressure of the woman's belly will expel the air. An artistic partner, by tugging the vulva in various directions, can just about make his gal's pussy talk. I recommend to the distressed lady who wrote you about this non-problem that she stop worrying and start playing.

A I must mention here that the gentle blowing of air into the vagina, as the above writer discusses, can be extremely dangerous if the woman is pregnant or recently given birth.

Comment: A well-known local writer and his charming muse approached me at the Bay Area Book Fair. Giggling about the column in which the original letter appeared, they shared with me her coinage of a term for the phenomenon and gave me permission to share it with you. Ladies and gentlemen, the subject under discussion is VARTS.

♂ ▲ ♀ ◀ ♂ ◀ ♀ ▲ ♂ ▼ ♀ ▲ ♂ ► ♀ ▼ ♂ ▲ ♀

Prong A, Slot B: Tips, Techniques and How-Tos

♂ ▲ ♀ ◀ ♂ ◀ ♀ ▲ ♂ ▼ ♀ ▲ ♂ ► ♀ ▼ ♂ ▲ ♀

Q One night a few months ago, I stumbled upon a discovery I thought might be of interest to you. My boyfriend and I had been out to a party that night, where he had a few glasses of wine. That night he fell asleep quickly, like a thud, bypassing our usual cuddles. Pretty soon he was snoring away like a steamship with me locked within his arms in tight embrace. I tried to wiggle free, to no avail. I figured if I was captive, I might as well try and make the most of it. I freed my hands and began to rub his penis. It immediately began to get hard, and as it did his breathing got shallower, and he actually quit snoring.

I was by then quite excited myself, but even more so at the idea that I had stumbled upon a simple solution to the snoring dilemma. Fortunately for me, he is neither a regular drinker or snorer, so my research has been limited. Do you know of any studies along this line of approach?

A Since you are not regularly sleeping with a snorer, you might not be aware of the enormous (and expensive) array of devices available for people with this problem. For the partners of such, there is little beyond ear plugs and ear phones and white noise producers. For the snorer, there are chin straps and slanted pillows, customized mouth pieces and surgical interventions. I'm all for your method for a variety of reasons, not the least of which is that it takes no special equipment beyond willing hands. As for research, those of you who sleep with snorers, let's get to it!

Q Is it possible to decrease the sensitivity of the clitoris, by masturbating with streams of hot water, for example? While I orgasm manually with myself and through intercourse, oral sex very rarely works for me. Do you have any suggestions about how a woman can learn to enjoy this? It would be wonderful for the times in my relationship when, for one reason or another, oral sex is the best option during lovemaking.

A I can't think when it would be the "best" option except by preference of either party. Oral sex is *an* alternative to penis-vagina intercourse, along with anal intercourse, manual stimulation by either party, vibrators, dildoes or other sex toys, or penis-vagina contact without penetration. It is possible to become habituated to any one type of stimulation to the exclusion of others, but it's my experience that the feeling of water directed at the clitoris is very similar to the feeling of receiving oral sex. The best way to learn to enjoy any sexual activity is practice and experimentation with a willing co-explorer — "Does it feel good like this? Is this better or less good?" A productive method is to start by combining the desired activity with one that has proven reliable, receiving oral stimulation at the same time you are using your own hand, for instance.

Q I always read with great interest letters in your column from men who crave the complete sensation of having their semen swallowed during fellatio. For me that's like trying for a home run when you can't even get a base hit. I've been married for two years, and although my wife loves oral sex when I perform it on her, she's never willing to reciprocate. Unfortunately, I know what I'm missing. When I was single, I had two different girlfriends who were crazy about giving head and were both really proficient.

I find myself desperately desiring a blow job, and I don't know what to do without going outside our otherwise wonderful marriage. I've tried taking it into my own hands, so to speak, but while I've read about men who can do it to themselves, I seem to come up short. Any suggestions as to how I can coax my wife into putting my "hankering" where her mouth is?

A The most frequently asked question I encounter is some variant of "How can I get my partner to..." If there were one sure-fire answer, I'd let you know, honest. The fact is, negotiating with one's partner is a learnable skill. If you have been able to reach a satisfactory solution on where to vacation, whom to entertain in your home, and how to spend disposable income, you can probably find a solution here, too. If not, you may have to start at the beginning in Negotiations 101. Tell her how important oral sex is to you and ask her to please be specific about her reluctance ("It smells or tastes bad," "I don't know how," "I'm afraid I'll gag."). Then counter a specific problem with a specific solution or two. If all else fails, try a trade-off (so many minutes of head for so many minutes of back rubbing or even wall washing) or outright bribery. Someone who is creative enough to try a do-it-yourself approach to oral sex will certainly be able to come up with some inducements.

Q I have a fairly prim exterior which I feel I need to maintain for professional reasons. My lovers have been uniformly enthusiastic about my energy and creativity in bed, but I'm concerned that some men I am interested in will never see past the buttoned-down exterior to consider me in a sexual light. So how can I seduce a man while wearing a business suit?

A There are classes on the art of flirting and it might be fun to take one, or you could watch the body language of women who you know to be flirting and see what you feel comfortable incorporating. Some specifics: Hold eye contact a beat or so longer than necessary. Make a point to talk to him, smile at him, and touch him casually in conversation. Get "caught" staring at his crotch. Arrange to notice in his presence that an extra button has become undone or your skirt has ridden up a bit too high. Caress your throat or arm or in some other manner touch yourself sensually in his presence. Comment upon his scent or notice something else personal about him. What you are wearing is of no importance if what you are doing is provocative.

Q Is it common for a woman to get an upset stomach after swallowing a man's semen? This did not happen to me when I first began going out with my husband, nor with any past lovers, but in the past few years I feel like death itself about an hour after we make love. I spoke with a sex counselor who told me the diarrhea might be caused by the same chemicals in my husband's semen that allow it to be ejaculated, so there's not much to be done except change our style, i.e., have him come elsewhere. What's the straight poop here? We already vary how we get off, and both of us would hate to eliminate that particular method. Can you shed any light on this? Do we have any other options?

A People can develop allergies of all sorts. Sure it could be the ejaculatory chemicals, whatever they are. It could also be the shellfish your man had for lunch. Explore food allergies first. A change in his diet could make a difference. Using condoms during oral sex or pulling out of your mouth and using your hand at the last moment are other options. But like the old saw — "Doc, it hurts when I do this — So don't do it," if swallowing his semen continues to make you sick, the solution is obvious.

To the woman who becomes nauseated from swallowing her husband's semen, you might have suggested a drug called Bonine, an over-the-counter, anti-travel-sickness medication without the drowsiness effect of Dramamine. I used to take this back in the '60s before ingesting peyote to counteract the inevitable nausea that preceded those great technicolor hallucinations. If it worked for peyote... It's an incredibly exciting turn-on to have a woman swallow my semen when I come, so I hope you won't discourage the practice.

Q How can my lover learn a gentler touch with me? Though he wants to and tries to, his hands are somewhat large and clumsy and he doesn't caress me softly the way I like. I've showed him what I mean, but he's not used to handling things gently. Any ideas?

A Even if your man is a stevedore used to handling baling wire, he can still — *if he is interested enough* — learn to touch you more pleasingly *if you communicate your wishes clearly.* Notice the two big "ifs?" If you lie there giving directions when you're both sexually aroused, such a lesson is doomed to failure and frustration for both of you. Take a massage class together, or rent an instructional video and lay out a sheet on your living room floor. Consider attending a sexuality seminar or one on improving couples' communication. Try to create a fun project out of enhancing your (joint) sensuality, rather than teaching old Ham Hands to satisfy the Bitch Goddess.

Q You had two letters that could have been from partners in the same relationship: (1) My girlfriend says she's too sensitive for oral sex, (2) My boyfriend just doesn't know how to touch things gently. You know what you should have said to him? "Start experimenting right away with the lightest possible touch. Err on the side of too faint to be felt. Don't touch the clitoris directly; move all around it. When you do approach it, use pressure through the labia at first, still not directly on it. Concentrate on the vaginal opening and leave the clitoris alone if she still feels insecure. Above all, SHAVE ahead of time or else grow a beard — smooth or soft, but not prickly." As for her, tell her to say, "Look, touch me as if you're touching your balls!"

A Well, I'm glad one of us said it.

Q My virgin friend recently met a man on a bus and they've been going together for a couple of months. She refuses to make love to him before marriage, but she has oral sex. She has pulled, poked, slapped, twisted, and sucked for hours on end, to no avail. He says he does not have a physical problem and that he finds her attractive. What can this poor girl do to make her man come?

A Has she tried whistling Dixie, would you know? This is not a question for Ask Isadora or even ask you, good friend of Poor Girl. It's possible that he's holding back on purpose. It's possible that she's awkward and so it's not sensual for him. It's possible that he never comes from this type of stimulation, and it's also possible that he requires a whistled chorus of some other tune in order to climax. She needs to ask him. Sexually active people need to become skilled at oral intercourse...and I don't mean fellatio or cunnilingus.

Q You often recommend counseling or therapy in your column. I can see from the way several friends of mine have turned their lives around for the better that it can work. I am willing to try but I am overwhelmed by the process of finding a "good" one, whatever that means. I was a Home Ec major. How would I know about the finer points of cognitive vs. behavioral, Reichian vs. Freudian, head work vs. body work? Do you have any suggestions on how I can find a good match between me and my problems and a counselor/ therapist and her or his preferred treatment methods? I don't want to ask my friends for a referral for a number of reasons.

A Early therapist Carl Rogers spoke of 10 traits he felt to be crucial in an effective therapist: empathy, respect, genuineness, warmth, concreteness (which I'd define as practicality), confrontiveness (which is not at all the same things as belligerence or dogmatic adherence to one specific treatment method exclusively), self-disclosure, and immediacy. I feel that anyone who possesses these traits — which can be assessed somewhat through an initial phone call — will be a good counselor regardless of his or her training or methodology. Tests with untrained peer counselors vs. professionals of many schools tend to bear this out. In any case, you might do a little reading. Knowing, for example, that one school emphasizes Family of Origin learning, while another focuses on present day problem solving, might engender some intuitive preference on your part. Whatever you believe will work is going to be more effective because of it.

✍ Recently you answered a question about the traits of an effective therapist. I'd like to add one more, if I may, and that is a sense of humor.

Q I am a 42-year-old man married for eight years to a great woman. I have always been sexually active, but one thing I have never been able to do is come in a woman's mouth. My wife gives great head, but feels neglected because I can't come that way. I've tried masturbating first and then letting her finish me off but it didn't work. Is there something else I can do?

A I know a whole lot of women who would think you a prize — no risk, no fuss, and no unpleasant aftertaste. Nonetheless, you are partnered with a woman who you say feels otherwise (isn't Nature perverse?), so let's see if we can problem-solve. This may be a case of insufficient or unfamiliar stimulation — oral stimulation just not being enough or too different from what it usually takes for you. In that case, you are on the right track with providing your own stimulation and offering her the finale; just keep at it. It also might be a case of no-longer-applicable proscriptions, such as "A gentleman never...," well, you know. If that's the case, you may need to hear your wife's request, her desire, how much it would turn her on, etc., many times before your head, your heart, *and* your ejaculatory mechanism can really believe it and let go.

✍ To the woman whose lover couldn't come during fellatio: Try using your hand at the base of his penis and your mouth at the tip. This is a technique I learned in order to avoid being deep-throated, and it's sent almost every man I've tried it with right into Happyland. Hand and mouth is a double treat that has a lot of room for exploration and variety.

Q You answered a question in your column from a man whose wife feels neglected because he cannot ejaculate in her mouth. My problem is just the opposite. My wife will not try this, and I feel disappointed in that I feel she is unwilling to see how important a part of sex this is for me. I love her dearly and have tried talking gently to her about it. I have also tried just being patient and waiting for her to come around, putting flavored oils on my penis, making a game out of it, and finally, giving up on it. This is the only noticeable difficulty we have in our sex life and our marriage. She refuses to see a therapist with me, believing the problem is solely in my expectations. Any suggestions?

A You've been quite creative in your attempted solutions. We now know a variety of things that won't work. To find something which might, both of you need to move from your position of "if only you change your mind there'd be no problem." Since you state this as the sole, um, bone of contention in your marriage (the rest of us should be so lucky), it's fairly evident that your struggle is not about where you ejaculate at all, it's about who will "win," who is "right," and who really wields the power in this relationship.

I have often recommended in this column several excellent books that deal with couple communication — by Tina Tessina, Susan Campbell, and Jordan and Margaret Paul. Here's another. Buy or borrow a copy of Hugh and Gayle Prather's *A Book for Couples* (Doubleday, 1988. $8.95 209 pages), and turn to page 106 for an exercise they call "The Six Rules of Arguing." If you follow their instructions and don't arrive at a solution, I promise that at the very least, your argument will move onto something a bit more challeng-ing than "I want you to" vs. "but I don't want to."

Q What do you know about fist-fucking vaginally? Is it dangerous, either physically or in terms of safe sex? My friend thinks she can get hurt. I don't really think so. It can be quite gentle. Are there any nicer terms for something this nice?

A The other common term for it is "fisting," not a whole lot better. It still sounds hostile, and, as you say, the activity at its best is most often slowly and gently done. How about "hand balling?" Vaginal fisting consists of a woman's partner slowly introducing one finger, two fingers, three, into her well-lubricated vagina until the hand, (fingers pressed narrowly together and covered with a latex glove) is engulfed. It can then be moved, again slowly and gently, in an in-and-out motion simulating intercourse, though not completely pulled from the body.

If the active person's nails are trimmed very short with no ragged edges, if latex gloves and plenty of lubrication and communication is used, with the recipient guiding the process and stopping if the sensations are too intense, this activity is unlikely to be dangerous. For a woman who likes a full feeling when penetrated and whose partner does not have a penis thick enough to stretch her to capacity — or any penis at all — the sensation of being filled in this way can be very satisfying.

Q I want to please my boyfriend as much as possible. Recently he asked me to perform oral sex. The thought of it repulses me, but I think I would like to try it. Can you please give me some tips on how to perform oral sex the safest and most satisfying way?

A I can't imagine how doing something you find repellent can satisfy you or someone who cares about you, so I'd first do a lot of soul searching to see if you can look at the activity in some other light...perhaps kissing a very important part of the body of the man you love. The safest way to proceed is by covering his penis with a nonlubricated condom, or by concentrating your mouth's caresses to the shaft area and away from the urethral opening. You might rent an explicit video, and have him comment on preferences as you both watch or page through a book such as Franklin's *Ultimate Kiss* (The Sexuality Library, 938 Howard Street, San Francisco, CA 94163-4114). If the two of you literally play, using a banana for him to instruct and you to practice, or by covering his genitals with something gooey and attractive like chocolate syrup, the whole procedure might become associated with fun, rather than any unpleasantness.

Q I read a letter in your column about a man whose girlfriend enjoys anal sex. As a woman, I was really happy to see that other women get off that way. For me it was a real discovery. For years I feared anal sex and now I really look forward to it. Several women I know with whom I've been able to talk freely also share my feelings. Is it becoming popular, or are we unusual?

A You're in the minority, but that doesn't mean you're weird. Far from becoming popular, anal intercourse has been proven to be a very efficient method of transmitting the AIDS virus. Since using condoms is only *safer* and not necessarily absolutely safe, many women (and men) who are not in monogamous relationships with a tested individual are discontinuing this particular activity.

Q Somehow I can't help but feel that these gals who are so coyly reluctant to give their guys head are really good business women. I should know, I had the reverse problem. Shortly after *The Sensuous Woman* was published 20 years ago, I wanted to give the best head I possibly could to my boyfriend. I lavished him with long sessions of "silky swirl" blow jobs topped off with digital prostate stimulation. I was wearing myself out every day and night and he was taking longer and longer to come. "To hell with *The Sensuous Woman's* silky swirl!" I said, and stopped.

I had been talking to several girlfriends with the same problem and they told me about The Snaky-Lick Trick. I was amazed at how fast I had his rocks off. The "trick" is simply to tease the underside of the penis head almost imperceptibly with the very tip of the tongue, just making ever so slight tongue contact with this most sensitive area in one light upward lick, and then backing off for about fifteen seconds between each lick. This creates an intense frustrating sensation in the male, which can result in a powerful ejaculation within a very short time. I suggest you carefully cover the penis head with either a "California Tip" rubber or hold some tissue over it right from the start, it can be that fast. I wish I had known about The Snaky-Lick Trick back in 1970, and I'm glad to share it with the wives and lovers who read your column.

A Wives, lovers, and all you other people, listen up. If this is an activity you ever want to do or have done to you, cut this column out and put in in your wallet RIGHT NOW. I can see the Snaky-Lick Trick column becoming another Coital Alignment Technique phenomenon (for which I am still stuffing self-addressed envelopes requesting reprints almost four months later!) And no, I never heard of a California Tip rubber either. I assume they are short-shafted ones that are designed to cover only the penis head, but I have not seen any like that around for some time.

✍ It was nice to see the Snaky-Lick Trick go public in your column. I wonder if your orally inclined readers all know that this technique can be used on the clitoris as successfully as the penis. I made this fortuitous discovery while going down on my girlfriend. We were both in a slowed-down state of consciousness on that occasion. It was all I could do to apply those light, upward, teasing licks to her tender button at 10- to 15-second intervals. The suddenness of her orgasm, its intensity and duration, took us both by surprise, considering how little I thought I was doing. Once again, the importance of subtlety in eroticism was made apparent.

A I'm wondering about the importance of whatever you both took to get you into that preliminary slowed-down state.

Q I was at wit's end. My boyfriend is 38 and, like a few more of his age I've known, has thrown in the towel on his sexuality. Sad, because I know there's a horny bastard in there. He claims there once was. So I tried the Snaky-Lick Trick and it was terrific. He went right through the roof. I was especially impressed that he showed me the article. That's initiative and I loved to see it.

A And I love hearing success stories.

Q I have a possible reason why some women don't want to perform oral sex on their male partners: HYGIENE. You would not believe the number of intelligent, socially acceptable men who do not bother to wash their penis, testicles, perineum, and rectum with a bit of soap and water every day. It's funny that women are so obsessed about vaginal odors, but men don't seem to believe that their groin sweat, etc. might be a little strong. Many men think that a rinse in the shower is good enough. Sorry guys, that doesn't always work!

A Suggesting a shared bath or shower before sex is a good way around the delicate problem of indelicate odors. Of course, if you discover the problem once proceedings have begun, you're on your own...and so may be the odoriferous one.

Q I was intrigued by a recent letter in your column. As a professional prostitute, I have come across a good cross section of American men. While men stereotypically tell women anything to "heighten the moment" (i.e. get laid), they often tell their wives or closest lovers very little about their emotional needs. Men tell and ask us, the pros, their innermost secrets (at least the weird ones), and ask us to act out what they don't even mention at home. When it comes to the sexual desires of the average client, I sometimes wonder about the validity of sex surveys. The johns ask most often for head. The next most frequent act is straight-up (fucking in a car or alley if a room can't be arranged). Then a close third is back-door stuff. (If you believe the sex surveys, especially with regard to the AIDS thing, hardly anybody does anal sex.) In my experience with tricks, anal penetration has little to do with clothing, sex, or gender identity.

A There are sex experts and there are sex experts. You now have it from both kinds.

Q Here's the situation: I want to try anal sex, but my girlfriend doesn't. She's absolutely convinced that it hurts more than it pleases, and snubs my argument that some women really like it and do it regularly (a woman described in one of your column's letters, for example. Unfortunately her desire for simultaneous hammer blows to the head didn't help my argument.) I say we at least try, and if it hurts too much we'll be done with it; if it's good we'll have added a new dimension to our usually very good sex life. Once she said if I'd try it myself with a cucumber, then she might do it, but she wasn't serious. Is there any literature or video tape she could look at by women who enjoy it? Is pain inevitable with anal sex? Does it lessen? Is this another thing I have to accept as something she's not that interested in, or do I just sort of try it and see if she's interested, which has worked with other things? Are there other problems with anal sex?

A I bet you tried the "but everybody else is doing it ploy" on your parents years ago and I'm sure it met with as much success then as with your girlfriend now. "Community standards" is just not a good argument when it comes to individual sexual conduct. Education can do a great deal to lessen fears, so reading books such as Jack Morin's *Anal Pleasure & Health* or watching videos together is a good beginning. So is allowing her to either do you or witness you doing yourself with a cucumber, dildo, fingers. She wasn't necessarily kidding. There are health concerns regarding anal play, and Morin's book can address them in detail. But how to "get" her to agree to do something she doesn't want to do? You have to know your adversary. Can she be bribed, seduced, taken unaware without feeling taken advantage of? Only she can tell you.

Q I am a relatively straight 33-year-old man. Recently, performing oral sex on women has become an obsession for me. It feels like a form of worship when I sit down to engage in my favorite form of foreplay. With my most recent sweetheart, I was always more than happy to go long enough to bring her to orgasm, which took me off the hook with the lovemaking that followed. Are there some interesting theories that explain my fascination? Also, given that I'm currently seeking a new lover, what's the latest on transmitting AIDS in this manner? Condoms are fine, but not on my tongue.

A If you read a delightfully engaging book and took pleasure in rereading it, would you need a theory to explain it? Humans are pleasure-seeking creatures. You like oral sex, it feels good to you, you want more of it. Why is that strange? There is also great pleasure in the power of giving pleasure, so that sexual philanthropy is in itself reenforcing. You imply that intercourse can be a challenge. If you feel more secure relying on your tongue rather than your penis to pleasure your partner, all the more reason to want to do it. We all enjoy doing what we do best.

Now, if a woman is infected with the HIV virus, it will be present in her vaginal secretions, but whether in sufficient concentration to be an infectious agent is not yet certain. There is a risk. Condoms on the tongue wouldn't offer enough protection, even if you were willing to use them. There are squares of latex originally manufactured as dental accouterments, called dams, which people who are concerned about disease transmission can put between their mouth and the body part of their choice. Some adult stores carry them or they can be ordered through most dentists or pharmacies, or regular plastic kitchen wrap in rolls have been used with success by many.

Q As a long-time masturbator, I love to be fondled and touched by a lover's hands on my genitals. Many men I've been with are reluctant to engage this way. Many men I've been with also do not enjoy performing oral sex but do enjoy getting it. Why is it so hard for a partner to realize that what they enjoy having done to them is equally enjoyed by their partner (me) when they do it to me?

A That's not always the case, that's why. If you're doing something to your partner in the hopes that he'll "get it" and so return the complement, obviously the message is not getting across. You may have to resort to more direct communication, such as "I love touching you this way and I'd love it even more if you did it to me."

Q I have recently encountered a small problem that probably isn't that uncommon, given men's general lack of knowledge of female sexual anatomy. I don't really feel anything when my partner is wagging his tongue around deep inside my vagina. I don't mind him doing this, of course, but it's not arousing — except maybe to him since he's not doing anything to my clit beside squashing it. I'm afraid that discussing this would make him feel self-conscious and inept anytime he puts his tongue on or in me. Is there any tactful way I can say "If you're doing that to help me come, don't bother?" Please remind your male readers that if the goal is an orgasm, the object of their attention and stimulation should ultimately be the clitoris.

A Let's personalize this very personal matter — your boyfriend's tongue, your clitoris, rather than men's general ignorance about women's general needs. "Tell me what it's like for you when you go down on me" or "Let me tell you what I feel when you do that" are openers to a discussion in which you can impart your preferences and discover his. "I'm afraid there are certain things you do only to please me and I want to check them out" is another, more direct way. Stressing what you like, rather than what you don't, is a more palatable way of telling a personal truth.

I must take issue with the woman who wrote about her inability to enjoy her partner "wagging his tongue around deep inside (her) vagina." Her letter strongly implied that this is something women in general do not enjoy, and which men perform only because of their "general lack of knowledge of female sexual anatomy." I am a man currently involved in an intense sexual/emotional relationship with a very erotic woman who absolutely loves when I wag my tongue around deep inside her vagina. This is important not as a rebuttal to your writer's implicit suggestion that women are indifferent to this practice, but rather because I learned my lover enjoys tongue penetration when she told me so! Your writer's problem is not men's lack of anatomical savvy, but rather her unwillingness or inability to communicate her sexual preferences to her lovers.

Q I've been in a relationship with a man for over a year; he moved in four months ago. He's 26 and I'm 27. I am a woman who enjoys oral sex a lot, giving as well as receiving. My lover refuses to perform it on me, even though I told him how important it is to me. He loves it when I do it to him, though, even requests it often, but he will not "return the favor." I feel very angry about my situation and just don't know what to do about it. I love him, but I feel unfulfilled, rejected, undesirable, and used. Is there any way I can change him? Do I have the right to try? How much longer do I put up with this? I desperately need help here.

A You wouldn't be human if you didn't try to change your partner...and you will be among a lucky minority if you succeed. Asking for what you want in a relationship is fair game for all. Most of us constantly, or periodically, weigh the pros and cons of any situation we're in. When the cons outweigh the pros is when the wise move on. You may have told your man how important receiving oral sex is to you, but did he hear you? I think it's time for a major "telling it like it is" session. From my audiotape "Let's Talk: A Guide To Improving Couples' Communication," (send $15 to 3145 Geary Blvd., #153, San Francisco, CA 94118) here are steps to take when conveying some difficult news (in this case, the depth of your unhappiness):
1. Make an appointment for a private conversation. ("Can we have a few minutes to talk before you go out this evening?") That way you are likelier to get his full attention.
2. Admit your difficulties in delivering the message.
3. Arrange yourselves physically so that you can be at eye level and within touching distance.
4. Make "I" statements. ("I'm very angry" rather than "You make me so mad!")
5. Give some positive strokes ("Most of the time sex with you is great...")

6. Make (or ask for) some specific suggestion for improving the situation. ("Is there anything I can do that would make doing oral sex on me more inviting? Can you tell me some of your considerations for not wanting to do oral sex?")

Q I married my husband a little over a year ago after knowing him for three months. During that time he was somewhat of an attentive lover. He does not kiss me passionately anymore, but instead gives me chaste kisses which, to say the least, are unfulfilling. I have tried on numerous occasions to get him to talk about it and also to explain why it is so important to me. I wouldn't push the issue, but sex isn't all that great to begin with, and without the kisses it seems to be pointless. What else can I do?

A Try humor, bribery, bargaining, tears, threats, counseling? Insisting that someone kiss you passionately seems pointless. Explore the possibility that his withholding precisely what you told him is important to you might be a sulky tactic to get something he wants in exchange. I'd say a heart-to-heart about your general relationship/sexual dissatisfaction is in order. Include whatever satisfactions you do have in this marriage so it doesn't sound like a bitch-and-blame session. The intent here is not to fingerpoint with "You never..." but to discover "What can *we* do to improve our situation?"

Q *Letter #1* My boyfriend told me he does not like kissing on the lips because of the transmission of germs. Other than when I have a contagious illness such as a cold, I see no reason to eliminate kissing from our lovemaking. He shows his affection in other ways, by kissing my forehead and cheeks and stroking my hair. He has never had a girlfriend before and I would like to help him learn to love kissing as much as I do. What do you recommend?
Letter #2 I'm a 30-year-old fellow who has never been very successful in any intimate relationship because of kissing. What seems to be an exciting and very natural act for almost everyone is a nightmare or a chore for me. It's not that I find it distasteful, no pun intended, but it isn't exactly fireworks. Could there be some physical defect along my erogenous connections that link my mouth and my brain, or am I just doing something wrong? If technique is my shortcoming, is there somewhere or some way I can be taught how to kiss to get more out of it than just wet lips?

A I put these letters together to better illustrate an assumption common in our society. "If you don't like what I like, or your likes differ from most people's, there must be something wrong with you." Heterosexual monogamy, monotheistic religion, and a preference for thinness are other shining examples of "everybody's doing it so anything else must be bizarre." Writer #1, odd as it may seem, your boyfriend may simply not enjoy kissing, which is pretty disgusting and ridiculous if you view it dispassionately. Think of explaining it to a martian. That it spreads germs is certainly a "good reason," but it isn't any reason at all in the face of either "I like it" or "I don't like it." You can try coaxing, teasing, bartering, threatening, seduction, or pouncing, or you can level: "I like to do this, I see that you don't. How might I induce you to change your mind?"

If you're lucky, he may admit to sharing the feelings of Writer #2. It may not be fireworks but it is a pleasant behavior for many people, all of whom had to wing it initially in their kissing careers. "Show me how you like to be kissed" is a reasonable request in any warm relationship. If you don't actively dislike it, you might find some pleasure in that of your partner.

Q My gentleman friend and I are two very physical people in our 50s and are most turned on by reading about positive, adventuresome appreciation of what nature gave us. I used to be able to find a small magazine called *Forum* that had articles and letters on new sexual ideas, things, positions, etc., that turn couples on. Besides *Playboy* or *Playgirl*, is there anything similar available today — a magazine on sexuality for ordinary people (not a scholarly journal)?

A *Forum* is still being published, by the same people who put out *Penthouse* in fact. (Forum International Ltd., 1965 Broadway, New York, NY 10023-5965, 800/333-0012). There is a small publication you might want to look at called *LIBIDO: The Journal of Sex and Sensibility*, published quarterly ($7 a copy, 5318 N. Paulina St., Chicago, IL 60640). Also, not scholarly in the sense of dense and dry, is the very informative "Sex Over Forty: A Practical Authoritative Newsletter Directed to the Sexual Concerns of the Mature Adult" (12 issues for $72 to PPA, Inc., P.O. Box 1600, Chapel Hill, NC 27515 or call 919-929-2148).

Q Could you do a review of the best sex-technique videos and where they can be bought? Books would be okay, too. How little I know, how little I know.

A Although they are mostly "to the trade," Multi-Focus Inc. (800-821-0514) has a catalog of sex education and therapy videos with brief explanations of their contents. Otherwise, The Sexuality Library (938 Howard St., San Francisco, CA 94103) carries an excellent selection of books for mail order, and offers entertainment videos that are subjectively rated in such areas as "woman-centered" and "primarily educational with erotic complement."

♂ ▲ ♀ ◀ ♂ ◀ ♀ ◀ ♂ ▼ ♀ ▶ ♂ ► ♀ ▼ ♂ ▲ ♀

The Old In and Out: Keeping Intercourse Interesting

♂ ▲ ♀ ◀ ♂ ◀ ♀ ◀ ♂ ▼ ♀ ▶ ♂ ► ♀ ▼ ♂ ▲ ♀

Q My friend and I have been debating about what is considered the average length of time for satisfying sexual intercourse. That is, what rates as an average performance for a male engaging in sexual intercourse and what can be judged as "inadequate" or as intercourse that ends prematurely? What do the experts say, if they say anything at all?

A Satisfying and average are two very different standards. This from the granddaddy of sex research, Kinsey (*Sexual Behavior in the Human Male*, W.B. Saunders, 1948): "For three-quarters of all males, orgasm is reached within two minutes after the initiation of the sexual relationship, and for a not inconsiderable number of males the climax may be reached within less than a minute or even 10 or 20 seconds." In more recent research — and we can only hope that things have improved in fortysome years — "How soon is too soon? Answers varied from one minute to a half hour." (*The Hite Report on Male Sexuality*, Knopf, 1981)

I prefer the current relative approach. Crooks and Bauer, authors of a constantly revised standard (and excellent) text called *Our Sexuality*, have this to say: "We define rapid ejaculation as consistently reaching orgasm so quickly that it either significantly lowers subjective enjoyment of the experience and/or impairs a partner's gratification. This definition eliminates arbitrary time goals, takes into account the partner's pleasure, and views the person's own subjective needs as an important determinant."

Q Intercourse with my new husband lasts approximately two minutes from the time of first insertion to his ejaculation when he grows soft. I've timed it on the clock. Is that normal?

A It's normal for him apparently. I infer that you are less than passionately transported if you're watching the clock during the proceedings. If you wish intercourse to be speeded up or slowed down, then state that to your husband...along with your willingness to assist in the process of learning how. Confronting the poor guy in battle stance, armed with statistics of what's "normal" for other people, is no way to encourage changes. Marital sex (and pre- or extra- too, for that matter) needs to be a cooperative effort for it to be much fun for either party.

Q I found the statement on the average man's two-to-three-minute staying power to be impossible. I am a man who usually goes for 15 minutes or so before my first climax and can handle multiples of that with no problem if that's mutually agreeable. I've had no complaints so far, but my point is neither do I get many comments on that being outside the woman's usual experience. Maybe you should ask for some more extensive input from your female readers before accepting those statistics.

A Why limit it to females? The statistics I quoted are accepted sexological truth, gathered from laboratory experiment reports and other scientific "fieldwork." Please, I beg you, do not turn into a clockwatcher even for the sake of science on what should be, after all, a delightful and intimate occasion, but if you are a person who has intercourse with men, you can write and tell me — briefly, please — what's your sense of how long the intercourse portion of a sexual encounter usually lasts, taking into account partners of years' standing (or laying) as well as hot initial couplings.

I was very interested in your discussion of length of erectile staying power. I have the pleasure of being close to a wonderful man who is quadriplegic. His condition, while somewhat complex and even changeable, essentially means that he has almost nil muscle control and surface skin sensation below his middle chest, but can gain exquisite sensation through pressure, emotion, and mind. This blessing in disguise creates a situation in which he maintains an erection for an hour and a half or more, which allows us to explore and experiment beyond our wildest dreams. Our only problem (others may wish for such problems) is that after an hour or so I may not continue to be as moist as we would like, but that can be taken care of. All of this may be one of the best kept secrets in the disabled community, and certainly refutes some of the naive and negative stereotypes regarding sexuality and the disabled.

Q My new boyfriend of two months has had a problem maintaining an erection for a long enough period to satisfy me during intercourse. He comes too soon and I end up frustrated. This past weekend he ate an enormous helping of cut-up onions, about the size of a cereal bowl. We made love that evening and not only did he stay hard, but he was able to get it up more than once. I climaxed two or three times. He was still hard after we finished! He claimed it's the onions that caused his libido to change so drastically. He's from Mexico, so some of the cultural stuff and/or dietary beliefs may be different. I praised his performance and joked about buying a 50 lb. bag of onions. He called me from work today to let me know he's eaten four onions so far. I'm curious as hell. Is there any connection between onions and a chemical body reaction?

A My guess would be that it was confidence engendered by such dramatic proof of your affection that enabled him to reach such sexual heights. I know I sure wouldn't be too eager to make love with someone who had recently consumed a bowlful of raw onions! Like beauty in the eye of the beholder, aphrodisiacs are in the belief system of the be-swallower. I wouldn't look a gift stallion in the mouth. Enjoy!

Q Unfortunately I missed the column in which the Coital Alignment Technique was described. Could you repeat the instructions for the technique, and could you also discuss how to deal with the inadequate feelings that arise when one is, as I am, unable to climax with intercourse? I am a single woman up against rigorous competition and often resort to hiding my difficulty (i.e., faking orgasm) so as not to make my lover uncomfortable. Not honest and not good, but I am not in a long-term relationship where I might work this out. Is there a better way to deal with this in the interim?

A I have received more mail about the Coital Alignment Technique than anything else I've written about in more than five years, even those damnable gerbils. I'm printing your letter to address the second issue — which is that so many women or their partners feel there is something abnormal in not having a climax during penis-vagina intercourse. A recent study indicates that fewer than 30% of women do. Those that can, often require a hand (of either person involved). Very few "lucked out" naturally, particularly in mainstream culture's customary missionary position.

With a new partner, you can say during or after intercourse what will do it for you, show him what is needed nonverbally, finish yourself off, or enjoy the proceedings without orgasm as a goal. There need be no more shame attached to what constitutes satisfying sex for you than in declaring what makes up a satisfying meal.

There is no need to feel broken or wrong if your preferences or predilections don't match the current prevailing cultural standard. Hang in there long enough and eventually society is likely to come around to your (preferred) position.

Q My husband and I have been married for a few years. During intercourse, he can't enter me without my assistance. He says he is "unable to find" my vagina. Indeed, when he occasionally slips out while thrusting, he can't reenter. Instead, he pushes his penis against any part of a large area of my pelvis until I help him reenter. Similarly, he "cannot remember" where my clitoris is. If I don't guide him, he will attempt to stimulate any area of my labia that he seems to choose at random. Over the years he has had ample opportunity to observe the locations of both my vagina and my clitoris, so I find his behavior hard to understand. I would be interested in your opinion and comments about this.

A If your husband plays stupid or helpless in other areas of his life, you could assume that's what's happening here as well. There is a possibility that when highly aroused he literally gets lost in his head, numbs out, or in some other way becomes situationally "stupid." Is it any different when he can see what he's doing? Not being able to recognize the feel of familiar objects by hand (and I suppose by penis or tongue, too) is one sign of neurological impairment. Suggest he discuss what you have described with his doctor. If he doesn't, I suggest that you do.

I read the letter from the wife whose husband slips out during intercourse and then cannot reenter, with sadness, shock, and recognition. If the problem is not neurological, it could be psychological. I went through the same situation with my former husband for 12 years. After two years of psychotherapy, I realized that he didn't want to be in the relationship. When I found myself at 36 with no children and with him resisting marriage counseling and artificial insemination, I got the picture. What I saw hurt, but after my divorce I have found myself more aware and definitely wiser.

Q I have been engaged in physical intimacies with a lovely, sexually aware, full-blown young lady. In our sexual activities, my partner has been able to reach multiple orgasm while she is astride me initiating her own movements. We also practice oral-genital exercises quite fruitfully. During these sessions my erection remains taut and I restrain my orgasm effectively, even when my penis is sheathed in her vagina or in her mouth. However, I noted with some regret that upon completion of intercourse when I have fully ejaculated, my member becomes flaccid and unresponsive toward a second performance. There she lies with her satisfying moans and groans of ecstasy, which motivate a measure of desire on my part to enter her again.

What is the capacity of the male to raise a second erection soon after ejaculating through intercourse? I realize I cannot match my partner's multiple orgasmic experiences, but certainly I would like to know if it is possible to nurture a second erection in the male.

A Come again? Oh, that's what you're asking about, isn't it? I was caught daydreaming about whether your "member" was as turgid and purple as your prose. The necessary recuperation period between ejaculations varies from man to man, time to time, and certainly from age to age. Some teenagers' recuperation periods are a matter of minutes, some elderly men's are a matter of days. Some men occasionally surprise themselves on "honeymoon weekends" (whether legal or not) by exceeding their usual abilities, whatever they customarily are.

Try continuing to "play" after your ejaculation and see what happens. Try continuing intercourse with your softening penis or recommencing intercourse by "stuffing" a still-soft one. If that's not possible or pleasurable switch to exciting activities that require no penis, and eventually you might get a big (or little, as the case may be) and pleasant surprise.

You had a question from a reader who wrote in purple prose about his desire to come again. Here is what works for me to achieve my second coming: I don't drink alcohol for three hours before I'm planning to have a double come. One hour or more before my estimated time of arrival, I drink two glasses of water. I don't take a leak before or during sex play. Using this technique, I can retain my erection as long as I want. After my partner has had her fill, I excuse myself, take a leak, return, and am ready for my second coming. Oh oh, the old piss hard-on ploy, you say? Well, it works. It's fun. Is this the good news the world has been waiting for, for one thousand nine hundred and eighty-nine years?

A Somehow I can't see a religion forming around the glories of a piss hard-on, however, stranger ones have been known. Thank you for your input, or should I say your outpouring?

Q I have a problem that is getting in the way of my enjoyment of sex. During sexual intercourse I reach a point of excitement very quickly, which prevents us from doing what we enjoy — screwing wildly. I have to stop, move slowly, stop, and so on or else I'll come. I have not had the problem previously, only in the past two years while I have been continuously involved with one woman. I have speculated that it may be connected to my use, or abuse, of phone fantasy lines. I had been using them for masturbation and usually do it quickly. Have I programmed my sexual responses, and if so, how can I deprogram them?

A There may be some dynamic in your relationship that is underlying your problem. (Often anger or defiance of performance pressure is expressed through a sudden inability to get or sustain an erection, a non-verbal "unfuck you"!) There might be a physical cause, such as your new lover having a tighter vagina that offers more intense stimulation then other lovers; but my guess is the same as yours. If you have become habituated to coming quickly with your masturbation, you can deprogram by practicing slower masturbation rites. Practice until you can again withstand intensity by your own hand (or whatever) similar to the desired "wild screwing. " Also consider masturbating beforehand on the days you plan intercourse. A second erection often naturally lasts longer.

Q Do you have some hints about techniques for stopping to put the condom on and not disturbing the erection in the process?

A I know one woman who boasts of being able to unroll a condom onto a penis with her lips and tongue without the man even being aware of what she's doing. Now there's a technique, unfortunately not available to all. If it's arousing for the man to have his partner smooth it on (most of us have to rely on hands), there's nothing wrong in asking her assistance. If he must or prefers to do it himself, he might place her hand on him somewhere that feels sexy or ask her to whisper to him or to watch, or whatever will maintain the erotic connection. The woman can also initiate the process when she's ready for intercourse.

In general, experiment with ways to keep it sexy, rather than have it be a furtive interruption of lovemaking. If the erection falters some, let that be okay. It will undoubtedly appear again.

Q My boyfriend is very sexy and a wonderful lover in many ways, but he only wants to make love in the missionary position. He says it's the only way we can kiss at the same time. I've tried suggesting an alternative for a second round, but still he refuses. I don't want to push to the point of making him uncomfortable, but I think we are in danger of falling into a rut. Can you suggest how I can get him interested in broadening our sexual horizons?

A Like some initial seductions (e.g., flirting) some arguments are best won nonverbally. Playfully but pointedly take over. Next time you both are ready, climb on top of him, or roll onto your side and pull him face-to-face with you. If you envelop him with your vagina and simply begin, he will find that there are other positions in which two can have intercourse and kiss at the same time.

Q You recommended a book called *For Yourself* (I don't remember whether it was in your column or on your radio show) and I found it helpful. What do you recommend for men? My boyfriend and I have been going out for a year now and I would like to prolong the enjoyment for both of us. All the five guys I have been with cannot keep their erection for more than two or three minutes MAX. My girlfriend says they're being selfish.

A Two or three minutes of sustained intercourse is really longer than average so, though it may not feel like it, you and your girlfriend are lucking out. I sincerely doubt that most men interrupt either their own or their partner's pleasure out of selfishness, orneriness, or any other purposeful spitefulness. Most men don't last longer because they don't know how! Good for you that you see it as a mutual learning process. Check out Zilbergeld's *Male Sexuality*, Castleman's *Sexual Solutions*, or any other good sex-ed book for practical exercises like "The Squeeze Technique," "Stop and Start," and "Quiet Vagina."

Q I'm getting increasingly horrified every time I read, in your column or elsewhere, that men on average last two to four minutes for intercourse. I like intercourse itself to last 15 to 20 minutes, not all continuous fast thrusting, of course, but slow, sensual bumping and grinding. I would prefer celibacy over having sex with a fast shooter. I suspect that men who come that fast don't truly enjoy or feel comfortable with sex, or else they wouldn't try to get it over with as quickly as possible. Some men have complained that I was too "intercourse oriented," but that's how I have my best orgasms. I tend to have several during intercourse, first a few small ones that build up to a big one that's really intense and long lasting.

Since in this age of AIDS, herpes, warts, etc., it is no longer practical to find a man who shares my sexual preferences by trial and error, I'm trying to find a way to bring this issue up, along with safe sex, before I go to bed with a man for the first time. For example, I could ask, along with "Have you read that X % of AIDS cases are transmitted by heterosexual intercourse?," "Have you read that purportedly men on average last only...?" and take it from there. What do you think?

A You could. But the same way, I'm sure, you do not rely on a man's report of previous safe practices to protect you and insist on condom use anyway, I wouldn't put 100% credence in a man's (or a woman's!) self report of how good he is and what he does in bed either. The proof is in the puttin'.

"To the woman who doesn't want to get sexually involved with men who can't sustain intercourse for at least 10 or 15 minutes: I'd strongly suggest investing in a dildo or two. Aside from the issues of objectification and performance anxiety, isn't it difficult enough finding a decent, sane, compatible, attractive, unattached man without adding yet another criterion to narrow down the field even more? With a dildo he can do you (or you can do yourself) until you're blue in the face; it'll never go down. If you like being held and cuddled while you're screwing, he can strap it on with a harness.

♀◀♂◀♀◀♂▼♀▲♂►♀▼♂

The Big O:
Men, Women,
and Orgasm

♀◀♂◀♀◀♂▼♀▲♂►♀▼♂

Q In the 25 years I've been sexually active, I've never experienced orgasm through intercourse. Tell me, are there actually women who can come during intercourse alone — like in books or movies — or do men write all these scenes? How do they do it?

A Here is one way. From *The Journal of Sex Education & Therapy*, Vol. 15, #4 1989 reported by Eichel, Eichel, and Kule: "Intercourse may be enhanced by a "coital alignment technique" that brings the penis and clitoris into sustained, rhythmic contact. A study of 86 participants suggests that (this technique) yields more frequent coital orgasms for women and more 'complete and satisfying' orgasms for both men and women.

"The woman lies on her back. The man positions himself between her legs, farther forward than in the conventional missionary position. He rests his upper body on her, possibly gripping her shoulders so that he doesn't slide backward. After insertion, the shaft of his penis presses up against her mons veneris. He does *not* thrust in and out, which produces little clitoral contact. Rather, both pelvises move together in short, rocking strokes. She initiates the upward strokes; he, the downward strokes. He directs his movement from the upper surface of the base of his penis. This primary erogenous zone thus remains in contact with the clitoris. As orgasm approaches, they should resist the impulse to break out of rhythm. They should breathe and vocalize freely."

Q I read with a great deal of teary nostalgia your description of the coital alignment technique. I am a 30-year-old heterosexual woman, and of the many lovers I've had, *ONE* knew that technique. Because of it, he is enshrined in a holy place in my heart.

I, too, am unable to climax through the usual thrusting in and out, and suffered feelings of inadequacy and shame when my partner expressed disapproval, chagrin, or guilt over the fact that "he couldn't make me come" and I did it myself manually. Also, I felt disappointed and like he didn't care. That's a lot to go through, all over orgasms or the lack thereof: but the one who knew The Technique did it without a word. I followed suit, and suddenly felt loved and worthy and womanly. And orgasmic!

I would like to share with you and, thus, I hope, with your readers, an extra trick he used on me that transformed me into all whirling arms and legs. He'd cup his hands around and under my ass cheeks and curve his fingers in so that he was exerting a slight pull on the skin of the inner crease of my thighs and the whole vulval area. The effect was that my clitoris was pulled down closer to his pubic bone. The whole area was exposed more so that sensation was heightened. A little tickle of my anus or a fingertip inserted into it, and then it was "Damn what the neighbors are thinking!" Was I ever sorry to see him go. It's such a lovely little trick, so useful for making lifetime friends and causing women to blush and smile to themselves as they go to work on the bus.

A If you are reading this column on public transportation, look around you and give a nod of recognition to that smiling woman across the aisle.

The letter from the woman about the Coital Alignment Technique almost brought tears to my eyes and made me feel great inside. I'm one of those men who care about women and have given many great orgasms. I'm glad to see that some women appreciate this and don't just see all men as greedy sex offenders. If a person deserves and wants a great lover, one will always magically appear. And, yes, it also makes me smile at the oddest times when I think about all the happiness and warmth I've shared with women between the sheets.

A I think everyone deserves a great lover, lifetimes full of them, for that matter. I wish I shared your faith in the universe to provide them. Rather than sit around waiting for that magical event, I suggest we go out there looking for the raw material from which great lovers are created — other folks like ourselves.

I'm an avid reader of your weekly column and usually enjoy and profit from your advice. However, I would like to comment about the letter from the formerly nonorgasmic woman who wrote about the coital alignment position, and all the follow-up letters. I am nonorgasmic through intercourse alone, although orgasmic with cunnilingus and masturbation. Therefore I read with great interest about a position that has lead to many women experiencing orgasm for the first time in intercourse. However, when my husband and I tried it — nothing.

What I found most frustrating about the letters was how this coital technique was initiated by one woman's lover without anyone saying a word. It is a common fantasy that a man should know what makes a women come, without being told, even better than she does herself. Oh good, now we can all feel inadequate again. Out there somewhere is a man who can make me come without me having to say a word. Seriously, while it may be true that one or two women had that experience, I think you should have pointed out that talking about different positions is usually necessary and actually desirable.

A Well, now, what is necessary and desirable is acknowledging the truth of "Different strokes for different folks." Verbal communication about sex is vastly entertaining as well as informative, but not always necessary. Sex itself is a very effective means of nonverbal communication and some people do just luck out in their sensual "conversations." I'm sure that there were other women disappointed that the coital alignment technique didn't produce the magic "correct" orgasm via penis/vagina thrusting. I made no promises, nor do I claim many, if any, "successes."

What little we all do know — that in this position the male "rides high" above the women, rocking the top of the penis shaft against the clitoral area, rather than thrusting in and out with its full length — works well for some couples, whether they talked about it or not. I'm sure that some readers will eventually incorporate this technique into their pleasure repertoire, and others will abandon attempts with it for other activities which, for them, are either more pleasurable and/or more productive of orgasms. One of the researchers into this technique is now writing a book about it. I promise to keep you all posted.

Q While I have read and heard much discussion about men who ejaculate before they or their partners would prefer, I have heard little about the opposite situation. My new lover is a man who can last for a very long time, but rarely has orgasms (through no apparent decision of his own). At first I just accepted this situation as a variation of male experience, and I told myself there was no reason that our sex should fit my notions of male response. He is a very sensual lover, far more attuned to nonsexual sensual exchanges than my other lovers have been.

However, I have discovered he is not holding back in order to last a long time, he is just not able to come with any predictability. He is clearly very aroused when we make love, though the intensity ebbs and flows for both of us due to the long time we spend indulging in lovemaking. Because of my own discomfort with lovers who focus all their attention on whether or not I have orgasms, I don't want to make him extremely self-conscious, though it seems unfair for him not to be able to come and also unfair for us to just give up and go to sleep. Any suggestions for remedying or resolving this situation?

A Where did you read that sex (or love or life) must be fair? It isn't. Your lover's sexual response is classified as a sexual dysfunction. The DSM-III-R (psychiatric diagnostic bible) says: "Persistent or recurrent delay in, or absence of, orgasm in a male following normal sexual excitement phase during sexual activity that the clinician, taking into account the person's age, judges to be adequate in focus, intensity, and duration. This failure to achieve orgasm is usually restricted to an inability to reach orgasm in the vagina, with orgasm possible with other types of stimulation, such as masturbation."

Setting aside the absurdity of "the clinician" being the sole judge of what is "adequate" stimulation, your man might want to see a therapist if his response is a problem to him. In that his response is beginning to be a problem for you, ask him how he would like the matter...er, handled. In order to climax, he may need some other form of stimulation which, until you express your interest, he is too embarrassed to request. If not, if he says his sexual response is okay with him, believe him and use your fine sense of justice in righting other, more fixable, instances of unfairness.

Q Recently I had a vacation in Great Britain and had a whirlwind romance with an Englishman of 25. I am 28. I was surprised to learn he was a virgin. He seemed to have all the right instincts and intentions, but he couldn't maintain an erection with me enough for intercourse. He could only achieve orgasm by masturbating himself because, he said, he guessed that was what he was accustomed to. In the two weeks I was there we seemed to make some progress in the right direction, but we didn't achieve intercourse. He's coming here for several months pretty soon and we plan to continue our romance and to have successful intercourse. What do you make of the situation? Is it the culture? Do you think he can transfer his m.o. from his hand to my body? I've never encountered anything like this.

A There are a great number of men in our culture and, I assume, others as well, who do not come through penis-vagina intercourse. Because most men can does not mean that all men do. My guess is the same as his — that the stimulation of intercourse is still unfamiliar and will take some getting used to, which may be the cause of his erection difficulties, too. If things don't improve with practice, enjoy what is possible. There are pluses to "outercourse," not the least of which is not having to deal with birth control.

Q My husband and I make love on an average of three times a week. I am orgasmic and have been with him and with others before him. The issue is what kind of orgasmic. When he and I started getting it on, most of my orgasms were from the standard penis-in-vagina action. It usually took a fairly long session of in and out for these to occur, but they eventually did and were quite nice. Over time, his ability to keep it up for that long is less and we both get a little tired of the in-and-out routine. Consequently, he is more likely to stimulate me manually or orally so I have an orgasm that way before placing his penis inside and getting off. Also nice.

I keep thinking that if I *can* have an orgasm the old "standard" way, I "should" do so. In other relationships I always had penis-vagina orgasms, achieved I can't remember how any more, but I think through heavy foreplay and lots of during-screwing playing. I guess my question is: are penis-in-vagina orgasms "better"? Should I have them as my goal? Or am I worrying too much about the means rather than simply enjoying the outcome? What do other people do and should I care, or is any orgasm in a storm okay?

A One of Freud's (now discredited) theories was that vaginal orgasms through penis-vagina intercourse were somehow more "mature" than those obtained in other ways. Research indicates differing types of orgasm with no good-better-best judgments attached. Other couples do all sorts of things that might be interesting for you to find out about. (Blumestein and Schwartz's *American Couples* is one place to start.)

The fact is, only you and your husband get to vote on what is good, better, or best for you, as a couple and as two individuals. The orgasms from efficient spousal sex are, as you say, nice. So are those from wild passion. They differ in form and content from each other as do those from hand vs. tongue. Personally, I'd hate to drop any from the menu of possibilities.

Q A few years ago was the first time I became orgasmic with the use of a vibrator. Since then it has stayed my very good and consistent friend! Now I am also involved in a great relationship with a man. The question may be a bit strange, but I am unsure sometimes if I indeed experience orgasm with my partner. Is it possible for my vibrator-caused orgasm to be much stronger than with a partner? Sometimes I think it is a head trip more than anything else, and the more I worry the less sure I become.

A Masters and Johnson have stated, and as Gertrude Stein might have said had she lived in our more liberated times, that an orgasm is an orgasm is an orgasm, by whatever means attained. That is not my experience or that of women I have spoken to. Orgasms are a result of fantasy and/or friction in different proportions at different times for different people. By virtue of the intensity and reliability of its stimulation, vibrators produce much stronger orgasms for some women who may also benefit from not having to worry about partners' feelings or thoughts. For others, orgasms within the context of a loving relationship or naughty one-night stand add a bigger kick. Trust your perceptions. If you find no plusses in sex with your man to offset the minus of a less-sizzling orgasm, think about bringing your vibrator to bed with the two of you and experiencing the best of both.

Q I have always had a great sex life until about a year and a half ago when I stopped having orgasms. Now I rarely have any feelings of sexual desire. My boyfriend of two years and I make love regularly, but we are both more and more disturbed by my growing lack of responsiveness. We feel that we have a relationship that could lead to marriage except for the state of our sex life. What is going on? What can we do?

A First of all, I would get a complete physical examination to rule out such possible causes as hormone irregularities, low-grade systemic or local infection. Once you are sure your physical health (and your psychological health, since depression often suppresses desire) is as it should be, I'd look to relationship dynamics between you and your boyfriend. Are you angry at him and not expressing it? Is there a power play going on between you about time or money or some other theoretically unrelated aspect of your relationship? If this possibility resonates, I'd look into couple counseling to bring whatever issues there are into the open so they can be dealt with in other ways than shutting down your sexuality. If you feel that what's going on between the two of you is not at cause, I would consider counseling on your own to investigate other possibilities.

Q I am now almost 32 and have worked on my inner attitude toward sex a lot. I was in therapy for two years and I have made good use of the tools I learned there. My question is how is it possible for me to have orgasms so easily in my dreams, when in my waking life it is usually difficult? The other night I was dreaming but I realized I was dreaming (I believe that's called "lucid" dreaming) and right before orgasm I got terribly frightened and stopped the orgasm. When I don't realize I am dreaming I have great orgasms. Is this normal, or is there still some residue of sexual repression going on that needs to be worked out?

A You have provided a perfect example of repression in psychoanalytic terms — "the rejection from consciousness of anything unpleasant." If orgasmic release of control is more often than not still so frightening to you that you can allow yourself to relax your guard only during sleep, I'd say there is definitely more work to be done in therapy.

Q I am a 45-year-old woman who was in a sexless marriage for 20 years. I learned to achieve orgasm with a vibrator and erotic fantasies. I've been single now for five years and have never had an orgasm with a man. No matter how skillful or patient men have been, none have been able to bring me to orgasm. I fake it in bed, and in solitude, return to the vibrator. I've never been able to tell any man I've been involved with about my orgasms with a vibrator. Is it too late for me with a man?

A There are at least two major factors here — physical and psychological. For 25 years you have been used to a certain kind of orgasm-producing stimulation. To change to other stimuli, whether from penis, mouth, or hand, would take some getting used to even if it were your own hand. That's the physical part.

Psychologically, all the energy you have expended keeping your secret could be redirected to something far more productive in bed — like having orgasms. Probably the easiest way would be to bring your vibrator to bed with the two of you so that the reliable stimulation you receive would be the same; you'd only have to get used to an altered set of circumstances — less of a change. So what I'm saying is that it's never too late *and* change is difficult under any condition. Are you willing to take the risk of self-disclosure for the potential benefit of increased intimacy and shared orgasms?

Q I am unable to have an orgasm in the missionary position. A man told me recently that this is because my clitoris is placed so high, "farther up than I've ever seen." I can have an orgasm if I am on top of a man, but only if there is contact between my clitoris and his pelvic area. I can also have an orgasm without any trouble during oral or manual stimulation. Is this man's theory correct? If my clitoris is placed too high, are there things that I could do to have an orgasm with a man in the missionary position anyway? I want very much to be able to be intimate in this way and I'm feeling frustrated and rather ignorant.

A I've said it before, that when *I* get to create human's bodies, I'm going to completely redesign the genitals. (My late father used to say that if he were in charge of such matters, he'd locate women's breasts in the middle of their back. While it might complicate the act of nursing an infant, it would add immeasurably to a man's pleasure while waltzing!) The exact figures are still in dispute, but probably fewer than 50% of heterosexually active women are able to reach orgasm through intercourse alone; that's in any position, top, bottom, or sideways. Penis-in-vagina sex often just doesn't provide the right stimulation to the clitoris — the source of most women's orgasms — and in most cases the missionary position provides the least of all. (I suspect this may not have been unknown to those antipleasure missionaries.)

By framing the situation in such terms as your clitoris being too high, your so-called friend managed to imply something wrong with you. (Couldn't it just as easily be that his penis is too low for optimal connection?) One way to learn to have orgasms in any particular position is to provide added and usually productive stimulation, such as someone's hands, until you can have the experience of a climax in this new situation. Eventually you might be able to achieve one without the added stimulation; this "bridging" technique is sort of a hardcore update of Pavlovian conditioning. Only you can decide if such an undertaking is worth the struggle.

Q For the last eight months I've had increasing difficulty achieving an erection, and when I ejaculate there is noticeably less fluid than before. I'm only 39 and know of no injury or psychological explanation for this. Should I worry?

A Having ruled out any obvious changes — new medication, or changes in job stress, health, or relationship — I would most definitely be checked out by a urologist. *Knowing*, even if you discover there is something physically wrong, beats worrying, I think.

Q Whenever I have intercourse, I secrete a white creamy substance that I can only describe as looking like Oil of Olay face cream. I know it's not my boyfriend's semen because it's much thicker and whiter and has no smell at all. We also know it can't be from him because we always use condoms and all his semen remains in their tip. This secretion doesn't happen when I have an orgasm myself and it isn't the normal clear secretion I make when I'm excited. It only happens after he has ejaculated. I wonder if there is some gland inside me that he rubs against that only secretes when it feels the contractions of his penis. Could I be one of those rare girls who ejaculates?

A Female ejaculate is clear, watery, slightly salty like tears, not as you describe, and I know of no gland that responds only to a male's ejaculatory contractions. Any vaginal secretion could be a symptom of bacterial imbalance like a yeast infection, but I've never known one to be so time-specific. As I said to the guy with the strangely calloused penis a few weeks ago, were it mine I'd take it to some experienced hands (in your case, perhaps a women's clinic) for an on-site inspection.

Q I have dated more than 70 women and only two of them could ejaculate that semenlike fluid from the urethra during orgasm. What kind of gland is responsible for this and why is it so rare?

A If this is what you discover while "dating," your sexual encounters must really be something else! Okay, sorry; let's get serious. That you found this response in less than 3% of the women you've been with is reflected in the fact that four out of five human sexuality texts I consulted for a good explanation don't even mention the phenomenon. The Grafenburg Spot is an area of glands and ducts located on the front wall of the vagina which develops from the same embryologic tissue as the male prostate, and is considered by some to be its female counterpart. When this area is stimulated directly it produces an orgasm accompanied by fluid expulsion from the urethra in *some* women. Why only in some women and not all? I guess for the same reason that only some people can wiggle their ears or pass a MENSA exam—Nature's perversity.

Q I have seen and heard a lot of info about male ejaculate, but what about female ejaculate? How is it different/similar? What is it made of? Given "female problems" like yeast, period, etc., I would be very interested in knowing if consuming this by mouth would be okay. P.S. She has herpes in a spot between her vagina and anus.

A Ernst Grafenberg, for whom the G Spot was named, wrote in 1950: "(female ejaculatory) fluid was examined and it had no urinary character. I am inclined to believe that 'urine' reported to be expelled during female orgasm is not urine, but only secretions of the intraurethral glands..." In *The G Spot* by Ladas, Whipple, and Perry, the authors report lab analyses to compare and contrast vasectomized (i.e., spermless) male ejaculate, female ejaculate, and urine: "Chemical analysis differentiated the ejaculatory fluids from urine on the basis of four chemical tests. Two substances, tartrate-inhibited acid phosphate, thought to be prostatic, and glucose (sugar) were substantially higher in the ejaculatory fluid than in the urine samples. Urea and creatinine (both end products of protein metabolism normally found in the urine) were substantially lower in the ejaculatory than in the urine specimens." All of this may tell you more about urine than you were interested in knowing, but I hope it addresses your question on the makeup and distinction of female ejaculation.

As for your other concerns: (1) The bacteria in a person's mouth are more numerous than those in a vagina. Thus oral sex puts her at greater risk of catching something from you than you from her. (2) A menstrual period is not a female problem in the sense of a communicable disease like a yeast infection. Of course, if the woman is HIV positive, her blood will be dangerous to you. And (3) A herpes lesion, as you can see, can have sites other than just genitals or mouth. Lesions can be infectious without being visible and any portion of your face in contact with shedding viruses puts you at substantial risk of getting herpes.

Q I can't seem to find a spot sensitive to stimulation anywhere in my vagina. Is the G Spot for real? Is it optional equipment?

A Just as there are women whose nipples are no more sensitive to stimulation than their knuckles, there are women who don't seem to have any such specific area in their vaginas. Bodies differ and change. Perhaps you might develop one. For some women, though, the G Spot is so real you can touch it.

Q I have a problem that has plagued many sexual relationships and caused the demise of one marriage. My problem is the inability to orgasm and ejaculate with a woman. This includes intercourse, oral sex, and mutual masturbation. I am, however, very capable of maintaining an erection during sex. During foreplay I get very stimulated, but as soon as intercourse starts the sensations in my penis go away. I feel as if I can't "just let go." I must add that solo masturbation is my only way to release sexual tension. Is there a way to treat this?

A The problem you describe is classified as a sexual dysfunction, and, while not totally uncommon in men, is, unfortunately, quite common with women. It is a problem only if both you and your partner *require* an orgasm and ejaculation with every sexual interaction. If you accept that none is likely but will take pleasure with each other anyway, you can enjoy a partnered sex life and a solitary one, as many people do. Otherwise, working with a competent sex therapist will likely produce techniques of both stimulation and relaxation that you can master to enable you to come to orgasm with a partner.

Q When I do leg lifts or sit-ups in a certain way, I begin to feel like I'm going to come. If I persist...you guessed it: splooey. I should point out that the sensation is not coming from direct rubbing or stimulation of my penis. Rather, it feels like some sort of switch is being turned on inside my lower abdomen. While I like an orgasm as much as the next person, context is important. Spontaneously coming in my shorts during an aerobics class is not my idea of a great sexual experience, although it is unique — or is it? I have never heard of anything like this from other men. Then again, it's not the first thing I bring up at a party, either.

Am I the only one who has experienced this? Should I be concerned? How can I acquire control over this process? I'm a little afraid that if I indulge in this explosive exercise to excess, it will become more ingrained and more difficult to control.

A What great motivation for a toned body! Beats the hell of the recently test-marketed antidepressant that produced yawn-induced orgasms. While I've heard of people sexually aroused by unorthodox stimuli, your experience is unique to me, too. One way to gain a feeling of control is to refrain from the specific exercises that trigger ejaculation, or switch to others at a certain pre-ejaculatory point. Better yet, thank the powers that be and simply enjoy the fruits of your labors. You can share the joy by reporting your experience next time you have a physical check-up. Then your doctor can enjoy the fame that results from writing you up in the professional journals.

This is in response to the "orgasm while doing sit-ups" letter. I was so excited to discover someone else who has experienced the same phenomenon. And then, reading on, the word "penis" surprised me. I am a woman and had assumed this was a female sensation somehow related to inner compression on the uterus or something. I become quite aroused when exercising at certain times. It's most pronounced in the evening after eating and drinking. I think a full stomach and/or bladder may create the feeling somehow. I have never felt this during an aerobics class, but in my own home I can manipulate it into a kind of masturbation. Let that guy know he's not alone.

Q I don't know where I got the idea, but in my mind there is a connection between blood pressure and ease of orgasm. Since I have very low blood pressure and come to orgasm very slowly, even when I masturbate, this idea makes sense to me. Since orgasm is brought on by blood filling the pubic area, does low pressure fill it slower? Are we hydraulic bodies in this way or, as you have said before, is it all in one's mind?

A Sexual mechanics aren't *all* in one's mind, obviously, or most of us would be getting it on varyingly and safely via telekinesis. Orgasm is not brought about by blood in the pelvic area, engorgement and erection are. Nonetheless, I have no idea about any correlation of blood pressure to erection time or ejaculatory speed. If you find out anything, I hope you'll let me know.

Q I am a male in my early thirties, in good health and engaged to be married, and in both my current relationship and my previous one I find it difficult to achieve orgasm. My sense of things is that it's simply a matter of being jaded, although I find my current lover attractive, sensitive, attentive, and sexually pleasing. I have no problem performing, only finishing in an orgasm. Is there any help for a man such as myself, short of a harem and/or extremely kinky strangeness? Any exercises, books, yoga postures? Any way I can regain the intense uncontrollable excitement of my teens?

A I wish I knew how to bring back the flat tummy of the teens, the dewy (when not acned) skin, the expectations of innocence. You want uncontrollable excitement, too? Anorgasmia, the lack of orgasm, or (subjectively) undue difficulty in achieving one, is usually due to insufficient stimulation, either physical or mental, or a psychological conflict such as fear of losing control. All these possibilities, and more importantly, solutions to them, can best be explored with a good sex therapist.

Q In August I'm going to marry to my boyfriend of five years. Of course we're very much in love, which I feel eliminates the possibility that my problem could be caused by a fear of intimacy. Four years ago I had four major orgasms while having sex with him in the missionary position. Unfortunately, that was the last time I had an orgasm during sex, and frankly, I miss it! I can achieve one through self-stimulation or with a vibrator. I have had other sexual relationships, but my fiancé is the only man who has ever given me an orgasm. According to my gynecologist, there is nothing physically wrong with me. I would certainly appreciate any suggestions about books, techniques, or special counselors.

A Browse through some sexual enhancement books in a good bookstore for suggestions on "techniques." Alex Comfort's classic series on *The Joy of Sex* or Patricia E. Raley's *Making Love: How To Be Your Own Sex Therapist* come to mind. Try whatever looks appealing, rather than "likely to be orgasm-producing."

If this is really troubling to you, however, I would suggest seeking out the services of a reputable sex counselor. Since there is no specific licensing for this, ask about her or his educational background and affiliations. AASECT (American Association of Sex Educators, Counselors, and Therapists) and SSSS (The Society for the Scientific Study of Sex) membership might be good indicators of special interest and training.

By the way, no man "gives" you an orgasm; you allow yourself to have it with him on those occasions. And, regarding possible fear of intimacy — would that love and marriage were proof of intimacy. Unfortunately, that's far from the truth.

Q I'm a healthy 22-year-old woman blessed with a stable, loving relationship with my boyfriend. The problem: In our two years of otherwise satisfactory intercourse, I've never come to orgasm. Yet in times past with other partners, I had frequent and even multiple orgasms. I know that mine is a common problem, but I can't comfort my beloved with statistics forever. How can I get the kettle boiling?

A It is a common condition for a woman to be unable to reach orgasm through intercourse alone, but not for someone who once was easily orgasmic to suddenly stop being so. Something else is going on here, so let's look at what has changed from when you were orgasmic. Something physical about you? Have you had a baby, an abortion, an operation, a major weight gain or loss? Something physical about your partners? All the other men with whom you were orgasmic had bigger, smaller, harder, softer, hairier, or smoother something than your present lover? A different situation? Then you were screwing around and now you're serious, or were you formerly often drunk or stoned and now you're sober? Do you see how to go about this detective work?

Do what you can to discover what is different and deal with it, changing it (yourself, him) if you can, accepting and accommodating if you can't. If it's more complicated than that, consider consulting a therapist, either with your lover or on your own.

Q You answered a question from a 22-year-old woman concerned about not having orgasms during intercourse. (She was able to with previous lovers.) In your answer, you asked about any physical changes, and one you mentioned was weight gain. I have gained a lot of weight in the past few years and that has hindered me psychologically in my ability to enjoy sex, but I don't understand how that would affect the ability to have orgasm during intercourse. Can you explain?

A Weight gain may be visible on the hips, for instance, but it also accretes on other body parts. Extra flesh on and around the external genitals will affect how a woman's body conjoins with her lover's — different angles, different stimulation. However, as I have said often before, orgasm is often more about what goes on between the ears than between the legs. If a woman's thoughts during sex focus on keeping her tummy tucked in or on not moving in a certain position that will display her in an unflattering light, how likely is it that she will surrender to climax?

Q My lover is having difficulty with ejaculation. He can get excited and have intercourse for a long period of time, but the final release rarely comes. Manual stimulation can do the trick, but this takes a lot of time and concentration. We're both relatively new to lovemaking and have little experience to fall back on. We're thinking the problem may be due to insufficient friction in a condom, inability to "let go," or too much focus on his being able to ejaculate. Any suggestions?

A All of your suppositions might be correct. My guess is that, being new to partnered sex, your lover might be used to ejaculating from a combination of his own friction and his own favorite fantasy. Perhaps if he incorporated one or both into your lovemaking so that some familiar trigger was present? Trust in one's partner builds over time. If he's used to ejaculating in private, he may need to accustom himself to your presence until he can let go without feeling too vulnerable. Adding a drop of lubricant to the inside of the condom, or changing to unlubricated condoms if he's already doing this, may provide different (better, to him) friction. And, there's always the distinct possibility that if he can relax and enjoy what is, without pressure to have it be something else, it will work itself out (and in, and out) eventually.

Do you know the fable of the centipede? Asked to explain exactly how he coordinated all 100 legs to move forward, he found that not only could he not offer the particulars, now that he was paying such careful attention to his actions, he could no longer move at all.

Q My lesbian lover and I have a problem: Contrary to *The Joy of Lesbian Sex* (Sisley & Harris), which gleefully assures that all lesbians have plenty of mutual orgasms, M. cannot reach orgasm when I orally stimulate her. I think our problem lies in the fact that she masturbates in what we think is an unusual fashion. She lies on her side with her palm between her thighs and applies direct pressure to her clitoris while tightening her pelvic and leg muscles. She reaches orgasm quickly this way. Would her form of pressing and tightening masturbation be the cause of M.'s inability to reach orgasm through oral stimulation, or am I just not getting it right? How do most women masturbate?

A Do I hear an inference here that in the situation as stated, someone must be at fault? Either the book (for raising false expectations), your lover (for not masturbating "correctly"), or you (for not giving good enough head). Of course lesbians, and any other women, are capable of heaps of juicy orgasms, together, separately, or in strange and wonderful combinations, but not all of them in the same manner. The more the partner can or will provide stimulation like the person is accustomed to, the more likely a person is to climax easily. (Penis-vagina intercourse mimics the penile stimulation that the majority of men provide for themselves with their hand, hence hetero men experience fewer failed orgasm attempts than do hetero women.)

In the chapter on masturbation in *The Hite Report* (MacMillan Publishing, 1976), the author outlines six basic masturbation types, although I could make a case for hundreds more with additional alternative variables such as sitting or standing, clothed or un-, reading erotica, thinking sexy thoughts, or even whistling "Dixie." Hite reports that 73% of her respondents customarily masturbate by stimulating the clitoral/vulval area with their hand while lying on their back, 5.5% do so while lying on their belly, 4% while pressing or thrusting against a soft object, 3% by pressing thighs together rhythmically, 2% using water, 1.5% with vaginal insertion, and 11% with more than one method. The book has more than 30 pages of quotes detailing precise descriptions of how, when, and where for many women.

Perhaps you might come to the conclusion that it's not absolutely essential for either you or your partner that she climax during oral sex, that both of you just enjoy it, and do what's "practical" when she wants to achieve orgasm. It might be a great deal easier than trying to mimic her usual doings with your mouth.

Q I learned to have my first orgasm with a vibrator. That was a long time ago and I'm getting bored with it. I would like to learn how to have an orgasm manually. I've been practicing and I do get very strong sensations (even pulsing and mini-contractions) but no orgasm. I don't want to deprive my body of orgasm while learning a new way to masturbate, yet if I keep falling back on the vibrator I'll never learn a new way. How can I learn how to orgasm manually without feeling frustrated when I don't come?

A You could come first by vibrator and practice manually for your second go-round if you can do two. You can agree to practice manually for, say, 15 minutes, and at the end of that time resort to the tried and true, gradually increasing the time of the manual sessions. You could have a practice session at night, with or without resulting orgasm, and use the vibrator for a satisfying quickie in the morning. You might also use both hand and vibrator, placing it at different spots than you're used to, or buy a new vibrator with attachments, accustoming yourself to the different-feeling orgasms different stimulation provides. Remember, keep this light. It's experimentation and exploration of self-*pleasuring* we're talking about here, not a matter of do or die. You may find, after all this, that you prefer the modern labor-saving device to the old-fashioned way. Many women do.

Q Is it possible for a man to fake an orgasm?

A Sure: gasp, shudder, aaah. If he wants to fake an ejaculation, that might be a bit tougher, but not impossible. With good pelvic muscle control, some men can make their penis contract voluntarily. If a condom was used or the partner particularly juicy, it's really very difficult to know exactly who is responsible for what wetness.

Q Why is it that some women orgasm so easily and others have a difficult time? Is it because some are repressed and others are not?

A How come some women have round bellies and others flat ones? How come some learn to roller skate, or masturbate, at an early age and some never do? Women differ as to their physical makeup, their natural aptitudes, and their life experiences. Who reaches orgasm how is a combination of nature (how prominent their clitoris or how sensitive they are to stimulation, for example) and environment (a lucky combination of partner, place, and practice). Feelings about sex could be a part of the equation, certainly, but not likely to be all of it.

Q Sometimes when having great sex with a partner, it is as if he can read my mind. He seems instinctively to know how to make touch electric. This happens rarely, but when it does it is sheer heaven. Isadora, what's going on? Telepathy?

A Perhaps. Perhaps it is the sheer happy coincidence of his wanting to give exactly what you want to receive. Good lovers, if such there be in the generic (meaning not only good for you at this moment but generally perceived by others that way), are so-called because they pay attention to subtle body cues. Your man may not be so much a mind reader as a body reader.

Q I spend approximately 30 to 45 minutes in foreplay — oral sex and fingering — to get my lover to come. I follow her directions as best I can — up a little, harder, give me head, etc. and I don't show disappointment nor anger as it's not warranted. Sometimes I feel like Sisyphus whose curse was to push a rock up a hill and let it role down repeatedly. Once she does come, she is too tired, sore, or exhausted to receive or masturbate me. If I come first, by the time I'm ready to help her she's lost interest or says it doesn't matter, or she takes twice as long, or fails, and I give up. Should I just accept "I don't feel like it now" after I come and forget about helping her? Who should come first?

A I think a discussion needs to take place between the two of you outside of bed, a committee of two on a problem-solving mission. There is no "should" here. Whatever you two arrive at as workable for the two of you, will work. I can't help but be struck by how laboriously joyless all this sounds. What about considering that, at least upon occasion, each of you will be responsible for her/his orgasm, if one is wanted, at the finale, but for the main event you will just roll around doing to each other whatever feels good to the doer. Touch her in ways that feel good to you to do, and encourage her to do the same to you. These caresses may not be orgasm-producing, but you'll probably have some fun.

Q My fiancé and I have very different sexual timing and have not been able to find a solution. It takes him a long time to climax. I, on the other hand, climax very easily, and lose all drive after I have an orgasm. I find myself getting angry, frustrated, and physically uncomfortable when it takes him 20 or more minutes to come. I also feel unexciting to him and deprived of enjoying his orgasms. I've asked for guidance, but he says it feels too contrived to talk about what he likes. We've tried counseling, massage, lingerie, and romantic settings. More and more often I avoid sex because it feels so unsatisfying emotionally. I might not be bothered by this, but he seems angry with me when I can't keep going, and I'm afraid this may lead to affairs once we're married. Any suggestions?

A I'm sure you know that your response cycle would be a delight to the majority of men and his to a great number of women. It's sheer perversity that must have brought the two of you together. He could, with determination, learn to quicken his pace, as you could learn to slow yours down. But since hating the other's sexual style is not a good beginning for a marriage, I'd shelve the lingerie bit for now and go back into counseling, concentrating on methods of negotiating your differences.

Q I am slowly reaching a pinnacle of frustration with my preorgasmic girlfriend who is 28. I am 33. I consider myself a fairly adept lover and am not lacking in experience. I've tried sexy hot baths; full body rubs by firelight; space music; hour-long oral sex from every conceivable angle, pressure, rate and rhythm; dirty talk; a new vibrator; a little porn. We're not getting much beyond a tremble. I chalk it up to a handful of previously inept partners, denying her sexuality in a vapid marriage, and lack of practice and assertion. She claims she masturbates when I'm not around, and I encourage her to do so and the various exercises which are good for such problems outlined in Barbach's book.

Ultimately, I suppose a woman's orgasm is her responsibility, but I truly want to do anything I can to help. A climax now and then would probably improve her erratic disposition. My only hint is her description of how, on occasion, this frustrating "almost" plateau is bordering on painful. So where do I/we go from here? Sex therapy?

A Yes, or couples' counseling. I don't know how she feels about her lack of orgasm, but it sounds to me like it has become a Joint Issue, a power struggle. Good couple therapy deals with sexual difficulties and with couple dynamics. Maybe it's the space music that's turning her off. It would me.

I just had to write about a column in which a guy wrote about his preorgasmic girlfriend. In order to tell what's really going on, check out his language. She "claims" she masturbates. Doesn't he believe her? Her disposition is "erratic." Isn't everyone's? From his tone you'd think he doesn't like her! And why does she have to have an orgasm? Is he using her to validate his self-image as "an adept lover," whatever that is?

In my own case, I think the main reason I failed to perform that particular trick for my former lover (who recently dumped me for the same reason) was that sex with him was so joyless and unsensual. Instead of just enjoying being together and accepting whatever happened or didn't happen, he worked on me with only one goal in mind. I can still see him kneeling over me with his vibrator, his jaw set in grim determination. I have some advice for that couple. To him: Lighten up, buddy. To her: Leave that creep and find someone who is on your side.

Q My boyfriend keeps asking me to repeat a strange technique to increase his orgasm intensity every time I perform oral sex on him. Just before he is about to come, he has me press my finger very hard just below his scrotum, half way between his testicles and anus. This very firm finger pressure actively reduces his normally powerful first spurts of ejaculation into a few fine mists. He has me continue the pressure while his penis seems to strain again and again to eject semen. When I release pressure he starts a cycle of intense ejaculations that seem to last twice as long as normal. He says the super-satisfying release is worth any possible risk, but I am worried. What do you think?

A What you're pressing on is the urethra, the conduit for semen (and urine). The worst that is likely to happen, beyond local bruising, says a urologist I consulted, is that the ejaculate could back up and be released into the bladder, with nothing issuing forth from his penis. This retrograde ejaculation happens to many men who have had prostate surgery. (One gets used to this initially surprising phenomenon, although at first it's something like encountering a barkless dog.) In other words, not to worry.

Beyond
the
Basics

♀◀♂◀♀▲♂▼♀▲♂►♀▼♂

Q Does jazz music stimulate sexual feelings or is it a myth?

A Many religious fundamentalists insist that it does. If it's down and dirty traditional jazz, you'd get no argument from me. My guess is that any rhythmic feel-good music puts people in the mood for other rhythmic feel-good activities, too.

Q I recently saw and had sex with an old lover. During foreplay I reached into his pants and discovered a small ring attached to his ridge. Please understand, I am not referring to a device known as a "cock ring," which usually encircles the penis. This ring was actually hanging off the edge like an earring. It startled me, but I didn't ask, and forgot about it until I felt it inside me during intercourse. Does the application of this ring produce pressure to ensure erection? (In the past he has experienced feelings of inadequacy because of his failure to maintain an erection during intercourse.) He said it was for my pleasure but I became afraid it might unfasten itself and injure me. I insisted he remove it. He was very reluctant. I was hoping for a ring, but this wasn't exactly what I had in mind! Have you ever heard of this kind of sexual aid? If so, is it dangerous to either partner?

A If it feels sexy to the wearer or his partner, as it does it some cases even if it didn't in yours, it can improve what happens in bed. In that sense it can be a sexual aid. However, a piercing and insertion such as you describe is generally only a fashion statement, and as such marks the wearer as a member of a particular subgroup, au courant, and in some cases, one who revels in intense feeling (a masochist, in popular parlance). Unless the site of the piercing becomes infected or it rubs either partner uncomfortably during penetration, I can't see it as posing any danger.

Q Some friends and I saw a VCR movie that was neither a porno flick nor a teenage sex flick but contained a great deal of nudity. The story, apparently a true one, is about a man who places an ad in the paper for a temporary wife for a long stay on a desert island. The ad is answered, the two of them live through injury, starvation, boredom, etc., but their biggest problem seems to be sex. Sometimes she rejected him and sometimes she gave in. Her desire for assistance and companionship on the island led her to force herself to allow sex. This movie frustrated me deeply. I felt she led him on with the display of her naked body and I also sympathize with her desire to be free of civilization's pressure to wear clothes. This movie made me feel like a pervert. I like seeking unclothed women but I get the message that I'm supposed to suppress that feeling. Are we supposed to link sex with nudity or not?

A I think part of your uneasiness comes from the moviemaker's double message: See this lovely actress's stunning body enhanced with lighting and makeup to create the ultimate sexual allure while I tell you a true story of adventure that, of course, has no intent to arouse you sexually. This double message is what sustains Madison Avenue: "Buy our product. No need to notice the bulging breasts of the woman draped smilingly around the display!" There are organizations of "naturists" who so decry the linkage of sex and nudity in our society that it is their avowed intent to create a conscious separation of the two. But by and large, our society is both prudish and sex-obsessed (not an unusual combination), so unless you do some major personal attitude adjustment you may continue to get disturbed by arousing messages that deny their intended effect.

Q For the past several years I have been unable to have sex with my husband without first pretending he is someone else. I fantasize that he's a coworker I find attractive, strangers I've seen on the street, even fictional characters in books — anyone but himself. Is this at all normal, or normal after ten years of monogamous marriage? Do other men and women do this? Is this the kind of thing that can happen in a healthy relationship or to people who should leave a marriage? Whether I stay in the marriage or get a divorce, I do not think I ever could tell him about this fantasizing thing.

A If you're not feeling turned on to the person in your bed and yet for reasons (such as being married to him) you choose to behave sexually anyway, I personally prefer the technique of summoning sexy images of *him*, such as the night you first made love, rather than thinking of other people, which strikes me as both sad and divisive. This is a personal opinion, and many reputable sex books disagree, since fantasizing about other people is quite normal for those in good relationships, bad ones, or none at all. I don't know why you would tell your husband in any case. "Hey, honey, remember that particularly hot session we had last week? Well, in my mind that wasn't you but some stranger I saw on the bus." Who would want to hear that? Having heard it, what could he do about it beside wonder ever after what or who you're thinking about? I suggest you consider ways of getting back in touch with the feelings you presumably had when you two first fell in love. Having your fantasies match your reality, or vice versa, is the best kind of sex there is.

Q I found myself full of empathy and distaste upon reading about "sexaholic" partners. That could have been me a year ago. I found my self-esteem eroded away by my partner's continual infidelity while I craved more dominant/submissive sex to prove to him how far I would go to love him and keep him. I have been single for over a year now, licking my wounds of rejection and betrayal, but find that I am still obsessed with sex with intimidation. It works to heighten my sexual stimulation to the extent that sex without "power play" has become disappointing. I find myself sabotaging relationships that do not have this intensely exciting feature, while thinking myself shallow for doing so. There seems to be a trust valve that won't open unless it's forced. Why does psychological battering create such loyal bonding? Is there any research being done on repatterning sexual drives?

A The questions you raise are multifaceted and can best be unraveled for you personally by working with a good psychotherapist. Briefly, I want to say that you are confusing a sadomasochistic *relationship* with dominant/submissive sex play. The latter can be a very exciting and stimulating part of an essentially egalitarian relationship. Unless such specific activities (like sex) are negotiated, with both parties understanding and agreeing to pre-set limits, you have an abusive relationship — which is not fun and exciting to a healthy individual, but degrading and demoralizing.

Q I am concerned about the fantasies I conjure up when my boyfriend and I are making love (or are we just having sex?). In order to achieve orgasm, I create mental images of being tied up and/or punished and being forced to have sex. There is no excessive violence in these fantasies. I am just overpowered by the man's physical strength and there is sometimes verbal abuse. The man in these fantasies is always my boyfriend playing different roles, e.g., a pirate (okay, corny), a burglar, etc. I usually try to substitute these fantasies with ones filled with positive, more romantic images just before I reach orgasm. Since I began masturbating at the age of 9 or so, I have used punishment, bondage, and forced sex fantasies, but I don't recall ever using these when making love with past partners.

I am familiar with the idea that the release of energy involved in violence is akin to and conducive of that involved in sex. However, I fear that my fantasies reflect generally a low self-esteem, a learned attitude that women are inferior to and should be dominated by men and, specifically, that the exclusiveness of these fantasies with my current lover indicate an inferiority complex with him on several levels. I feel bad about having these fantasies and wish I could supplant them with positive ones. Comments? Suggestions?

A I'm wondering whether you're a graduate student in psychology or a therapy client of many years standing, or perhaps you *are* a dyed-in-the-wool masochist to torture yourself so with the real meaning of your subconscious messages. My suggestion? Carry whatever fantasies arrive when you're alone or with a partner to the most elaborate extent possible as often as possible. Eventually they may become less hot and so you will achieve your aim in doing away with them. Experiments with sex offenders and homosexuals wishing to change their orientation in which attempts are made to extinguish unacceptable arousal stimuli by administering simultaneous electric shocks have met with dubious success. Forbidding something often makes it more rather than less sexually exciting, so that's why I suggest the opposite tack of encouragement.

Please do read through some of the many collections of peoples' sexual fantasies, e.g., Nancy Friday's, or P. & E. Kronhausen. Once you see how common this theme of being overcome into sexual submission is to both women and men, you might give yourself permission to join the throng.

Q I'm a male in my forties. I'm not able to get involved physically with a woman but I would like to talk dirty with her on the phone. I don't like the $2 type phone fantasies. At work, there are two young ladies who enjoy talking dirty — maybe I should say "sexy" — with me. What are the feelings of a woman about live phone sex and so-called dirty words? Also, are there books on sexy talk?

A Some women enjoy such talk face-to-face, some women like it over the phone — some like both and some women do not like it at all. Be very sure that anyone with whom you initiate such a call is a willing participant. Phoning a strange women to talk dirty can be not only objectionable and frightening, but also against the law. If you have found someone who enjoys doing this with you, great. If not, some of the phone fantasy lines and conference bulletin boards have live people, rather than recordings, with whom you can engage in sexy talk. Even if you prefer a noncommercial partner, this would be a better place to learn some good techniques than a book.

Q In real life I go to church to meet people, yet in my fantasy life I'm having sleazy sex with tattooed hunks in black leather...definitely unsafe sex like water sports, rimming, and fisting. Do we all fanta-size about sex acts we are too afraid, or too prudent, to try? Or am I a schizoid pervert?

A You are extremely normal...just more honest than some.

Q I've been spending a lot of time solo lately, but unlike many single people I know, my sex life has never been better. What excites me most is self-sex at, or perhaps beyond, the cutting edge. There's something about flirting with death that thrills me. While covered in latex from head to toe, I tighten a leather belt around my neck, feeling an incredible rush throughout my body. I pull the belt tighter and tighter until I can barely breathe. I bring myself to an outrageous orgasm and then loosen the belt around my neck. I am in control the whole time, though I'm also definitely in an altered state of con-sciousness. I haven't quite got up the nerve to say to others: "Try it, you'll like it," but it sure beats calling up 976 numbers and listening to heavy breathing, don't you think?

A You are not just flirting with death, you are actively courting it! Nobody is in complete control of anything during an orgasm, let alone all the many essential blood-carrying arteries that could blow, causing instant death. If you are feeling suicidal, acknowledge that to yourself, and then please look into psychotherapy. (If nothing else, motivate yourself by thinking of the embarrassment of being found dead in your fetish wear.) If there were ever a candidate for finding exciting methods of Safer Sex, you're it.

Q As a widow of several years and still young enough to enjoy and want sex, I have a problem. My husband was quite a few years my senior, so my sex life toward the end of his life was not what you would call perfect. When he had trouble with an erection, I felt it was my duty to help him orally, even though I personally do not enjoy this act. Still, he was my husband and his troubles were my troubles. I purchased a vibrator and learned to bring myself to orgasm thinking of him.

Eventually I met a widower who I thought could be a friend and sex partner to me. (With the present threat of AIDS, I was careful in my choice.) This friend is going through the same condition my husband did. I decided not to enter into any relationship in which I would receive incomplete satisfaction unless I indulged in practices I disliked, so I have gone back to masturbation using the vibrator and porn films on late night TV. I do this occasionally and only when I feel the need. My question is: Is it terribly unnatural? Am I hurting my character? Am I the only one in such a situation?

A Let me assure you that you, and only you, can be the judge of what is appropriate sexual behavior for you. Providing yourself with orgasms is very natural, seems only sensible, and hurts no one except you, and then only if you feel bad about it. Please reexamine your beliefs about self-satisfaction so you may enjoy yourself guilt-lessly. I urge you also to look at other methods of assisting a partner with erectile difficulties. Not all men expect, require or even want oral sex. It seems a shame to forgo the many other benefits of an intimate relationship under the mistaken belief that performing oral sex would be a requirement.

Q My lover has a masturbation technique which seems dangerous to me. He wraps a thick rubber band around the base of his penis, which then turns purple and looks like it's about to explode. He says the orgasm is much more intense. He wants to try it during intercourse, but first I want to make sure he's not hurting himself. Do you think there's any harm in this?

A Your lover has reinvented the cock ring, not as momentous as reinventing the wheel, but still very creative. The purpose of any band so placed, rubber, metal, or leather, is to keep the blood that has flowed into the area upon arousal from draining back. All that trapped blood does provide a firmer erection and perhaps a heightened sense of arousal, but there is some danger of "blowing a valve" or creating an aneurysm. Commercial cock rings of leather with adjustable snaps (which some kids wear as bracelets) would be a great deal easier to get off than a rubber band in an emergency, and thus, safer.

Q I am a 26-year-old female and I'm wondering if you know how common it is for females to be orgasmic only by oral stimulation. Several girlfriends of mine say they can only orgasm by oral means, and therefore are always in need of a partner to get off. I feel bad for them, since I know how satisfying masturbation can be and wish they had the ability to enjoy orgasms by themselves. I wonder if they just don't have the right frame of mind. Do you have advice for them on how to reach orgasm by manual means?

A Not if they don't want advice, I don't. Shere Hite's often disputed and sometimes confusing statistics state that 42% of her respondents climaxed regularly (not necessarily solely) through oral stimulation vs. 44% who did so regularly by hand (theirs or their partner's is not made clear). I think all women can reach orgasm on their own if, big if, they are motivated to take the time and trouble to learn. There are excellently written how-to books on this topic; Betty Dodson's and Lonnie Barbach's books come immediately to mind.

However, it is my experience that streams of water — such as from a hand-held shower, a douche bag, a bidet or a spa jet — when pulsed and sprayed against the clitoris and surrounding area, do a good job of mimicking the feel of a human tongue and would be a good way for your friends to begin getting used to a different type of stimulation.

Q I occasionally use a rubber dildo in my solo sexual practice. It's from England, courtesy of an ex-lover. It occurs to me that this could be a carcinogenic material and not worth the occasional pleasure it offers. Do you know if there are any documented problems?

A I'm the wrong one to ask about lurking carcinogens. I still eat bacon. If you're concerned, cover the dildo with a condom when you use it.

Q I read somewhere that sex burns 300 calories. Is the same true of masturbation?

A Whose sexual encounter are we comparing? The soldier coming home after a year of enforced celibacy, the couple celebrating their 25th year together, the one-night stand of two sexual athletes? And whose solo sex — the one who does it during TV commercials, and still has time to fix a snack, or the one who makes it the main entertainment for Sunday afternoon?

Q I'm sure I read in your column that homosexual fantasies are common among heterosexuals. You leave me wondering how common you believe this to be. How could anyone begin to guess, and how is it that one is a heterosexual if one is aroused by homosexual fantasies?

A Alfred Kinsey, of the famous Report, interviewed more than 1000 women and men (which is how we begin to guess about such things) and devised a labeling system for fantasies and activities that is called, appropriately enough, the Kinsey Scale. It goes from 0 to 6. Reading from left to right and having nothing to do with politics, a 0 is a person who is totally heterosexual in thought and deed and a 6 is a person whose fantasies and behavior are completely homosexual. While there are people who fall at either end of the scale, the majority of folk are, for at least some periods in their lives, a 1 through 5 — meaning that whatever the individual's avowed orientation, she/he will sometimes fantasize and/or behave sexually with a same-sex individual if hetero, an opposite-sex individual if gay. Because of this human versatility, more and more people are choosing to call themselves bisexual.

In his historic research, Kinsey assigned rating numbers to his subjects. Current researchers often let these ratings be subjective, and separate out thoughts from activities. A person could then be a 2 in fantasy and a 0 in behavior, or any other disparate set of numbers.

Orientation is the direction you're facing even if you haven't taken a single step.

Q Would you please remind the ladies to draw their curtains before they disrobe? I've got things to do, and I can't get much accomplished when the anticipation of a nightly display of delicious femininity keeps crowding out thoughts of anything else.

A A discrete worded anonymous note to the neighbors in question may nip this problem in the bud. If it does not, keeping custody of your eyes and your thoughts is your problem to deal with as best you can. Given a woman unconsciously undressing in her home vs. a man consciously looking through her windows, public sympathy (and the law) is going to look much harder at you than at her.

Q Help! This problem may break us up. My boyfriend of three years uses pornography whenever he gets a chance. He knows I hate it and he hides it. The more I complain, the more he does it. He says I have to accept him the way he is. He just has to go through every porno magazine out each month, like he might miss something not knowing what these women look like naked!

A An important clue here is "the more you complain, the more he does it." Complaining louder and more often leads to...what? Perhaps you might consider another response — indifference or amusement at his stubborn prurience. If you change your behavior, I'd be willing to bet that his changes, too. That's the way it usually works in power struggles...which is defined by such positions as, "I don't want you to feel the way you feel" and "I want you to do things the right way, which is my way."

Q I've always subscribed to the guidelines of "nobody hurt/mutual consent" in determining parameters in sex play, but recently I've come up against a situation that throws that into question. My lover, a woman who has moved from a place of ultra-shyness and unwillingness to experiment to a more adventuresome realm over the eight months of our relationship, enjoys anal intercourse, which is fine with me. Recently, though, she has requested "small pains," as she calls them, to amplify her pleasure. At first this involved pinching at pressure point stimulation. Then she asked that while we were engaged in anal intercourse, I tap the back of her skull with a small hammer. My problem with this activity is (1) I worry that the application of a hammer, however lightly, is dangerous, and (2) on the occasions we have done this, I find I slip into repulsive (to me) sadomasochistic fantasies. Please share your thoughts on this.

A (1) The application of hammer to skull, no matter how lightly, is a very bad idea. You are right; it is dangerous and would be even if you were not in an aroused state, when anyone's ability to judge anything is seriously impaired. I urge you to refuse such requests. (2) You are already engaged in sadomasochistic behavior — pushing the limits of pleasure and pain. If in your fantasies you go beyond your own limits of behavior, well, that's what fantasy is, a mental testing ground for limits. If your fantasies repel you because you are afraid you might act on them, wittingly or not, it's time for further exploration, perhaps with a therapist. A group in San Francisco called QSM has been putting on a series of Saturday workshops in S/M education. Recent topics dealt with defining and demystifying S/M and what S/M people do and how they do it. For more info write P.O.Box 882242, San Francisco, CA 94188.

Q I am currently involved in a wonderful relationship with my sister. I'm 24; she's 20. For many years we tried to deny our mutual attraction. However, in the last year we have come to realize that societal restrictions are less important than a true meeting of souls. What started as gentle strokes and fondling has escalated into the most caring sexual relationship I have ever experienced. Last month she mentioned how nice it would be if we only could have a child. Last night, as we were snuggling, she brought up the idea again. I felt that although it's a nice idea, the risk of genetic disease outweighs the benefits. On the other hand, I'm no medical expert. What are the odds of having a healthy child?

A If that is your only concern, the person to address it is a genetic counselor who will need to take an extremely thorough family medical history to come up with an educated guess. In my opinion there needs to be a few other considerations as well. Your existing family, for one, and how they might deal with such an open acknowledgment of your relationship. Not that they need to be happy about your choice, but your sister is still underage and your relationship is flat out illegal (therefore punishable) in most, if not all, states. You really must evaluate how you two (or three or more) would live in a world that views violation of the incest taboo as a crime, a sickness, and/or a sin before you plan any family additions.

Q My lover has put an interesting twist on the current trend of carrying one's culinary condiments with her when she goes out to eat. She says it turns her on to sprinkle my come onto her salad when lunching with her girlfriends and business associates. She transfers it to a little antique bottle after I come in her mouth; then we insure its viscosity by adding a tad of chardonnay. My question concerns safety. How long is it safe to store this concoction? She keeps it refrigerated and carries it in her purse the next day. Incidentally, I followed her lead and doused my Reuben sandwich with the stuff at a downtown deli with my raquetball pals and got a worldclass hard-on. I'm not sure if it was from holding the secret ("It's a vitamin supplement, guys") or it has something to do with latent desires to suck cock. Life's interesting, isn't it?

A Umm hmm. I'm nodding because my mouth is full with my lunch and now I'm not quite sure what to do with it. Ejaculate is a perishable commodity, so refrigerating it and using it as promptly as possible is a good idea. Other than that, all I can say to either you or she is if you plan to share your food, put a condom on it first. Bon appetit!

Q I'm a single man in my mid-thirties. I've also been a secret transvestite since childhood. Recently a woman friend, my best friend's wife actually, seems to have guessed. I think the idea really turns her on. Several times recently she's suggested that I dress up in her clothes. At the moment, these suggestions center around my attending a

Halloween party dressed as her and she as me. Her husband says he doesn't have a problem with this, but I'm afraid of the possible consequences. On the other hand, I would love to realize this fantasy. Suggestions?

A Yes, if it's not too late, think this one through quite carefully. The possible consequences of having your best friend's wife as a coconspirator in erotic activities, even though those activities may not constitute adultery as most define it, sounds dangerous to me. So does being forced out of the closet sooner than you might wish to an audience not hand-picked by you; since she has guessed, others may, too. If you are not absolutely sure you can keep this one-time event as a secretly titillating but harmless occasion, I would forgo the pleasure and look for other places and playmates with which to experiment.

Q Several months ago I met my current girlfriend on vacation. Anyway, we "hit it off." She shared with me her joy in being spanked. As our relationship has developed, I found I enjoy spanking her as much as she enjoys my spankings. Here's my concern: I want her to spank me but I'm concerned about "role reversal" if she does. What should I do?

A Discuss it with her and see how the idea sounds when brought out in the open. Does it excite her, too? Might the role reversal which concerns you be part of what makes the situation hot for you and/ or her? If you decide to try it, agree upon some guidelines — such as a "safe word," something you can use other than the obvious "No! Stop!" which might be part of the game when and if you want to change the scenario. ("Yellow" for slow down, "Red" for stop are common ones.) With as many safeguards as you can think of agreed upon beforehand, she may then surprise you with taking over at some point in the future. If you don't like it, you don't have to repeat it. If you do, you may have to rethink your equations of being active with being in control.

Q We're a cohabiting couple, with two regular day jobs and a young child, searching for imaginative solutions to our DINS (double income, no sex) syndrome. One idea we have is to meet during lunchtime somewhere between our Civic Center and Financial District jobs for a noontime erotic encounter — which is also a great way to diet. However, we can't afford to pay a full day's rate at a legitimate hotel, and we're leery of delving unguided into the Tenderloin to find a hotel offering hourly rates. Is there a source that we could consult to assist in securing a clean, discrete, affordable space? Cable TV with adult movies would be a plus.

A You might check out the local sex paper and swingers mags to see who advertises there. Otherwise, I'd phone likely looking hotels/motels in your preferred area and ask about rates for "a business client periodically in town for the day who needs a place to shower and change." Many places will offer such legitimate short-term rentals who do not want to be represented as hot-sheet hostelries. If a made-up bed with mattress is not a necessity and a hot tub will do as an entertainment substitute for a TV set, check out hot tub clubs and spas, often found in hotels.

In reference to the letter about where to go for an afternoon quickie: Advise your readers to go to any large downtown bank that offers safe deposit box services. A careful search will show that privacy can be guaranteed within the intimacy of some safe-deposit customer rooms if you avoid those with half doors or glass enclosures. To avoid nasty stares, it would be wise to rent a larger, more expensive box, rather than the minimum cheapskate container. In it, place your love lubricants, condoms, and sexual toys. For convenience sake, the parties may wish to carry a towel with them in a heavy-duty manila envelope. Be aware that unless both parties are named on the signature card, a special form must be used if an additional party is taken into the private room.

A Hey, I bet you're the kind of guy who never gets caught without ice cubes in the tray or correct change for the bus, either. I thank you, my readers thank you, but downtown branch managers are going to be cursing your name.

Q Although I'm married, I am a regular customer of massage parlors. I enjoy being masturbated. It's always safe and, in the right hands, both relaxing and exciting. Recently, out of curiosity I decided to see what it was like to be massaged by another man. To my pleasant surprise, the experience resulted in one of the most satisfying orgasms of my life. Now I'm hooked on masseurs as well as masseuses, but ads in the mainstream press offer very few options for this type of service. Could you suggest some resources for this otherwise straight man to explore this new dimension of his sexuality?

A If you were offering services primarily sought by gay men, where would you put your advertising dollars? Ads for "complete" massage by men and for men abound in all the gay-oriented newspapers.

Q I am a 26-year-old woman who desperately wants your advice. I'm afraid that anyone else would think I was crazy. My questions concern my unusual sexual fantasies. Whenever I masturbate, I think about someone — either a man or a woman — having an "accident" by wetting their pants in public. This did happen to me a few months ago waiting in a long bathroom line at a concert. As it was happening I found it embarrassing, but when it was over and I was standing there in a puddle in my soaked jeans I suddenly found it arousing! Now I think about it happening to others and it turns me on. Am I "sick"? Do others have this secret fantasy? Should I seek counseling? Where do I go to find out more?

A Urine and the act of urinating is such a relatively common sexual turn-on that one of the twelve chapters in Nancy Friday's 1980 book on men's sexual fantasies, *Men in Love*, is devoted to the topic. She uses the popular phrase "water sports." Urinating as a sexual act is also often referred to as "golden showers." If you think about it, it's a logical source of sexual fantasy, combining, as it does, early memory associations of both pleasure (warmth and bladder pressure release) and the erotic appeal of the forbidden (associated with toilet training). You only need counseling if your feelings about your fantasies continue to disturb you greatly.

This is to the woman who had the fantasy about involuntary urinating. Since the topic of her letter is so rarely discussed, it is no wonder that people who have these fantasies wonder if they're crazy. I think that in many ways I am not unusual. During the early days of my relationship with my girlfriend, we explored these fantasies. Now we have let it drop and become more reserved with each other about this. My sex life with her is fulfilling, but I still find myself often preoccupied with fantasies not too different from the letter writer.

The chapter in Nancy Friday's *Men In Love*, "Water Sports," is only partly on the mark about this phenomenon and she sounds faintly disapproving. Friday does not believe that women have such fantasies, but my guess is that women are socialized to suppress such strongly forbidden feelings. I think part of the appeal of such fantasies, as opposed to such overt acts as "golden showers," has to do with the involuntary release of everybody's hidden sexuality. Many people regularly suppress their sexuality, particularly during adolescence (when I first discovered this fantasy), yet we all release hot liquid from our genital areas on a regular basis. I would include this point along with yours and Friday's about men's fantasies of women who are out of control.

Enclosed is a stamped envelope. I would be very grateful if you would please forward it to the woman who wrote you about this to let her know she is not the only one with such fantasies.

A I cannot forward mail, I am sorry. But by your writing and by my publishing, she and probably some others as well, will feel less uncomfortable about themselves.

Q My lover and I are still hot for each other after 30 years. This isn't a problem! We want to have someone take a black-and-white photograph of us nude in an embrace, rather like the classic sculpture by Rodin. We don't know enough about light and shadows to get a good result by tripod and cable release. Who could do it for us so that the result is so timeless and beautiful we could hang it in a museum (but won't)? It will go in our home and be loved for what it means — thirty years of horny bliss.

A Make a tour of art galleries and shows, find a photographer whose work you both like, even if the subject matter is nonerotic. Take her or his card and one of you phone and state your wants. No photographer will be insulted to hear you appreciate the work you saw and to be asked about a possible commission. If she or he would not take such a special project, a knowledgeable referral could follow. There are photographers who specialize in "boudoir portraits" and so advertise in papers just like this one. (By the way, congratulations. I love hearing about success stories like yours.)

Q I'm a woman in my mid-thirties who's been single for almost two years. I've always found masturbation a decent substitute when there's no lover in my life. However, recently I have discovered a frighteningly wonderful substitute. Since my chow, Mr. T, was a puppy, I trained him to perform cunnilingus by enticing him by rubbing a bit of Alpo on my inner thigh. He took to this immediately and now performs the act with no Alpo. I've been engaging in this activity weekly for almost a year and I am concerned that I will have problems breaking this habit. Do you believe that this could be keeping me from having normal sexual relations with a person? And is there any possibility that I may contract any weird diseases? Please answer in your column as I am too ashamed to discuss this with anyone.

A First you need to know that sexually assaulting an animal (which is not defined) "for the purpose of arousing or gratifying the sexual desire of a person" is listed as a misdemeanor in the California penal code, punishable by up to a year in the county jail. Second, the SPCA and animal-rights-advocate readers need to know that by answering you (or any of the other letters in this column), I am not endorsing the behavior in question; for many people there is a very real issue of nonconsent and power abuse in any human/animal sexual contacts. That said, your disease concern can be handled by having your vet check the animal for any parasite condition which might be transmissible. As for a dog (or a vibrator or any other nonhuman stimulant) being a substitute for a person-to-person connection — good as the critter might be at giving head—when the two of you can giggle together, when he brings you chicken soup if you're laid up with a cold, when he proffers flowers, a backrub, or a goodnight kiss, then I'd worry.

I can't believe that woman would feed her dog Alpo. It has artificial coloring.*

---

*This letter gets my vote for the briefest and most "Berkeley" quibble of the year.

Q At my lover's request, I shaved all the hair off my pubic area, and now I have a few qualms and questions. First, how unusual is this? Do a lot of women shave their vaginas to have better sex? Second, are there any adverse health effects? Are there preferred shaving methods? Finally, are there creams or oils particularly suited to such sensitive skin after shaving?

A First of all, you could not possibly shave your vagina since that's inside your body. What you shaved was your mons and outer labia. Look at any pin-up magazine and you'll see women pubicly shorn in varying degrees, from completely bald to neatly trimmed little topiary puffs. You won't see many totally natural pubic patches since our culture frowns on hair growth outside the "bikini area" and very few adult females manage that feat without help. Like the shaving of armpits, another very sensitive area, who does this and who doesn't is a matter of personal preference. If seeing you shaven there turns your lover on, I suppose it would lead to "better sex." Any newly defuzzed body part will be more sensitive to touch and subject to skin irritations and ingrown hairs. Whatever has worked for you on other sensitive skin areas will probably work there. You can also experiment with different razors, depilatory creams, or waxing. To soothe any minor irritations, I usually recommend unscented cornstarch.

Q Honey and I met at a swing party house about a year ago. He's 26, I'm 24, and we do the parties once or twice a month. Kinky I like, but weird is weird. He wants to go down on me right after I make it with a guy, especially if the guy is black. He's talked to me about a fantasy of another guy doing me from behind and him going down on me so he can get the load sooner. Another fantasy is he wants me to give a guy head and then swap the load from my mouth while we make it. Other women he's been with have talked to me about his interests and I learned he is not the only man with this interest. He is not bisexual that I know of and we are totally up front about who we are with one another. I tried to find reference to this action in the U.C. library which has some pretty exotic stuff. Honey says it has been written about since the Romans. I would like your thoughts here.

A Regarding unusual sexual practices, it usually goes something like, "If I enjoy it, it's creative; if I don't, it's weird and perverted." The word "kinky" can be either positive or negative but usually refers to "practices which I personally have never engaged in." While I can't quote you reference chapter and verse about Honey's turn-on, it is familiar to all the sex educators, players, and sexual sophisticates I spoke to about it. As you surmised, most agree that the erotic charge carries with it a strong homosexual — or at least phallocentric — component. All other considerations aside, I'm sure you're aware that dealing with the ejaculate of unknowns — vaginally, orally, or anally — is very risky business these days.

Q My wife and I recently attended a play with another couple. In the darkened theater with my coat in my lap, I unzipped my fly and took out my cock. I made it throb and move up and down by moving my muscles. I pushed my coat down on the left side exposing myself to the possible view of the woman, but hiding it from my wife's vision. In the dim light I could see what I was doing, and I'm sure the woman could have seen if she had looked at my crotch. After a moment, after the thrill of potential exposure satisfactorily registered with me, I pulled the coat back, covering up my actions, and I finished jerking off.

I realize this is not acceptable social behavior and I don't want to break the law, but I have a need to have a woman watch me jerk off. I don't want it to be my wife (to whom I am sexually faithful), and I don't want to go to a prostitute, nor do I want it to be some shocked screaming woman who calls the police. Would a sex therapist allow me to jerk off in front of her while in a therapy session discussing my problem? I don't want her to be involved with me in any sexual contact. I only want her to be a consenting adult witness to my activity. I believe the need to have a woman watch is rooted in some childhood event.

A No, a reputable therapist will not be party to a sexual act, which your masturbation is. Nonconsensual flashing is not only unacceptable social behavior, it is illegal, so your social friends won't do (unless you ask and they agree). You say your wife won't do, nor a commercial partner. You leave yourself few options. Have you considered the live "girlie" shows in porn movie houses where women dance and tease while men watch and jerk off? You can rent a private booth where you can see and be seen, or sit in the theater seating, which now may have an additional erotic charge for you.

Q I am writing to you because I want to break into the sex industry and I'd like your advice and referrals. I want to be a high-class hooker for women, perhaps "call boy" or "courtier" (rather than courtesan). I want to bring to this profession sophistication, good taste, plus genuine caring for my clients. I am an attractive bisexual man, very experienced sexually, sensual and sexy, adventurous and passionate. My goal is to find sex work where I can serve women's needs and fulfill their most outrageous desires in a compassionate and considerate way. I don't want to work the streets. I want to get paid very well. How can I get connected with a high-class bordello that serves women, or luxury hotels or cruises or tropical resorts? Got any ideas?

A I was unable to locate any bordello in Nevada (the only state they are legal) which caters to women. I doubt there is a fast-track management traineeship in the profession you describe. You just go out there and be an entrepreneur. Hanging out at resorts, hotels, cruises, where there are women with money and leisure and vacation devil-may-care attitudes, is an excellent way to begin, but that costs, so you are betting on the come, so to speak. These places won't hire you to service their clients, so negotiating with any individual women — who may be shocked at the idea of paying for male services — is up to you. For more info on the sex "industry," you might write to U.S. Prostitutes Collective, P.O.Box 14512 San Francisco, CA 94114 (include SASE).

Q Perhaps you have heard the rumor about a famous male movie star who was recently admitted to Cedars of Lebanon Hospital to have a gerbil removed from his rectum. Perhaps it is just a rumor and this movie star did not really do this, but my asking around has made it clear to me that this practice does indeed go on in certain circles.

My questions are: What sort of people engage in this practice? Do the animals have a chance of getting out alive? Gerbils bite. Does this mean their teeth are removed? Ecccch. I thought I'd heard of everything. (Gerbils cannot be purchased in California, by the way, because of the impact they would have on our environment if they got loose. This means that someone must be breeding them or importing them illegally.) I am hoping you will say this is all a fabrication, and it really doesn't occur at all; or if it does occur, that the people who do this take really good care of the little critters who are not harmed by it one bit.

A I wonder why gerbils are so often the theoretical "partner" of choice, and not, say, moles or gophers, or even common field mice. I thought the reason there were so few gerbils around California was that no one wanted to leave her/himself open to accusations of nefarious sexual doings. If one is so inclined, the same objective could be accomplished with a less notorious small fuzzy rodent. (Just kidding, animal rights folks.) There is no doubt that people put the most astonishing array of objects into their body orifices, just ask any emergency room worker, so I suppose furry critters are among the found objects; however, I sincerely doubt that any type or class of people make this a regular practice. Of course, any critter so used would die; it's almost impossible to train them to snorkel.

Q A few months ago my girlfriend asked me to help her take an enema, which I did. I held the bag and inserted the nozzle and controlled the flow — the whole thing. She taught me how to do it. In the process I was aroused. I assumed it was because I was looking at her naked body. A few days later I saw the syringe hanging on the back of her bathroom door and I was aroused again at the sight of it. Then recently I saw a syringe in the drug store and became aroused one more time...just by looking at it! Now I find myself fantasizing about giving her another enema and am thinking about it for myself. Any comments about this fixation I seem to have now?

A I bet that when you were little and received a toy that appealed to you, you thought about it and played with it and checked out similar ones that belonged to other kids. That's not a "fixation," it's a turn-on. It usually diminishes with time, but sometimes not. Sometimes those with a favorite red truck grow up to be a fire fighter with a lifelong fascination. Enema play is a turn-on for many people — having to do with the secretive and forbidden, perhaps with early childhood memories, with dominance and submission, with "naughty" parts and products. My only caution here is that you be aware of cleanliness concerns should you or she come into contact with each other's feces.

Q My boyfriend recently gave me a set of Ben-Wa balls for my birthday. I eagerly tried them according to the instructions: "Insert deep into the vagina and rock gently." Inserting them deeply was no problem. Even when I tried not to they migrated there of their own accord. Unfortunately, once they were in, I couldn't feel them at all. No sensations. Sexual response is not usually a problem for me. As my boyfriend diplomatically puts it, I am "medium to large"; in fact, extra large. Could the balls just be too small for my vagina size? What should I do to increase pleasure? And are there any risks associated with Ben-Wa balls — getting stuck, lost, infections?

A Checking with the knowledgeable folks at Good Vibrations, the grownups' toy store, corroborated my own experience and yours, that there is more mystique than muscle in those little metal balls. Maybe ancient Asian women were built differently then modern women of all races. Maybe larger ones would do something different than a super tampon would, but I doubt it. Anyone interested in experimenting nonetheless, sterilize them before insertion. They can't get lost. The vagina is finite. Standing up and walking around will allow the balls to drop down to easy reach, if not out onto the floor.

Q I am a 35-year-old professional, married for 7 years and in a monogamous relationship with my wife. I have had very little sexual experience except with her. My fantasy is voyeurism. Since puberty I have been attracted to nonviolent, straight hardcore pornography. Although I enjoy a pleasant sex life with my wife, because my libido exceeds hers a bit, I fill the gap with masturbation. I would love to watch hetero sex in person with no participation. The only time I've done this was when I accidentally walked in on a friend and that time I immediately left the room. Are there any safe places where I can indulge in my fantasy without sleaziness, fear of exposure, etc.? I'd like this to be very private. Should I stick to the VCR?

A You have a very explicit fantasy which you might (I hear some doubt) like to enact, but only under very specific conditions. Would paying someone who does sex for money to arrange such a show for you be acceptable? What about attending a swing party where there are often people who enjoy being watched? Could you put an ad in an alternative paper or answer one? Would arranging to go away for a weekend with another couple of your acquaintance, and then leveling about your wishes, be possible for you? If you did stick to your VCR, would it be more exciting to watch amateur films wherein the couple being filmed are doing what they like to do, rather than acting out a commercially typical script? What you want is harmless enough and fairly easy to accomplish. Consider each of your requirements and then what you are willing to do to accomplish them.

Q The very first time my girlfriend and I had sex together was in the walk-in refrigerator at the restaurant where we both worked at the time. Since then we have done it in many other cold places, most notably in a snow drift several feet deep in her parents' Vermont backyard during last year's Christmas visit. During that same trip she also wanted to make love on the surface of a frozen lake, but I declined on the grounds that it was too dangerous.

Our sex life in more conventional places (like a nice warm bed) is just fine. It's just that she likes to supplement this every few weeks with sex in a cold (and usually semipublic) place. I've always been cooperative when she suggests these little outings; after all, she's usually game for my new sexual ideas, but I can't honestly say that the act itself is physically pleasurable for me under these cold circumstances. Getting and maintaining an erection requires a concerted effort of will, and an orgasm, for me at least, is usually out of the question. The primary appeal for me is just seeing how excited and happy it makes my girlfriend.

My question is: Have you ever encountered any other people, male or female, with this particular preference? Is there a name for it? What do you suppose causes it? Is it dangerous? (After the snowdrift incident, during which we were completely naked and almost entirely submerged in snow for almost an hour, I had some concerns about hypothermia and frostbite, although the constant physical exertion probably helped.) Please reply soon, Isadora. The weather is getting colder and my girlfriend is getting hotter.

A Sheesh, and some guys complain because their girlfriends want 10 minutes of head! How about calling it cryoerotica or (doubly appropriate) frigiphilia? Have I ever heard of such a preference? Not specifically, although I'd guess the semipublic part, which is quite common, plays a major part in the turn-on. But if an object, act, or combination thereof exists anywhere in human imagination, you can bet that someone somewhere gets off on it. Why is anybody's guess. I can't think of any other dangers beside the obvious one of hanging out in subfreezing weather, which you are already aware of. Did your mother ever tell you not to make funny faces or odd body positions because you might freeze that way? If so, who are you going to believe?

♀◀♂◀♀▲♂▼♀▲♂►♀▼♂

Who's Who:
Read the Labels

♀◀♂◀♀▲♂▼♀▲♂►♀▼♂

Q The man I'm dating admitted to me once, back when we were just friends, that he liked to wear women's clothing and that he would make a good lesbian. After we started dating and I asked him about it, he claimed he wasn't serious. His roommate is a closeted gay, so should I assume this man is a bisexual? Gay? Heterosexual with a twist? I love him and I don't understand the denial of something I absolutely know he once told me. Once a transvestite always a transvestite? Do people change that much in a year? Please help.

A Liking to wear women's clothes does not make a man gay or bisexual or anything other than a man who likes to wear women's clothes, in this case, might even be *did* like. Of course, people's activities can change, even their preferences. Perhaps his current reticence is due to the scarier risk of your disapproval now that you two are lovers. Rather than reduce this issue to a "You said it!" "No I didn't" argument, remind him again of your willingness to discuss the topic should he ever want to, of your interest in it (if you genuinely have one), and then, if you can, let it be. Everyone is entitled to his or her secrets.

Q The guy I lived with and I broke up several months ago. I was upset and had sex with his best friend. Not a good idea, I know. When I phoned my old boyfriend to see if we could get back together again, I found out that he and the friend of his I had sex with are now lovers. He never mentioned any homosexual feelings to me before. My question is, how much of that do you think is my fault?

A Do you think your boyfriend said "That's it, I've had it with women because of the way she treated me so now I'm turning to men?" It doesn't usually work that way. My guess is that in dealing, as friends, with each man's feelings about you and your behavior, the subject of their feelings toward each other also got brought up...and acted upon. You may have been a catalyst, but certainly not the cause of their turning to each other.

Q I am a mature biological female with an orientation toward gay males. The term "Fag Hag" doesn't seem to fit my male self-image or the dominant male sexual role I prefer. Finding partners hasn't been impossible, even though straight men go running into the night and gay men always return to male lovers. What would you call me? It would be helpful for me to know if I have a label and if there are others.

A You might be a transsexual (a man in a woman's body, in this case a gay man) or you might be perversely creative. I'd have to know more about both your fantasies and your preferred activities in order to classify you according to The American Psychiatric Association's DSM-III (R), a standard diagnostic tool I try to avoid. If you are troubled by your sexuality seek the services of a sex counselor/ therapist and the two of you can explore the possibilities. Whatever you come up with, I assure you that you are not the only.

✍I appreciate your efforts to avoid DSM-III (R) classification of the woman who wrote to you describing her "dominant male sexual role" preferences. Her status or condition is no more than that, a status or condition, not an illness or disorder, and no, she is definitely not alone. She can find kindred spirits in ETVC which, though primarily oriented toward male-to-female TVs and TSs, also includes female-to-male TSs and those like your writer who are attracted to sexually feminine males. (ETVC, P.O.Box 426486, San Francisco, CA 94142-6486)

✍You published a letter from a female who wondered if she was a "fag hag." Miraculously, you suggested she might be a female-to-gay male transsexual, which is exactly what I am. I think the writer of that letter would benefit from knowing other females who are attracted to gay men and what they have done about it. The illustrated paperback book *Information for the Female-to-Male Trans-sexual* by Lou Sullivan is $10. (FTM 1827 Haight St., #164, San Francisco, CA 94117)

A Thank you for letting me know about this fascinating new resource. May I add that all females who have a tendency to be attracted to gay males, or all females who want to play the sexually dominant role with men (or even gay men in particular) do not fall into the category of transvestites or transsexuals. Some are heterosexual women who have a vested interest in not getting what they want, and some are women who simply like a challenge.

Q Is homosexuality a genuine form of sexuality equivalent to hetero-sexuality, or is it a perversion that people are pretending is an acceptable sexual alternative because that is the socially correct opinion these days? If two men rubbing up against each other can be considered sex, then why not a man and a tree or a man and a bicycle?

A Why not indeed? If you are a man who gets off on bark, bikes, or buttocks (male or female or gender unknown), then rubbing against the object of your choice will probably be very sexy for you. There isn't An Answer to your question. Societal norm *is* what defines what is okay sex and what is perversion for most people. Look at the Golden Age of Greece where homosexual love was seen as noble, and heterosexual sex only as pragmatic baby making. In the matter of partnered sex, by the way, there are only a limited number of body-part innies and outies, so what any two people do together sexually is likely to be similar to whatever any other twosome can and will do regardless of whether the pair is mixed or matched. Therefore, many homosexual couples do more than rub against each other and many heterosexual couples do less.

Q I've been in the process of coming out to my relatives in the Bible Belt. As "a bachelor living in San Francisco," it ought to be pretty obvious. Oddly, the relatives I expected to reject me have not, but my intellectual relatives, whom I thought would be accepting, have given me the cold shoulder. Of course, the AIDS epidemic has put a strain on all gay-straight relationships, but wouldn't you expect college professors to be more worldly and tolerant of sexual diver-sity?

A Alas, no, not even more educated. A psychiatrist (that's an M.D.) at a recent party voiced aloud his concern about catching AIDS from the vegetable dip. He feared someone infected might dip, munch, and then have the temerity to redip. Stupidity is no respecter of degrees. There's a reason for the popularity of such phrases as "You never know who your friends are." Those who embrace you, will do so because of their feelings for you, not homosexuality in the abstract. Those who shun you may be doing so because of their feelings for homosexuality in the concrete. Since you're unlikely to know the whys of their cold shoulder, you might write them off as closet cases.

Q Please bear with me while I gripe about something inextricably linked to sexuality: the availability of housing. Very often while looking for a shared rental, I am asked about my sexuality. I always feel like yelling "What the hell business is it of yours?" I recently called a place that was looking for a lesbian housemate and the man who answered said that the sexuality issue was pretty non-negotiable. Do they monitor all possible contacts or have a camera installed over the bed? I could see specifying "Discrete people only" or "Non-monogamous need not apply" or anything that directly affects a shared living situation. I really don't understand this obsession with knowing and controlling the gender of the housemate's sleeping partners. Do you?

A A gay householder may be hetero- or bi-phobic as easily as the other way around and may expect prejudice from anyone else not of their stripe. They may be making assumptions that one group is neater, more reliable, less promiscuous, whatever, than another. The ad placers you encounter may be confusing labels with behavior. Rather than argue the premise or the stated requirements, I'd investigate any promising ad. Then, if you like the set-up, ask what their reasons were for specifying a particular sexuality and then refute those specifically: "I am not a ____, but I am very comfortable with the ____ lifestyle" or "I don't call myself a ____ but since I don't generally entertain overnight guests, it's unlikely to affect our homelife." You may not encounter much better luck in finding a living space than you already have, but at least you will be doing your bit for values clarification.

Q I once heard that if your first sexual experience is homosexual, then you will be prone to homosexual fantasies without being gay. This seems to be the case with me. What have you heard?

A Our sexual patterning is not that simple. We are not ducklings who imprint and attach to the first visible moving object. Sexologist John Money has written several books on the whys and wherefores of our individual "love maps," as he calls them, and I suppose his guesses are as good as any. Certainly our earliest (not necessarily our first remembered) sexual experiences color our sexuality forever, but if your theory were correct what would we make of people whose first sexual experiences were same-sex and who continued to be homosexual?

Q My wife for 20 years, although orgasmic, has never shown the slightest interest in sex, never initiates it, and is almost totally passive during it. This has always been very distressful to me, but my frequently expressed concerns have no effect. I always thought this was an individual problem. Recently I saw one of those ethnic-humor joke books. A good number of the jokes about Jewish women revolved around the theme of lack of interest in sex and passivity during sex. I had never been aware of this particular ethnic stereotype, but the image does fit my wife who is Jewish. Is there some cultural basis for such an attitude toward sex?

A I suppose I could come up with one — such as a traditionally persecuted people directing their daughters to marry for reasons of physical and financial security, resulting in depressed women in loveless marriages. But I could also dispute that as so much socio-logical horse pucky about a totally baseless stereotype. As opposed to the Catholic position of sex being confined to the function of procreation, Jewish tradition has always emphasized the joy, indeed the "blessedness" of enthusiastic conjugal sex.

Q My coworkers and I have been debating homosexual relationships, in particular male homosexuality. We feel the best route to being understanding is to try to understand. The question is: do gay men take turns in the bedroom? Does each one find his sexual niche (i.e., giving) and stick to it? One prevailing theory in my office is that in long-term homosexual relationships one person consistently gives and the other likes to receive. Any info would be most appreciated as we have no one else to ask.

A Your question seems to presume that "they," gay men, are different from "us," whatever the gender and orientation of you and your coworkers (straight men? gay women? bisexual women and men? everything but gay men?). By and large the arrangements couples work out about who always, never, or sometimes does what to the other is far more a product of the preferences of the individuals, than of their sex or orientation. For instance, Person A usually initiates because that person is more assertive or has a greater desire, Person B blisses out and forgets to do anything at all unless re-minded. That's one pattern, and can appear as often in hetero couples as in same-sex ones, and maybe, due to cultural conditioning, even more frequently. Variations abound, preferences can change, and while leopards seldom change their spots, occasionally a constant "giver" in one relationship can be the predominant "taker" in another.

Q I want to get right to the point and ask the difference between liking someone a great deal and being in love. I am a 20-year-old man who has never been in a relationship with a woman. The Other is around my age and I believe enjoys my company as well as I enjoy his. We have common interests. Often I find myself just standing and talking with him for at least an hour and never getting bored or tired. When I am with him something extraordinary clicks between us and I feel energized. Each time we do separate I feel a twinge of regret and a void. I wish I could spend the rest of eternity with him. I do not see myself as gay (being a virgin I can't prove or disprove that, can I?) nor does he present himself as gay. Do I find myself liking him because I have not found his female equivalent? What's going on? Have I found love or just my best friend?

A Defining sexual orientation is no more a simple either/or than like/ love is. Thinking of both concepts as a continuum (from not liking at all to being head-over-heels besotted, from thinking only and always of women to thinking only and always of men) might be closer to the truth, but it's really not an ideal analogy either. Your virginity is not an essential issue, since had you slept once with a woman, it isn't as if you would have been be inoculated against same-sex feelings. Personally, when I am drawn to someone, male or female, it feels similar. The same qualities of wit, intelligence, self-acceptance attract me in people of both sexes. I long to spend great amounts of time with this new object of my interest — talking, listening, gazing, touching. What makes me define as heterosexual, rather than bisexual, is that expressions of affection for my male friends usually includes a desire for body contact that either doesn't exist or isn't as compelling with the female friends. To me that is a small but important difference.

Be honest with yourself. Avoid labels and cosmic absolutes. Do you want to do sexual things to and with this man? If so, how much a part of your attraction to him is that? Have you ever had strong feelings for other people, men or women? How did they differ? If you're really brave, you might direct some conversations with your friend to the nature of love and friendship. Finding out his feelings may help you clarify your own.

Q I am a 20-year-old male, very attractive. I've been with a lot of women and it's sometimes played out. I've thought of being Bi. Then I thought I was going crazy. Should I try being with a guy to find out what is going on with my hormones?

A Whether you are having sex with men, women, or fruits and vegetables has nothing to do with hormones, nor does turning toward men for sex have to do with being bored with sex with women. Most people find enough happy surprises in sex with one gender or the other to keep them pleasantly amused for a lifetime. My suggestion would be to take a sexual education and enhancement course at a community college or elsewhere for more information on what people do together for pleasure. I also suggest looking into psychotherapy. No matter how busy you've been, being "played out" at 20 just doesn't wash.

Q I feel as if I have been plagued with this problem most of my adult life and still have not reached a comfortable solution even after years of therapy. Every time I start a new relationship (and these have been predominately with women) I end up fantasizing about men. I have a number of close men friends, both gay and straight, so it's not just the company of men I long for. In fact, I'm not sure what it is I'm missing when I'm in a relationship with a woman. I have been fairly honest about my conflict with my honey, but even this admission does not alleviate the pain I go through. The same conflict has occurred when I have had relationships with men: I miss women. Any insights?

A Several possibilities do occur, but I try to refrain from psychologizing (e.g., "The trouble with you is ...") in favor of seeking solutions. The most obvious one is to refrain from monogamous relationships and aim instead for having a male lover and a female lover at all times. Another is to commit to your honey and simply enjoy your fantasies as fantasies, the way most people who have exclusive sexual agreements do, regardless of who else they fantasize about. Perversely wanting precisely what one does not have, however, is a wonderful way to keep oneself in a state of perpetual unhappiness, so if you are not still in therapy I'd consider re-entering it; if you are, I'd consider the possibilities of other therapists.

Q I am a fairly happily married woman in my thirties. When I was single I had an active heterosexual social life. However, ever since I was a small child I have been attracted to women, especially those with very large breasts. I have never had a lesbian relationship, but often fantasize about large-breasted women, even during sex with my husband. I find men attractive as well, but nothing turns me on like large breasts. It has taken me years to face this part of myself and quite some time to actually tell anyone about it (you). My question is this: am I a lesbian, a bisexual, a woman with a strange fixation? I would also like to know if there are other women who feel the same way as I do. I'm beginning to really wonder about myself.

A I firmly believe that what label you wear regarding your sexual behavior, whether strange or normal for you, heterosexual, bi-sexual, or homosexual, is entirely up to you. Whatever best fits your sense of yourself is a good way to categorize yourself in your own mind. Many women who see themselves as heterosexual are so obsessed with the attractiveness of large breasts that they undergo expensive, painful and risky surgery to have them. I see the key question for you being not what to call yourself, but what to do about your feelings. Reading and learning more about other women's sexual fantasies may help you place yourself comfortably in relation to other women, and to decide what, if anything, your next step might be.

I am writing in response to the letter from the woman who fanta-sized about large breasts while making love to her husband. I, too, am a married heterosexual woman just turning 30 and I know I am not a lesbian. I have never let that beautiful part of my sexual fantasizing make me feel strange or indifferent to my husband. I feel there is nothing wrong with it, I've been doing it for years. At one time I wondered why, but attributed it to thumbing through my father's Playboy magazines as a child and fondling my own breasts during masturbation. So you are not alone, nor should you feel like you have to classify yourself into some sexual niche. Enjoy it!

A Read on for more support.

I, too, fantasize about large-breasted women, particularly during masturbation. As a 36-year-old heterosexual woman, this is something I've never dared discuss with anybody. Aside from the enjoyment I derive from my private imaginings, I also experience feelings of envy and longing. My breasts, although cute as buttons, are just about button-sized. Since my very early teens, I've desired at least a mid- to full-sized B cup. I value my health and my body, but when I see teenagers who have larger breasts than me I feel cheated. You wrote "many women are so obsessed with the attractiveness of large breasts that they undergo expensive, painful, and risky surgery to have them." Are you opposed to this surgery?

A Not necessarily. While it is painful, risky, and expensive, there are many women who feel the results are worth it all.

Q We are having a discussion in our office about the ability of an individual to achieve orgasm after having surgical sexual reassignment. Do males who have been transformed into females have vaginal sensations and orgasms? If so, how is this physically possible? Conversely, do females-into-males have erections and ejaculations? If so, how?

A This is very basic anatomy, so those of you in the know, forgive me if I oversimplify. Orgasms are a product more of fantasy than of friction. (You may have heard me say that before.) Many paraplegics who have lost all genital sensation are capable of having orgasms through stimulation of other body parts, as are some others who, while having genital sensation, also have other exquisitely erogenous zones as well, such as nipples or neck. Males-to-female TSs usually have their new vaginas constructed from the nerve-abundant flesh of their former penises and their labia from scrotal skin. For many, genital sensitivity is eventually regainable after the surgical trauma. For those who permanently lose sensation, the psychological charge of experiencing penis-vagina intercourse, along with focusing on hitherto secondary erogenous zones, may combine to enable them to be orgasmic. Females-to-males most often have intact clitorises enlarged through hormone therapy, which, of course, continue to be erectile. They don't ejaculate through the clitoris, but many genetic men don't ejaculate upon orgasms, either.

I must ask you to elaborate on your response to the question about the ability of an individual to achieve orgasm after having surgical sexual reassignment. First you stated that orgasms are a product more of fantasy than of friction. You followed that by giving examples of how friction of other erogenous zones can produce orgasm even when genital sensations are lost.

If fantasy is more important than friction in achieving orgasm, why didn't you support your initial statement by giving examples of how? How do you explain the fact that people who do not fantasize during sex do achieve orgasm? How do you explain the fact that intensifying physical stimulation (i.e., with a vibrator) produces a more intense orgasm, regardless of whether or not the person fantasizes?

A I have said this isn't an easy topic. Fantasy, in the sense I used it in my response, meant "beliefs" rather than an elaborate scripted scenario of events. An example: One woman who consulted me decided to call what she experienced during penis-vagina intercourse an orgasm even though it did not correspond to the recognizable orgasm she knew from self-stimulation. Once she relabeled her experience (altered her beliefs), she became orgasmic in a way which supersedes verbal juggling. She experienced herself as orgasmic through intercourse, increasing her pleasure and changing her image of her own sexuality.

Another example: In a recent meeting of the Society for the Scientific Study of Sex, Beverly Whipple, one of *The G Spot* authors, reported on several experimental subjects who were apparently able to think themselves into orgasm, some with and some without accompanying fantasies. She called it "thinking off" and was as eager to understand the phenomenon as, undoubtedly, you and I are.

What I might have said that would not have added to the confusion — and which I will so state now — is that having an orgasm is much more for most people than rubbing on the correct area of sensitive skin, although for some that is all that is required.

Q I am a 36-year-old hetero male puzzled about what happened during a routine prostate exam. My doctor, a woman, was massaging the prostate gland, a procedure that normally causes me great discomfort. Initially, this occasion was no different, but then some sort of "tumbler" tumbled and I got a major hard-on and began to experience real pleasure, as well as pain. There was no disguising my erection, but the doctor mercifully ignored it. I am not attracted to the doctor (as far as I know) and am wondering what this experience is all about. Am I leaning toward gay?

A Why would getting turned on by a female doing things to your male body imply gay desires on your part? If you believe that only gay men respond to prostate stimulation, think about whether that makes sense. Some men do, some don't. Body parts don't have sexual orientations. If it feels good, a body responds, until or unless one's sense of propriety overrules that response — whether the stimulus is male, female, animal, vegetable, or medical.

Q I am a good-looking young man with feminine tendencies. Although I enjoy my masculine-shaped muscles and stiff hard-on, I also like feminine attributes in myself of shaved body hair and soft, smooth skin. I find it exciting to wear sexy lingerie, garters, G string, and make-up. I want women to see me as sexy, so I don't think I'm gay. I don't know how to be a transvestite and don't really know what a transsexual is. Do I need psychiatric help? Are there other men like me and women that can appreciate me?

A Ah, labels. Maybe the compilers of the Diagnostic and Statistical Manual of Mental Disorders should have followed in Kinsey's original footsteps and studied wasps. Only you can judge whether you need psychiatric help. If you feel miserable, by all means. Are there others like you? Of course. There are only so many people designs to go around and then Nature starts repeating herself. Are there women who will find you sexy? Undoubtedly.

    If you desire women and, more importantly, if you do not desire men, gay is not an appropriate label. "Androgynous" means "having the characteristic of both sexes." Would that fit? A transvestite is a person who gets erotic pleasure (as opposed to a Halloween giggle) when cross (*trans* in Latin) dressing (vest, as in vestments). There's nothing you have to *do* to qualify. A transsexual is a person whose sense of gender identity (Do I feel I am a man or a woman?)

does not match the apparent sex of the body. Whatever you call yourself (I suggest by your first name), when you are comfortable with who you are in all your wondrous complexities, other people will respond to that positively.

Q I occasionally pick up a swingers' paper as well as subscribe to Penthouse *Variations*. There are aspects of transvestism I find puzzling. Most articles and letters on or about the subject claimed that these men who enjoy wearing women's clothing were not homosexuals, although certain homosexuals do dress as women. However, other letters and articles, as well as advertisements by transvestites and services catering to transvestites, stress several aspects of the lifestyle that I find disturbing...like the wearing of bras, when the male anatomy does not lend itself to this. It doesn't make sense — nor does the wearing of make-up — if the transvestite's desire is merely to enjoy greater variety and pleasure in clothing not bound by socially determined standards. Female domination, verbal humiliation, sadomasochism, bondage and discipline, all seem essential for the transvestite to enjoy his "role" as a woman. And if a man is not gay, why is anal intercourse (either by a female partner using a dildo or by a male) an essential part of the letter, article, or ad?

A There are some huge and erroneous assumptions here. Sexuality is neither simple nor logical, so don't look for simplicity or logic. There are an amazing variety of sexual turn-ons available to us all. At different times and in different combinations, a person can be hot or not about breasts, buns, boys, beasts, even bagels. Being anally penetrated is one of those hot or not turn-ons available to men and women of various orientations. So is being dominated, humiliated, and bound, or dominating, humiliating, and binding. People cross-dress for various reasons — a broader range of clothing options being one of many possibilities. Some might enhance the arousal factor of donning clothing our society currently deems feminine by using make-up and bras — which, of course, can be filled with other than natural breast tissue by either males or females.

Some men who do this are playing, some are acting out fantasies, some are dramatically expressing their feminine aspects, and some may be experimenting with actually living as a female. Some are *also* into sexual power play or anal stimulation or other activities, which they might do along with, before, after, or instead of cross-dressing.

Q My lover is very attracted to the shape of pregnant women and I am supportive of that attraction, so that's no problem. The nude photo collections have only a few pregnant women in them. The only picture books of naked pregnant women we've been able to find are at adult bookstores where the photos are lewd and distasteful, not to mention very disrespectful of women. Do you know where one could find a tasteful, artful book of pregnant nudes?

A Adult bookstore's special-interest magazines are your best bet for variety if not necessarily good taste. Valentine's Day is coming up. Why not make him a made-to-order scrapbook of the best you've been able to find?

Q We have had a perplexing incident in the medical office where I am employed. Perhaps you can shed some light on the matter. A young man came into the office complaining of pain and discharge following intercourse. A culture proved to be positive for gonorrhea. An antibiotic was prescribed and he promised to send his girlfriend into the office. She did come in but declined to submit to a pelvic examination. She at this point had something confidential to tell the physician. She confessed that she was "an incomplete transsexual" which she explained meant she is taking female hormones but has not yet had surgery of the sexual organs. In other words, "she" has a penis and no vagina. The patient insisted that her male partner is unaware of this. Our question is what did they do and why didn't the young man realize his girlfriend has an intact male member? We are trying hard, but are unable to visualize such a mistake being made.

A If the patient asked for her disclosure to be kept confidential, I'm wondering why the whole office is discussing it. I think the examining physician here is in need of some information on ethical as well as sexual practices.

Okay, you and the doctor heard "intercourse" and assumed penis/vagina when the young man and his lover obviously had penis/mouth or penis/anus or even penis/armpit intercourse (though I've never heard of catching an STD in this latter fashion). The preoperative transsexual might have declined to be touched "there," or postponed the event until "after her period," or "after their marriage." She probably tucked her external genitalia toward the back and taped them there and/or wore "sexy underwear" to bed.

If enough interesting activities were going on elsewhere, it's relatively easy to distract a partner from looking or touching any particular spot. I can assure you that there exist many, many heterosexual couples where not only has he never really paid attention to the particulars of what she has between her legs, she herself hasn't either. Our society's message that vaginas are embarrassing unmentionables is still very strong.

Playing it Safe: STCs

Sexually Transmitted Conditions

♀◀♂◀♀▲♂▼♀▲♂►♀▼♂

Q Jack and Jill are HIV negative and monogamous. So are Hansel and Gretel. Jack and Hansel want to start a physical fairy tale of their own. Are they still in danger of contracting AIDS, and will it be necessary for them to use a bookmark between their pages?

A When two individuals who are HIV negative get together, their activities will not spontaneously combust the AIDS-causing agent. At issue is the reliability of the test results of each of the partners. If one of them is wrong, they are not only putting themselves at risk, but also putting Jill, Gretel, and any possible future offspring. Let us hope they all lived and loved happily ever after and that Mother Goose never gets wind of such carryings on.

Q In all their talk of monogamy, the media often fails to notice that one can have sex with many people, and as long as everyone is screened and sex is limited to within the group, the act is as safe as true monogamy and far safer than serial monogamy with unscreened partners. The key word to use in conjunction with safe sex should be "screened" rather than "monogamous." For this reason, people who believe in responsible nonmonogamy advocate using the term "screened group."

A As long as the word "responsible " is in there with the word sex, I'm willing to support it — whatever its conformation. Personally, however, I see trust issues as a paramount problem in many one-on-one relationships. To rely on "one of the lovers of one of my lovers" to keep you safe is asking a great deal.

You said you thought screened nonmonogamy was okay as long as participants were responsible — meaning, I suppose, that they honestly do stay within the group. Unfortunately, recent experiments have shown that some HIV carriers do not respond positively to an antibody test for years after infectious contact. No one knows how often or why these delays occur. But this long and unpredictable window period means that even people who have been screened and do not have sex outside the group can unknowingly infect their partners. Condom use is only safER sex. The only sensible alternative to nonpenetrative sex is monogamy with both partners as aware as possible (given testing limitations) of each other's status.

A I don't see where sex with one person whose screened HIV status is not to be completely relied upon is a whole lot different than sex with more than one in the same situation. I have abridged your letter in which you make other arguments in support of your position. You and I agree there is still much to be learned about the HIV virus, its incubation, and transmission. Your solution is monogamy, which is neither practical nor possible for many people. Therefore, I urge people to educate themselves about what risks are known and to take what precautions they are willing to take to protect themselves. If your choice is monogamy I'll support you in it if you will support others in differing choices.

If I willingly have unprotected sex with you who either do not know or do not disclose your disease status, and I get infected, I see the fault as mine. That's called "personal responsibility for one's actions" and I wholeheartedly endorse it. In the meantime, let's both of us do our best in educating the unknowing, so that more people will make responsible decisions.

Q I'd like to use condoms to cut down on my sensitivity and thus prolong an erection, but my wife hates them. Which ones have the least latex/chemical smell?

A Two excellent breakdowns of varieties of condoms and their various properties can be found in "Condom Sense" (send $2 to The Condom Resource Center, Box 30564, Oakland, CA 94604) and in the March, 1989 issue (and perhaps by now a later one) of *Consumer Reports* magazine. You might also try introducing her to ones with colors or flavors so that condoms can be perceived as a fun enhancer, rather than as a "marital aid."

Q Being newly arrived on the dating scene, I'm rather nervous about sex, or more accurately, AIDS. A lot of what is called safe sex seems like "sorta safe sex": French kissing is an exchange of bodily fluids yet "it's very unlikely" that French kissing will give you AIDS. Intercourse with a condom is "safer," but what if the condom breaks? And is it true that you have to take the AIDS test and then wait six months and take it again to make sure it wasn't dormant? Do you know of any free or low-cost safe sex information classes? I'm not planning on getting into a sexual relationship unless I feel that it's going to be a long-term monogamous one, but I do have my eye on someone, so please hurry with your answers!

A Activities like French kissing don't "give you AIDS." What is under discussion with safer sex practices are the more or less effective means of impeding the transmission of the HIV virus, which causes a number of lethal conditions, all lumped under the name of AIDS. Many community colleges, universities, and social service organizations sponsor safe-sex workshops and seminars from time to time. The Institute for the Advanced Study of Human Sexuality has published an easy to read set of "Guidelines for reducing the risk of contracting AIDS during sexual contact" called *Safe Sex in the Age of AIDS for Men and Women.* (Citadel Press, 120 Enterprise Avenue, Secaucus, NJ 07094, $3.95 in paperback)

Q I sure hope you got the phone number of the straight man who wrote you about loving oral sex! You could sell it. Do you have any information on the possibility/probability of AIDS transmission in the opposite direction — to a heterosexual woman from the loving mouth of a man?

A I don't dare say that anything is impossible, but transmission via saliva has all but been ruled out by most medical experts.

Q Can one get a sore throat or a cold by swallowing someone else's come? What virus other than the AIDS virus might it carry?

A Any virus that's being incubated in the body can be excreted through the ejaculate. If the contact with a virus-harborer is close enough for you to engage in come-swallowing, you may possibly have kissed or shaken hands (first? at the conclusion?), which is an even more efficient way to transmit a flu virus, for example.

Q It seems that any sane, intelligent individual these days who is sexually active must be armed with patience, condoms, dental dams, rubber gloves, a love of latex, and a great deal of forbearance. My experience of sex is that it's a lot like swimming — in other words, a whole-body experience. I'm very uncomfortable with the type of barrier/protective sex that is called for in the Age of AIDS, and so for the last three years I have been celibate by choice due to a combination of a fear of AIDS and a preference for no sex over "latex sex." I thought I'd find a woman who was both as sexual as I am and as fearful. We'd date for nine months or so, get tested when we both felt the potential for more, wait another nine months, and then have at it hammer and tongs sans latex. Then comes the scientific announcement that the AIDS-causing virus can remain undetected for up to three years. Is cruising the parochial schools for a virgin my only protection?

A If you think certain safety lies between the thighs of a parochial school girl, things have changed even more dramatically than you imagined. My suggestion is to go on about your life, meet whomever you meet, and when you find yourself in a developing relationship with a woman, bring up the topic of safety for mutual discussion and problem-solving. There are many safe-sex classes being offered (by hospitals, clinics, colleges, community centers). The two of you might attend together and together assess your options. There may even exist a woman in the world for whose "hand" you might be willing to don latex armor.

Q I am HIV negative and I've never had herpes, not even a cold sore. I realize how very lucky I am. Is it being selfish to require the same health status in a significant other? Friends tell me I am asking for too much. Self-preservation is no longer the first law of the jungle?

A About this self-preservation: People can be herpes carriers without ever having had an outbreak, and it's not a lethal condition; but for *absolute* safety stay home and stay celibate. When and if you find yourself partnerless for whatever you deem to be "too long," or when and if you reluctantly disqualify a significant other candidate who "seemed perfect except for...," than you can decide if your standards are unrealistic. When else could a person be selfish (i.e., "concerned unduly over personal pleasure") than in choosing a partner for pleasure? That "unduly" business is someone else's judgment.

Q Does the regular use of condoms that contain benzocaine as a desensitizing agent, or the use of over-the-counter desensitizing ointments that contain up to 20% benzocaine by volume, cause any long-term side effects? Most importantly, by using these local anesthetics regularly, could the human body absorb enough toxin to cause birth defects or any adverse effects on fetal development?

A I have heard nothing about such adverse physical effects. Benzocaine is topical and not easily absorbed into the body. Since pregnant women are asked to eschew even an occasional aspirin during fetal development, it makes sense to keep any chemical or drug away from the birthing area. For more information on the chemical properties of benzocaine, please check with a pharmacologist or toxicologist. Long-term use of desensitizers would have psychological effects, however. Besides (re)learning different signals of ejaculatory control, if one is used to having sex with a numb penis, feeling all the feelings of sex would take some getting used to, and may feel so different as be interpreted as "unsatisfying."

Q I am a man in my 60s who has had genital herpes for five years. Initially, the outbreaks reoccurred every four months. For the past four years, I have taken three grams of Lysine daily and have had no outbreaks. My questions: Is it possible that a partner infected by me would have a similar mild case? I have heard that the herpes virus is so small that it can pass through rubber. Are condoms of any real value in preventing the spread of herpes? Finally, I would like to advise prospective partners as accurately as possible about their risk of becoming infected. What should I say?

A There is no reason to suggest that a partner infected by you would respond as you do to the herpes virus. The decisive factor would be her or his body's ability to marshal resistance, not the strength or weakness of the herpes strain. Tests do prove that an intact latex condom is an effective barrier against the herpes virus if used correctly. Nonoxynol-9 in lubricant and/or spermicide increases the protection for both parties. For maximum safety, the National Herpes Information Center (919/361-8418) and the National STD Hotline (1-800-227-8922) both recommend refraining from intercourse during the active phase of a genital herpes outbreak, which includes the prodromal symptoms through the return of new skin after skin blistering.

Tell a prospective partner what you know to be true about your condition ("I have had occasional outbreaks of genital herpes, which for the past few years seem to be under control") and point him or her toward these resources for the latest information on the subject.

Q Now that condoms are the thing, I thought I'd pass along an experience of mine. I was getting frequent vaginal infections, not yeast, but the medical folks couldn't diagnose it. Then by chance, I switched to non-lubricated condoms and now everything's okay. I must have had an allergic reaction to the lubricant. What the heck do they use anyway?

A Most lubricants are — if you'll excuse the expression — impregnated with nonoxynol-9. It's a very effective antiviral agent and spermicide, but it is a chemical. With many people having adverse reactions to substances as "nonthreatening" as milk, you can imagine that more people react to more complicated substances. Thank you for the tip.

Q I'm a sexually active woman who is not unintelligent. I read the papers and know that since I am not in a monogamous relationship, I should be protecting myself better from the possibility of disease, but trying to talk some unwilling guy into putting on a rubber or, worse yet, trying to put one on him myself seems beyond me. Is there any hope?

A There are several good, clear books on practical tips and assertiveness techniques, but I think you will be more motivated with some hands-on experience. You could convene several friends in the same boat (anyone who may be sexually active with men or who is a man), buy a bunch of condoms and a bunch of bananas, and have a "fuckerware" party with prizes for the most and least adept or the most creative approach. Make learning fun!

Should you be moved to add to the body of popular wisdom, The Condom Resource Center (P.O. Box 30564, Oakland, CA 94604) is always looking for good rhymed couplets having to do with condoms. (Non-English majors, what that means is two lines of verse, each with the same number of syllables and with the last syllable of each line rhyming with each other.) A kind reader has sent along some possibilities, without attribution, unfortunately, but they were too good not to share. So, what the hay, maybe you'll be inspired.

Cover your stump
before you hump.

Don't be silly,
protect your willy.

When in doubt,
shroud your spout.

You can't go wrong
if you shield your dong.

S/he won't get sick
if you cap your dick.

If you go into heat,
package your meat.

While you're undressing Venus,
dress up that penis.

When you take off her pants and blouse,
suit up that trouser mouse.

Don't be a fool,
vulcanize your tool.

A night in armor
is unlikely to harm her.

It'll be sweeter
if you wrap your peter.

If you're not going to sack it,
go home and whack it.

✍ I remember how funny your little "poems" were that encourage the use of condoms. I believe you help women a great deal by publishing such propaganda. From what I've read, many women can be intimidated into not protecting themselves. How sad! I think the humorous touch helps in delicate situations like this. Therefore, I'm wondering if it would be possible to publish in your column the funnier results of musical condom contest run by Terry McGovern, a San Francisco disc jockey.

A The little poems I published in this column were entries in the Condom Couplet Contest held in mid-February in celebration of National Condom Week. Some examples: "Don't be silly, protect your willy," "You can't go wrong if you shield your dong," "In December gift wrap your member." Terry McGovern read a newspaper article about the invention of a condom implanted with a microchip which, upon "agitation," plays a little tune. Terry invited his listeners to send in something appropriate and received the following suggestions: "The Minute Waltz," "Raindrops Keep Falling On My Head," the Beatles' "Love, Love Me Do," "Feelings," and one which he says won his "ouch, too true" award — "Staying Alive." My personal favorite of those he told me about was "How Deep Is Your Love"; his was The Star Spangled Banner (think about it).

Q My partner and I are enjoying our new redwood hot tub. Not only is the water hot, but, on occasion, so are we. The only thing stopping us from making love is the fear of infection. PH increaser and chlorine concentrate are in use according to the chemical booklet we got at the spa store, but answers to our questions are not at the back of the booklet. What are the risks of infecting my honey's vagina or my penis if we have intercourse under water? Would bromine be better for us than chlorine?

A Driving unsterile water up her vagina and into your urethra, as the movements of underwater intercourse will do, is not a great idea. There is some risk of infection. Just how bad the infection could be, how great the risk, vs. how great the pleasure, is a matter for others' expertise.

Q It is delightful when the young lady who invites me home has condoms in her apartment. Putting on a condom has become part of an erotic ritual; it enhances the mood and the anticipation. However, what to do when we're done with it? I would like to pass along this helpful hostess hint: Ladies, be certain that tissues and a waste paper basket are near your bed (or wherever you plan on enjoying each other). Without nearby means of disposal, your gentleman caller has a sticky problem on his hands...and elsewhere. He can't drop it on the furniture or the floor. Lubricated condoms stain the finish. Put it in an ash tray? Exceedingly gross. It would be a sin to break off the warmth of a post-orgasmic embrace to dispose of a prophylactic. A damp washcloth and a soft towel are also very handy. Freshening each other up is the best way to instigate a fresh start.

A Thank you, Miss Manners. It is you writing, isn't it?

Thanks for the etiquette tips on condoms. Special thanks for not even suggesting those items be flushed. Many urban sewage departments have reported problems with latex-clogged pipes. Condoms are beginning to wash up on beaches everywhere like anorectic jellyfish. The solution to one set of world health problems shouldn't make another set of problems worse.

A When I was a kid, we referred to used condoms washed ashore as Hudson River cuddle fish.

Q I am a single, currently celibate, woman. I am trying to keep up on the latest safe-sex practices and info. It's something to do until I am with a partner again. I understand there is a chemical in most spermicides that also kills the AIDS virus, true? That's all well and good, and I know we all should be using a good new condom before intercourse, but aren't spermicides and condoms together a bad combination? Aren't the condoms more likely to tear? Can you recommend some reading on the latest preventive measures? (I'm so glad you're out there! In this day of complex sexual questions it's nice to know there's someone to turn to. I certainly can't ask my mother like I did back in 1961 when I was 10!)

A Spermicide manufacturers know their product is likely to be used with latex — if not with condoms, then with diaphragms — and insure its compatibility. It's those seemingly innocent "household" lubricants like Vaseline or hand cream or vegetable oil, anything oil- or petroleum-based, that can have an instant and devastating effect on latex. Here are three safer-sex primers that may be available in bookstores; if not, order directly, *The Complete Guide to Safe Sex* ($6.95 + postage to Exodus Trust, 1523 Franklin St., San Francisco, CA 94109), *Safe Sex in the Age of AIDS* ($3.95 + postage to Citadel Press, 120 Enterprise Ave., Secaucus, NJ 07094), and *Play Safe* ($4.95 + postage to Center For Health Information, P.O. Box 4636, Foster City, CA 94404).

Q I saw an ad for a magazine that referred to "suppressed research that women cannot sexually transmit the AIDS virus." Do you know anything about this? Is there any evidence that women can sexually transmit AIDS?

A Conspiracy theories abound. Also, working hypotheses are abandoned as more about the human immune deficiency virus is discovered. Even such pros as Masters & Johnson can be wrong. What we know now is that HIV is most effectively transmitted via blood transfusions, shared needles, etc.; slightly less efficiently by semen; and less efficiently — but, if acquired, just as deadly — through vaginal fluids.

Q Until the start of my current relationship, I was celibate for more than six months; not so my new boyfriend. When he tried to go down on me, I said "Uh uh, not safe sex." But in fact if I were to test HIV negative and as long as he doesn't bite, would cunnilingus be any more dangerous than deep kissing, which we already do without protection?

A Let's hope he doesn't bite while going down on you, regardless of anyone's HIV status! The most likely potential virus transmitter here is your vaginal secretions, not his saliva. The AIDS Foundation lists deep kissing as "probably safe." If you both would like cunnilingus to be a part of your repertoire without waiting another six months for your test results, use a barrier between your genitals and his mouth. Latex squares called dental dams are available at sex shops, some drugstores, and through dentists, or in a pinch, try kitchen plastic wrap.

Q I prefer lambskin condoms with my girlfriend and understand that the passage of viruses and bacteria can be demonstrated in vitro through lambskin. I've read that for the transmission of HIV to occur, a fairly profuse exchange of fluids is required. Clearly a lambskin condom prevents this. Is there any hard evidence of VD transmission through lambskin? Would you think them safe for heterosexual sex?

A "Hard evidence" is conflicting. I remember reading a study which validated the efficacy of lambskin condoms, but I can't quote it. The AIDS Foundation Hotline in San Francisco cites studies at UCLA that "prove" their unreliability, and so recommend only latex condoms. These are lab studies, as you point out, and what happens between two hot and fallible humans in actuality may be entirely different. If you use a lubricant with nonoxynol-9 with your lambskins, you will be adding another layer of protection, but hetero sex or homo sex, you may not be getting the best protection available. You could don latex over lambskin if that isn't "guilding the lily."

Q Now that I have begun using rubbers again, the dread occurrence of the '50s is happening again — rubbing through and shredding reservoir-end latex rubbers. I believe the problem comes from trying to ram a dick head into that useless tip hundreds of useless times. As a reservoir, it's a joke. Come on, a good load in that tiny tip? It has become part of the look of a rubber, that's all. I've never had this problem with equipment without reservoir ends. What do you think? What do you know? What is it with the rubber makers?

A I sympathize with your frustration, but smooth-end condoms are still being manufactured. Buy those and forget about the ones that cause you such grief. They do work for some men or there wouldn't be so many of them on the market. I don't think "style" is sufficient explanation.

Q I've finally found a tender, good, sexy, adorable man with whom I want to spend the rest of my life...or at least the next few months. While I use a diaphragm and jelly for birth control, I also want to use condoms as disease protection. He agrees, but he tends to lose his erection the moment he puts one on. He wants us to be tested for HIV infection but I foresee problems. Even if we both tested negative, I wouldn't feel secure unless he tested negative again six months later, and I have no idea whether we'll be together that long. If either of us tested positive, the relationship would probably end. I certainly would not have sex with him if he were, and if I was I would be devastated. I wish we could use condoms until the relationship solidifies. Does the spermicidal jelly offer any protection?

A Your protection increases with every barrier against pregnancy or disease. Spermicide with nonoxynol-9 is some protection, and the diaphragm is much more, but only against pregnancy. Condoms would add another level of security and the only one against most STDs. Your relationship would "solidify" into something more reliable and trustworthy if you were to share your fears with your partner, and together work out both an interim and long-term solution. He can learn to become comfortable enough with condoms to not lose his erection, and you can learn to become more familiar with voicing your wishes and fears. You'll both feel a lot safer, physically and emotionally, when you do.

Q I love to perform oral sex on my boyfriend. Is it wise to use a condom even if he does not come in my mouth? What are the chances of picking up the HIV virus from pre-come? I've tried to ask doctors these questions but they either don't know, treat them as symptoms of a neurosis, or are too embarrassed to answer. One just told me not to "let" any man come in my mouth. It never dawned on him that a woman could love giving oral sex. Please, Isadora, tell me what I need to know.

A What you need to know is the phone number of the AIDS Hotline (1- 800-342-AIDS)...and apparently, so do your doctors. (When my own was unwilling or unable to answer my sexual questions, I changed doctors.) The AIDS Hotline volunteer I spoke to quoted tests confirming the presence of the HIV virus in the pre-ejaculate of infected individuals. What is at issue is whether it exists in sufficient quantity to be an infectious agent. Most health educators do recommend using a condom for oral sex. If you choose ones which are unlubricated or otherwise untreated, Gold Circle, for instance, they are not as intrusive as you might think. You can still get most — if not all — the pleasant sensations associated with giving oral sex.

Q There is a certain popular hair gel which contains nonoxynol-9. We were wondering if people use hair gel as a lubricant, or does nonoxynol-9 have other applications?

A People do all sorts of wondrously inventive things, but nonoxynol-9 has other uses than as a barrier to disease-causing agents. It is also a surfactant, a substance useful for its cleansing, wetting, and dispersing properties, in this case, a detergent to be used head to (something like a) toe.

Q My lover and I enjoy a giving and mutually rewarding sex life in which fellatio and cunnilingus play a major part. I very much enjoy going down on her, and have found that when we use her diaphragm, my lips and tongue become slightly numb. I am almost sure that this is caused by the contraceptive jelly we use. I wouldn't mind at all as long as I knew it was safe. So what's the poop on the goop?

A The FDA purports to certify the safety of all pharmaceuticals but new discoveries are made constantly that add to, and sometimes contradict, previous beliefs. Manufacturers of products used during sex want to avoid lawsuits, so they too are concerned about safety in the multiple ways their products might be used....we hope. You wouldn't think they've heard about oral sex, however, from the taste and smell of so many spermicides and lubricants. Read the label on your lover's contraceptive jelly, ask the pharmacist about unfamiliar chemical polysyllabics, and maybe experiment with other brands. If the stuff she's using now numbs your lips, it might be doing the same to hers, a side effect not generally conducive to good sex.

Q Can genital warts be transmitted orally? In other words, can cunnilingus or fellatio result in the warts appearing in the giver's mouth? Or can the wart virus be transmitted by mouth to genitals?

A Yes. Transmission need not be mouth to mouth, genitals to genitals or even foot to foot. The papilloma virus, like those of herpes, is no longer even classified as to its point of origin, but simply as a disease-causing agent.

Q My doctor, soon to be my ex-doctor, was abysmally ignorant about chlamydia. Though my girlfriend tested positive at the clinic, he claimed he could not test to verify my infection without a discharge, which I did not have. I am told a good percentage of infected men do not have one. After some insensitive comment about it being caused by "promiscuity," he gave me a blood test, which I was later informed is not effective in dealing with chlamydia.

A The health care workers at STD clinics are often the most well-informed on the subject. Your doctor is not only an ostrich ("I don't want to know about these things that smack of promiscuity"), he is also a dodo, and a dangerous one at that.

Q I've been involved with a wonderful man for over two years. We have spoken of marriage. I've made some mistakes before and he's always forgiven me. This, however, is almost unforgivable and I can't blame him for hating me: He's contacted herpes from me.

The main problem is that he's angry I never told him I had it. I was told by my doctor that it could not be transmitted if the sores are not there. Since I've been with him I've only had two outbreaks — once while he was away for a week, and once a year later when it was gone two days before we had intercourse. I never thought I was putting him at risk. I was never with him when I had an outbreak. I know he's been faithful to me. I am extremely angry at my doctor for misinforming me. I can't stand the thought of him hating me and remembering our relationship as the one that gave him herpes. Are there any cures at all? In other countries? Is there anything I can say to alleviate his hurt and anger toward me?

A I'm sorry, there are no known cures for herpes. Let's assume your doctor informed you to the best of her/his ability. What you were told was the prevailing belief about herpes transmission until recently. Anger at getting herpes is not the same as anger at being deceived, but at present, anger feels like anger without any fine distinctions. There is a possibility that your lover already harbored the herpes virus from an earlier cold sore and it expressed itself at this time, so that his infection did not for sure come from you. He may be too upset to hear you now, but write him what you wrote me and suggest that, when he is calmer, he get his facts from the National Herpes Information Line (919/361-8488) and perhaps re-evaluate his upset.

Q After six years of marriage, I am single again. Partly because I want no emotional involvements right now, and partly because I have never experienced pay-as-you-come sex, I went to two different prostitutes last month. Far from feeling empty or depraved, I walked away (drove actually) feeling pretty chipper. My question has to do with AIDS. So far, I have only experienced blow jobs from these working ladies. I am fearful of intercourse even with condoms. Is it safe to have oral sex without a rubber? I called the county health office but their answer sounded like "overkill." They recommended latex even for oral sex. For myself, I can't imagine a vulcanized blow.

A The person who ingests infected semen can become infected by it. It is still unknown whether the person who ingests infected vaginal secretions can, although menstrual blood must be avoided. The receiver of oral sex is thought to be safe from possible infection since saliva is not a good transmittal agent. There are oral artistes so adept that they can put a condom on an unsuspecting recipient with their tongue, so I am told. Next time you pay for play, you might suggest a trial vulcanized blow for curiosity's (and your playmate's safety's) sake.

Q My partner doesn't like to use rubbers. I find myself insisting on them lately for several reasons. First, he broke our monogamous agreement a few years ago by having unsafe sex elsewhere, and then for a brief time continued to have unsafe sex with me. This shattered my trust and I resented the fact that, unbeknownst to me, my health was potentially at risk. Second, he has herpes (although fairly dormant), and we both have been treated for venereal warts. Third, we have been pregnant several times, resulting in abortions. Diaphragms are a disaster, and it seems that condom and foam are the most reliable method for me.

Given all my reasons for wanting to use condoms, is it really fair if he finds them so uncomfortable, etc.? I don't know where to draw the line. I'm even hesitant to give him oral sex without a condom, which infuriates him. I used to not care about any of these things and I'm beginning to feel like a prude. I love him, but I also care about myself. He feels hurt and rejected and I wonder what the options are — if any.

A What options there may be are up to the two of you to discover via a joint brain-storming, problem-solving session. Start with exactly what you told me: "I feel unsafe in our bed. I find myself unwilling to risk another pregnancy, more warts, herpes, with your un-sheathed penis." While he may not necessarily have the language for it, I hear your partner saying that to him, insisting on a latex barrier between you creates an emotional barrier for him, too. Perhaps he feels resentful because it acts as a reminder to you both that he has broken your monogamous agreement. Perhaps it feels like a punishment each time you mention the need for protection. Maybe it's simply an inconvenience he feels "he shouldn't have to put up with" if life were perfect.

Ask him for his feelings about condom use, state yours. Honor what you hear. (No "That's ridiculous" or "Don't feel that way.") Since the ideal outcome of wanting to be unsafe and not sorry is just not possible, remain clear that security — both physical and emotional — must take precedence over comfort or preference in whatever compromises you make.

The problem of the condom that just won't stay on is one that my lover and I have solved quite nicely. You know those good old rubber plumber's O rings? They're used as washers to keep faucets from leaking and they do the same for condoms, too. These rubber circles come in a variety of sizes, cost about 50 cents, and are reusable. Use one by stretching it over the already-in-place condom and position it near the body at the penis's base so that it fits snugly — not so tight as to be uncomfortable, but not so loose as to slip off with the condom.

We use two for extra safety, and my lover says he even enjoys the feeling which seems to increase the sensitivity of his penis and delay orgasm. We keep quite a few on hand so we don't need to wash the used ones immediately, and leaving them out in the air for several days helps insure the death of any nasty viruses. We've heard they come in different colors but we've only found them in basic black. Available at your favorite neighborhood hardware store!

▲ Creativity lives!

♂ ▲ ♀ ◀ ♂ ◀ ♀ ▲ ♂ ▼ ♀ ▲ ♂ ▶ ♀ ▼ ♂ ▲ ♀

Me, Myself and I:
Solo Sex

♂ ▲ ♀ ◀ ♂ ◀ ♀ ▲ ♂ ▼ ♀ ▲ ♂ ▶ ♀ ▼ ♂ ▲ ♀

Q I masturbate every three days or so, but while I was in high school I whacked off daily. I'm 23. Sometimes I wonder if my well-functioning "come mechanism" will wear out, or not function well later in life when I have a partner. Do we get only so many ejaculations, the same way a car gets so many miles? Is there a danger in masturbating this much?

A Some drivers baby their autos and are driving what are now 500,000 mile classics, while others junk theirs as wrecks after a mere 50,000 miles. It has to do with the quality of the original car, as well as the care given it by its owners. You will not wear out your pleasure parts. Your body will tell you when you've momentarily had enough by simply not doing what it generally does. After a period of recuperation (which may be minutes or days at various times in your life), it will be up and functioning as always.

The only dangers to enthusiastic masturbation are — one, that you may stay home playing with yourself rather than going out and about meeting potential play partners, and two, you may accustom yourself to a particular touch and timing when alone, which will make it harder to accommodate a partner whose needs or preferences will differ.

Q I am a 72-year-old woman alone. I can't bring myself to a satisfying orgasm. Help!

A I'm left with several questions from your all-too-brief letter. Many women of your generation were so thoroughly inculcated in the evils of masturbation that doing so creates more guilt than pleasure. If that's the issue, or if you have no idea where, what, or how to stimulate your body to produce orgasm, reading about the joys of self-pleasuring may help. Look for Dodson's *Sex for One*, Barbach's *For Yourself*, or Blank's *Good Vibrations*.

If the issue is that your sexual responses have changed over time (or since taking some medications) so that your body no longer responds as it once did, you might (after speaking with your health care provider about what is now different) seek out two newsletters on health and aging: *Hot Flash* c/o Dr. Jane Porcino, School of Allied Health Professions, SUNY, Stony Brook, NY 11794, or PMZ Newsletter (*Post-Menopausal Zest*), Volcano Press, 330 Ellis St., San Francsico, CA 94102.

If you're having orgasms but they aren't satisfying, perhaps due to loneliness or social isolation, seek friends through the logical means of neighborhood, family, community activities, or through such national common-interest groups as The Gray Panthers and Options for Women Over Forty.

Q The only time I feel relaxed enough to feel horny is right before I drop off to sleep. At that point I have an internal fight with myself: masturbate vs. "if you don't let yourself fall asleep now, you'll never get to sleep." I think that side of me is afraid I will take too long to come and that I won't get relaxed enough to fall asleep, so most of the time the side that wants sleep wins. Since I don't like the choice between being sleepless or sexless, what can I do about this?

A I see two issues here, and neither of them has to do with sex. First is time management. Go to bed earlier, or else wake up earlier if your masturbation must take place in bed! The other issue is what sounds like insomnia — worrying so much about getting enough sleep that you lose sleep worrying. Learn some effective self-relaxation techniques, hypnosis, self-talk, or biofeedback, so that when and if you "get relaxed enough to fall asleep" is just not a subject of worry. By the way, the most effective relaxant I know is a good orgasm.

Q You rightfully discouraged self-strangulation methods of masturbation. This is, in fact, a touchy sleeper issue among today's teenagers. I wouldn't think of discouraging any nonhazardous self-pleasuring techniques, and I'm certain that neither would you, but the fact is that a certain undisclosed percentage of reported "suicides" seen in today's obituaries are the results of this practice. The method seems to have achieved a certain word-of-mouth popularity among many teens, and when, on occasion, they are found strangulated in their own bedrooms, in deference to the delicate feelings of the victim's families, police reports routinely leave out the presence of masturbatory materials at the scene of the "crime." The downside of this otherwise sensitive handling is that the word does not get out that this is a dangerous and potentially fatal form of self-play.

A Any form of recreational activity whose aim is to achieve numbness or unconsciousness — whether it is self-strangulation, injecting, sniffing, eating, or drinking to stupification — is potentially fatal. You want a real high? Tune into life, not out of it!

Your column is always informative and entertaining, but in a recent one you have perpetuated a misconception that may have dangerous consequences. Those who engage in self-strangulation to induce heightened orgasm may unwisely consider themselves safe and continue this dangerous practice if cleared by a professional of suicidal propensities, since invariably arousal is the intent and suicide need not be a factor, even on an unconscious level. The claim is that such practices can produce extraordinary exciting orgasms and altered states of consciousness. I have no intention of finding out personally or of encouraging experimentation. Those who feel compelled to engage in this practice should do so only in the presence of a buddy who should not, of course, be experiencing the altered-states phenomenon at the same time. Safer than doing it solo, but the buddy runs the risk of being charged with murder or accessory to suicide if things go wrong. I recommend to you a comprehensive overview, *Autoerotic Fatalities*, published by Lexington Press in Lexington, MA in 1983.

A This letter came from a New York therapist who is a director of *Lifestyles*, "a counseling service for those engaged in, or affected by, unconventional sexual and social styles." An excellent service no doubt, and I do appreciate the input. However, I cannot imagine a therapist worth his/her salt having the chutzpah to unequivocally "clear" someone of suicidal propensities. Life is not a board game whereby visiting the lucky right psychologist you get a Free Card that entitles you to eat and drink to excess, inject the drug of choice, jaywalk, or take other risks with impunity. What would you call people who continue to engage in life-threatening behavior after they have been informed of the risks, if not suicidal on some level?

Q Is it bad for a man to masturbate without a hard-on? I am a mid-fifties gay man who's had no sex with another person for many years. I've never been very active sexually with other guys, but until I was well past 40, I jacked off at least once a day. Now all that has sort of petered out (ahem). I rarely get a hard-on except when I look at some particularly exciting porn. Still, once in three weeks or so I get the urge, and by "shaking" everything around a lot I can still come. Sometimes I place a pestle with its blunt end against my prostate, which helps and feels good, too. But what if that Shining Knight on the Slow Horse finally shows up?! What if he's not into shaking? Or pestles? Will everything just magically fall into place, or am I ruining myself for life?

A What pleasure you have now is actual, realtime, feelable pleasure. Why would one want to forgo that for theoretical potential pleasure? Anyway, by all the dictates of my fairy-tale books, should that knight rein up on your doorstep, he's got to like shaking and pestles, or else he wouldn't be your knight, but an impostor. On a more prosaic note, it would be unrealistic to suddenly expect a physiological response that you haven't felt in years, but love — and Grand Passion — creates their own miracles. If you don't find yourself having the firm erections of your teens, or even of your forties, I'm sure you and an eventual lover will discover something the two of you can do together that can feel even better than a pestle.

On an even more prosaic note, in the meantime please find something other than a pestle for applying prostatic pressure — something that can be sterilized, for one, and something with a flange to prevent it from getting lost in your innards. If the stark reality of sex shop dildos is too much, the Japanese make flanged phallic-shaped silicon objects in decorator colors that are a bit more free-form.

♂ ▲ ♀ ◀ ♂ ◀ ♀ ▲ ♂ ▼ ♀ ▲ ♂ ▶ ♀ ▼ ♂ ▲ ♀

The Social
Squaredance:
Meeting, Mingling,
and Finding Partners

♂ ▲ ♀ ◀ ♂ ◀ ♀ ▲ ♂ ▼ ♀ ▲ ♂ ▶ ♀ ▼ ♂ ▲ ♀

Q I used to be very comfortable and calm around women, but lately that's changed. Now I frequently feel awkward, nervous, and ill at ease, particularly around woman I am attracted to. I probably come across as shy and neurotic, not exactly the masculine ideal. Interestingly enough, I have been told (without my asking) that I am not just good in bed, but "great." I suppose there are two reasons why I am writing to you: One is to tell the women out there that a shy nervous guy could be more of a man than they might think. The other is to ask you for some advice on my anxiety problem. I am in therapy and it seems to help, but I like your column and I'm interested in what you have to say about it.

A Social skills (as opposed to talents) are so-called because they are learnable, not innate. If you're not yet ready to go out there mixing and mingling, or would like to take a momentary breather to remuster your courage, I can recommend my audio tape workshop, New Ways to Meet New People ($15 to 3145 Geary, #153, San Fransisco, CA 94118) for assistance in clarifying and overcoming various common stumbling blocks. Otherwise, classes and groups abound that offer not only practical suggestions, but opportunities to give and take support from others who share your feelings, which includes every single person to a greater or lesser degree.

Here in San Francisco current issues of freebie papers *Common Ground* list a course in "Learning to Speak Without Fear," The *Learning Annex* lists "How to Begin and Continue a Conversation," as well as "50 Ways to Get a Date," and *Open Exchange* has several sections of resources for connecting. In other cities, good places to look for such offerings are community bulletin boards, alternative newspapers, and singles' publications.

Q I'm 17 years old and have a few problems with my social life. My first problem is I really want a boyfriend who is a sex maniac. I have joined some social groups but I can't find anyone. Also, I have a friend who is a prostitute. She tells me I should try it so I could find someone. I think about sex most of the time. During those times, I *want* sex. I am attracted to movies with sex scenes. I really want to know what is happening to me. Do you have any references such as phone numbers or addresses that could help me cope with my problem?

A Your hormones are your problem, as well as friends with dumb ideas. Thinking about sex, looking at sexy pictures, and feeling desire for sex are all normal feelings. Gratifying those feelings with a "sex maniac" or finding a partner through prostitution are way out in left field solutions. First of all, do a little reading on adolescent sexuality — Eleanor Hamilton's *Sex With Love* or Sol Gordon's *The Teenage Survival Book* for some insight into your dilemma and some expert suggestions on coping mechanisms. If you want to learn to pleasure yourself, to give yourself orgasms, the lessons in Betty Dodson's *Sex for One* will help remove the edge of desperation. As for your social skills, joining clubs and teenage discussion groups is definitely going in the right direction. Hang in there, you'll get it all together eventually.

Q What about having a contest about creative ways to meet people? So far, I have gathered leftover mini Xmas trees from supermarkets to donate to the forestry service for replanting burned areas. My main hope was meeting a nice ranger, spending time talking about the darned trees, then getting on to better things — like us. I am now "researching" replacing my car. I have stopped many cute guys to ask information like "How does your car drive? Does your wife enjoy it? Is there room enough for the kids and dog?" They love talking cars with me, I guess, since they have knowledge and it's a safe subject. I am now starting riding lessons. Once a week I get on a large, sweaty, hairy beast and trek out into nature for an hour with a very nice guy. My fantasies race faster than the horses.

A Anybody who wants to send me your creative ones, I'll print them. That is, I will print ways to meet people, Ducks, not your fantasies.

Q I have a problem I'm too embarrassed to tell even my best friends. I am 21 years old and I have never had any kind of physical contact with a girl, not even a French kiss. I am definitely not gay. All through high school I was popular and athletic and I never worried about sex because I figured it would come when it would happen. Now that I'm in college, my lack of any kind of experience makes conversation with my friends very awkward. If they talk about sex I have nothing to contribute. I would rather keep people thinking I am a cool guy then to take a risk on losing this reputation. In addition, I don't participate in many social situations or date any more, because I don't know what to do and I am deathly afraid of embarrassment. As you can see, I am digging myself a hole I can't get out of. I don't know if I'm writing to find out if I'm not alone, to ask for advice, or to find out if I need help.

A How about if I offer input on all three? You are certainly not alone in being sexually inexperienced at the age of 21. At other times in this century, such premarital chastity was the norm, and many did not marry until their 30s, or at all. While your total inexperience is atypical in the U.S. today, it isn't necessarily abnormal. What you do need help with is your "deathly fear." Nobody enjoys being embarrassed, but most people will risk all sorts of discomfort if the potential gain is attractive enough. (Animal experiments show that female rats will cross an electrified grid to get to their young, and male rats will do so to get to a female in heat. We all have our priorities!)

The obvious routes to a solution for you is to change your feelings, your behavior, or both. Read some human sexuality books, call some talk hot lines. Watch carefully for signs of unease in other guys when the talk turns to sex. Reassure yourself that you are not alone in this, and that you are okay for now being where you are. You can take classes in assertiveness or massage to increase your social and sensual skills, and you can consider working with a sexual surrogate through referral from a relationship counselor. Social avoidance only compounds the problem, as you know. Begin making some changes soon and the process will go much easier for you.

Q My wife is 70, I'm 68. She's been through with sex for three years. I still need sex once or twice a week. I've heard that older people often have sex with the same gender. I would like to do this instead of getting involved with another woman. The question is where and how do I do this?

A Most metropolitan areas have several gay-oriented newsweeklies that list clubs, social events, discussion groups, meetings, etc., which would appeal to gay men and to those who wish to meet and mingle with them. Have you discussed your intentions with your wife? Unless same-sex experience is something you've long been interested in, I'm sure you and she — perhaps with the aid of a marriage counselor or sex therapist — could come up with some other possible solutions to your dilemma.

Q I am a woman unapologetically into S/M. If I found my partners only within "the community," Society of Janus meetings, for instance, there would be no problem. I find that limiting, however. My problem is that when I honestly and directly tell someone I'm interested in that I do S/M, it's usually as well received as if I said I do dead babies. I hear something like "Heh, heh, that's nice," and they're gone. I can't very well not tell a prospective partner, but there's got to be a better way of doing this or I'm never going to get it on. What do you suggest?

A There is hang-it-all-out honesty like "I am into S/M" (or "That new hairdo makes you look like the Bride of Frankenstein!") and there is honesty with discretion (e.g., "I prefer your hair when it's more contained" and "I find playing with power exchange extremely erotic.") I did a recent market survey, at a Media Alliance Soiree actually, and found that most people's associations to "S/M" or "S & M" were very negative: pain, whips, chains, sicko. Those people whose responses were neutral or positive (e.g., leather, power, fantasy, control, surrender) generally volunteered that they "had a friend who...," in other words; they had received some education on the subject. I strongly suggest finding some softer words and more appropriate time (Why do I get the sense that you're jumping the gun?) to talk about "playing with erotic power exchange." After all, if it is not a consensual erotic power exchange for both parties, what you have is not sexual play, but assault...and very few people would find that sexy.

I was especially interested in a letter in a recent column from a lady talking about S/M. I too think this lady should try the softer, slower approach. There are many people out there who are curious and yearning deep-down to try it out, but think it's taboo. If approached correctly and openly and taken as fun, it can be very exciting. The actual S/M activity can just be fantasy play — maybe some bondage, or the threat of pain with clothes and atmosphere. S/M has a bad image. I agree that people prefer words like leather (fashion), power (dominance) and surrender. I have been lucky in that I have been able to find women who, once introduced gradually, begin to enjoy such activities. I am submissive and usually look for dominant qualities in a woman. Also, in conversation I drop a very slight mention of bondage, S/M, etc., and wait for a reaction.

✍ In response to the woman who wrote that her admission of interest in S/M sends prospective partners scurrying away, here are two possible strategies: Engaging in a sharing conversation with a possible partner about fantasies in general can allow her to gauge the person's state of openmindedness and creativity, as well as the prospects for expanding boundaries of acceptance in the future. Nancy Friday's books on male and female fantasies would be excellent "props" around which to center such a discussion. She might also consider placing a personal ad in publications with S/M readerships such as (depending on her orientation) "On Our Backs" (526 Castro St., San Francisco, CA 94114) or "The SandMutopia Guardian and Dungeon Journal" (c/o Desmodus, P.O. Box 11314, San Francisco, CA 94101-1314). A personal ad may reach someone she has simply never bumped into at a social S/M event, as well as someone who is not an actively social member of the S/M community...like me.

✍ That woman who was interested in an S/M partner is welcome to correspond with me, should she wish. She can write to...

✍ I enjoy your work very much. You can do a kind thing by giving that woman interested in S/M my phone number. It is...

✍ I don't know whether you ever do this, but if that women who is into S/M wants to...

A I don't think I have seen such an outpouring of Good Samaritanism since the letter from the woman wanting a man with a large penis.

Q I've occasionally answered personal ads and met interesting people. But I have no idea how to respond to a personal ad that requests a telephone response.

A Some ads offer a choice whether to answer by letter or phone, so write if you prefer that. If the mechanics of a phone response elude you, phone the advertising department and ask someone to explain. This goes for the new telephone bulletin boards, which advertise in the personal sections as well. If it's what to say that puzzles you, write out a personal ad for yourself and read that onto the tape recorder. After that, if the person phones you back or you them, you carry on the way you would on any blind date, conducting the verbal show and tell until you decide whether or not to take the next step of meeting in person.

Q I am a heterosexual man whose personality incorporates many positive traits normally associated with women. I am caring, nonaggressive, and nurturing. I have throughout my life suppressed these characteristics and have instead attempted to be a "manly" man, strong and aggressive. I have never enjoyed this role and I have never filled it very well. I have not succeeded in changing my nature and have also not had much happiness in life or in relationships with women.

At 30, I want to change my life. I want — dare I even admit this anonymously? — to be *feminine*. I want to admit to someone that I want her to defend me, to lead me, to support me, to make sexual advances toward me. I think body hair and muscles on a woman are sexy. I want women to admire my body. I want to wear sexy clothing. Call me a transvestite, but I want to grow my hair long and wild and wear make-up. I want to have my awful ugly body hair removed and feel silk panties against my skin.

If I admit these desires to most women and men, I am sure I will be ridiculed. But I am just as sure there are places and organizations where I can meet women who are strong and dominant and want to be the protector in the relationship. I am also sure there are groups of men who would like to be my friend. Can you please tell me, and everyone like me, where we can find women and men who will love and understand us.

A There are organizations who support alternatives to traditional sex roles among whose members you might feel more comfortable being who you are. A good central clearing house is the International Foundation for Gender Education (P.O. Box 367, Wayland, MA 01778). Personal ads may net you a core group of friends and/ or potential lovers as well. If you go ahead and begin instituting your desired changes, you may indeed receive some rejection, but you will also begin to naturally attract those people who are sympathetic to your style. And, even if you do nothing but wait, society will eventually catch up and encompass you.

Q My problem with finding prospective dating partners is huge and painful. The prospect of expert help in this gives me a little more hope. I have what is called "an invisible handicap"; it is pulmonary and allergenic. It has kept me from working for quite some years. My most visible handicaps, therefore, are impoverishment and loneliness. I'm a sensitive intellectual with some years of college, not unattractive, and yet the last several times I've met a woman and there has been the proper chemistry, she widened her eyes and ran upon hearing of my situation — almost *just* like that.

Is it true that the bottom line for women in loving relationships with a man must always be money? I include the deadly euphemisms "good provider," "can take care of himself," "knows what he wants and gets it," as well as the more blatant ones of the personal ads: "successful professional" and "independent means," which appear in print so often that when they don't, it seems like an oversight. I certainly don't want to think that women are all basically whores. Is it more complex than that? More simple? What am I overlooking? What options ought to be open for a man in my position?

A Not to make light of your health problems, but every person you'll meet has an invisible handicap. It usually takes the form of a secret certainty that "once she/he finds out about my (knobby knees, flatulence, neediness — you fill in the blanks), I will be rejected and abandoned." I don't think Gordon Getty has a job either, but if asked what he does, my guess is that his answer is "I am a composer" or I volunteer with..." rather than "I live off my inherited wealth."

Yes, being poor and ill and jobless is not only awful for you, it's not very attractive to other people, men or women. So, find another, more positive, way to present who you are and how you live, show yourself to be understanding and supportive of others' failings in ongoing contacts, and don't look for love in a Yuppie newspaper but instead in places and activities where a person is judged by standards you can attain and perhaps at which you can excel.

Q What advice would you have for a divorced, single mom with two teen-aged sons, celibate several years since the divorce, who is unmoved by men, more comfortable with women, and even turned on by some; yet because of a conservative religious upbringing and motherhood, is not interested in a lesbian lifestyle? What sort of social life, lifestyle, relationships, etc., will work for such a person? Anyone else like me out there?

A Having friends, or even an occasional or more than occasional sexual bounce, does not constitute a lifestyle. You can be heterosexual, lesbian, bisexual, and/or celibate without making it a public crusade. Start exploring the possibilities. Attend discussion groups or events based on who you are and what you know to start with — Parents Without Partner meetings, support groups for the newly single, political or religious events, women's groups. See who you connect with, explore what's possible in the way of friendship or more with an individual as an individual. Of course there are women like you out there, many of them. If you simply "start walking," you'll soon find your way, and undoubtedly some fine traveling companions as well.

✍ I read your letter from a single mother of teenagers looking to make a life for herself. I sympathize, but feel it's even harder on parents of little ones, whether single or coupled, the price of baby-sitters being what it is. Is Parents Without Partners the only resource? What if you have a partner, but want a better social life any way?

A Cooperative nursery schools, where the parents participate in some way on a regular schedule, is a wonderful way to connect with others in your position. So is starting conversations with the grownups on the benches in public park playgrounds. Any newspaper or magazine devoted to parenting or family life might be a helpful publication to look into. A recent ad in one such local publication called for the formation of a social group for gay, lesbian, unbiased heterosexuals, and other alternative families of kids under two for "monthly romps, park-hopping, and baby-sitting exchange." If you can't find an ad for what you want, consider placing one.

Q I am a young man with what I think are average looks, but all my life I have felt unattractive to women. Women rarely introduce themselves to me. My main problem is that I am extremely nervous and shy around them, especially ones I find attractive. If I walk into a room and see one that attracts me I can't get myself to get anywhere near her. If she glances my way, I look away instinctively, although I try to fight this. I haven't the slightest clue about what to say to a woman I've never been introduced to, or to any others, for that matter. All my current female friends have become friends through introductions by my male friends, and these girls aren't interested in a relationship with me. I've never had a girlfriend. Do I have femaphobia? What's my problem? What should I do?

A I can't tell you how many letters like yours I receive a week. Your problem is that you lack social skills, which are learnable. Since you do have some female friends, you're off to a good start. Allow them to be your research resource. Ask them what they find attractive, what interests and amuses them, what's the first thing they notice about a man, etc. I often urge shy counseling clients of mine to read popular women's magazines aimed at the type, and age group they are interested in — from *Seventeen* to *Lear*. From the focus of their articles, you can learn what's of interest to many women of that category. Now, armed with information such as "Mostly everyone responds to a friendly smile" and "Most people want to feel understood and appreciated," or even the knowledge that most women think they're overweight, go out there and practice, practice, practice the art of meeting another person's eyes, of smiling, of being a good listener, of moving more gracefully in your body. Classes that involve shared physical activity, from dancing to martial arts are also good places to begin. If you are concentrating on learning something, you can forget about the unnecessary shame and self-consciousness that stand in the way of expressing your natural, friendly self.

Q My third personal ad is appearing this week. I am an attractive woman, upper 30s, who gets cold feet at the time of actually meeting a person. I'm great at writing and can talk on the phone for hours, but something comes up when trying to set a date to meet — "That's not a good day, okay, then I have to cancel, I'll get back to you." Once I actually stood up a man. I'm all too aware that my father issues come up at these times. Please don't say get into therapy; I've been in lots of therapy. I am making a commitment to push myself to carefully screen this next batch of responses, make a meeting commitment, and keep it. But if my feet get cold again, what should I do?

A I have in my office a framed Ashleigh Brilliant card that states, "If you can't go around it, over it, or through it, you had better negotiate with it." Whatever happened with your father or with previous therapists, the behavior you have decided to change is in the here and now. If a face-to-face, one-on-one blind date is difficult for you, you can "force yourself" by threats (the Stick Method of motivation), or you can bribe yourself with rewards (the Carrot School), or you can be gentle and negotiate with yourself. Wouldn't going to social events, where meetings occur more naturally, be easier for you? If you're positively convinced that personal ads are the only way to go, what about placing an ad in conjunction with a friend, and then you two meeting two others simultaneously? Counseling can be used as a problem-solving tool in this way, so if you do get cold feet again, reconsider further counseling with that aim in mind.

Q There is a woman in my office who is very nice, intelligent with a great sense of humor and a cute face. She is also quite overweight, at least 40 to 50 pounds. I get the feeling she would like me to ask her out, which I have thought about doing, only her heaviness turns me off. I've had relationships with woman who were "plump," but she's too much. Is there a polite way of saying "You seem interesting but I'd feel more attracted to you if you lost weight?" I don't want to hurt her feelings.

A Good, then don't ask her out until and unless you can do so with the intention of enjoying her company without her having to qualify for yours. If she ever asks you what it would take for you to become attracted to her, you have permission to say your "if you lost weight" speech. Until then, such uninvited commentary is rude in the extreme. If she's as intelligent as you say, she knows what she looks like. You either accept that she does not fit your preferred body type but you will explore further anyway, or you sigh a sigh of regret that all her appealing qualities do not outweigh that fact.

Regarding office man who was attracted to an office cutie but didn't want to go out with her unless she lost weight: I'm an attractive, physically fit woman whose man is 100 pounds overweight. He has all the qualities a person would want in a friend and lover, and I'm pleased to be with him. Office man's letter only points out the pressure society puts on people, especially women, to have great bodies. However, a warm day at the ball park where men and woman are walking around in tank tops and shorts will show that most folks have no room to talk about body shape, let alone judge other people's. I'm not saying that all overweight people are nice people, but I learned the hard way that it is impossible to judge how emotionally and sexually wonderful a person is by what he looks like. I've been with men whose great bodies turned out later to be 99% asshole. Maybe office man will reach a point in the future when he won't write off a woman he's attracted to simply because she's large.

A Should he miraculously make a complete turnaround, there exist two fascinating resources he, and others, should know about. One is The Big Board, a computer bulletin board (BBS) with information about goods, services, personal ads, and other items of interest for large people and their admirers. If you have a 300, 1200, or 2400 Baud modem, the 24-hour-a-day number is 415/824-7952. The other is a fanzine called *Dimensions*, a publication for admirers of the large figure. (send $18 for 6 issues to them at 7247 Capitol Station, Albany, NY 12224)

Q I'm a night worker for the Post Office. I'm not interested in making friends with the other people on my shift, but it seems like my choice is them or nothing. When I'm available, I don't know anybody else who is. Most social mixers take place on Friday and Saturday nights. What else is left?

A Various parks and public places. Whoever else is there when you are is also off work. Be friendly. For a less haphazard method, there are groups and classes that meet weeknights (if you don't work seven nights a week) or weekend afternoons. You might just have to look harder for resources, but I assure you there are many. Don't make the fact that it's not as easy for you as it might be for a 9-to-5er be the excuse to be alone if you don't want to be.

Q Here's a question most people probably learned the answer to in Dating 101 back in junior high school, but I apparently missed it. If you agree to a blind date and the other person turns out to be someone who puts you off completely the moment you lay eyes on him/her, are you obligated to go through with the date? If not, what do you say or do? If so, how do you get through the evening without letting your revulsion show, and also without letting the other person get a false impression of even the remotest interest on your part?

A Not finding someone instantly attractive, or even more strongly, finding them unattractive, cannot be an excuse for rudeness. The ideal solution would be not to allow yourself to get into such a position in the first place. Screen your blind dates over the phone, or through the intermediary who's setting you up, to exclude whatever characteristics you find so revolting (drunkenness or bodily filth are the only qualities I can think of to cause such a strong instant aversion). Always set up a brief first meeting, coffee or cocktails, so that there's not a whole evening to get through, but an hour at most. If the person asks you out again, either through a false impression of your interest or just incurable optimism, all you need do is refuse. If her/his behavior is objectionable, refuse less delicately.

Q I seem to have forgotten some guidelines for the world of dating. How does one gently let an over-eager suitor know that there's not enough interest for a romance? I think most people get the idea when the other person offers multitudinous excuses for not being able to get together. But what about the person who's persistent, who even (ackk!) asks for the truth? Would men like to hear a gentle, maybe nebulous, brush off or the cold facts? I hate hurting people's feelings but that's certainly not a reason to continue seeing someone you don't feel right about.

A Someone who asks for the truth is entitled to hear it, I think. The news that there's no romantic future can best be imparted with lots of positive strokes, literal ones like a pat on the hand, if that's possible. "We've had some interesting conversations," or "You're a very attractive person...however, I don't see any romantic possibilities here and I don't want to waste your time." If you really can't bring yourself to be that straightforward, you can fall back on the social nicety of outside forces: "I'm so sorry, but my life is just too busy these days for any new friendships," or personal failings, "I'm afraid I'm just not completely over my last romance." Please, oh please, don't say "Let's be friends" unless you mean that you do want this person in your life, and if you do, make the next social overture so he knows you meant it.

Q Only a precious few of my partners have seemed to realize that kissing is both a dialogue and a dance. For me a good kisser can enhance what seems like an otherwise average sexual experience while a bad one can be a total turnoff. Do some kissers have naturally good rhythm and others two left feet, so to speak? Can you teach someone to kiss better? I've tried with some partners without a whole lot of success, even though they were willing students. Please comment.

A Some people love to kiss, others see it as a mildly to extremely unpleasant means to an end. I think most people would classify the former as "good" kissers and the later as "bad," no matter how labile the lips or talented the tongue. Enthusiasm lends itself to artistry, I believe.

As for teaching, you can certainly request a specific change ("Don't pucker your lips; relax them") or demonstrate a technique ("Rather than thrusting with it, try using your tongue lazily like this...") but one cannot make a silk purse from a sow's ear, teach a pig to whistle or create an instant sensualist out of a germ-avoiding, anxiety-ridden, anal retentive — to coin a new phrase.

Comment: A resource to be shared: Writer Jay Wiseman has published a handy-dandy little book called *Personal Adventures; How to meet people through personal ads.* Valuable stuff here for first-timers or those with disappointing results from other forays into this increasingly popular social form. It covers such concerns as what constitutes an appealing ad in one type of paper vs. another, ideas on arranging the first contact safely and gracefully, how to proceed or kindly indicate disinterest, and so forth. (send $10 postpaid to P.O. Box 1261, Berkeley, CA 94701-1261)

♂ ▲ ♀ ▼ ◄ ♂ ◄ ♀ ▲ ◄ ♂ ▼ ♀ ▲ ♂ ► ♀ ▼ ♂ ▲ ♀

Two's Company, Three Can Be Fun, Too: Non-Monogamous Arrangements

♂ ▲ ♀ ▼ ◄ ♂ ◄ ♀ ▲ ◄ ♂ ▼ ♀ ▲ ♂ ► ♀ ▼ ♂ ▲ ♀

Q My boyfriend and I often fantasize about the excitement of another woman joining us in lovemaking. However, we don't know how to find the type of woman we're looking for. We certainly don't want a street prostitute; the venereal disease situation is too dangerous. My question is: Is there an organization that can match us with the type of woman we're looking for?

A You don't say what type of woman you are looking for, so I can't specifically direct you. If what you mean is someone who is willing to play in a threesome, I don't believe they are organized! You will see personal ads for couples seeking other playmates in this very paper. Far more explicit ads for such are available in magazines geared to finding sexual partners, such as The Odyessy (P.O. Box 1879, Los Angeles, CA 90007). Commercial party houses, wherein people may negotiate various sexual arrangements with other willing singles and couples, are a viable alternative. I've also noticed that the telephone bulletin boards that offer various arrangements now also have some for couples. Last but not least, look around you at people you already know for possibilities. If you can't do your friends, who do you do?

I've got an alternate resource for the couple looking for a third person. It's a group marriage newsletter put out by Polyfidelitous Educational Productions (PEP) (P.O. Box 6306, Captain Cook, HI 96704-6306) called "Peptalk." Supporting membership of $25 annually entitles one to the quarterly newsletter, a free entry in Network, a membership directory, roster of personal ads, and *The Primer*, a reference book on living in group marriage.

A *The New Faithful: A Polyfidelity Primer* has chapters that cover personal lifestyle evaluation, finding like-minded partners, negotiating the relationship (sex, health, money, parenting), and the personal stories of several believers. Even if this isn't everyone's cup of tea, it is a fascinating look at one alternative to serial monogamy.

Q I am 23 years old, and after several dozen lovers, and meaningless relationships, I am engaged to a wonderful, beautiful man who I respect, care for, and love very much. However, as of late, I have cheated on him on two occasions. Our sex life is fine. I don't understand my actions and have been feeling terribly guilty. Is it possible to be truly in love with one person and be able to enjoy sex with someone else?

A Someone wise said it is impossible to be happy if your actions do not mirror your beliefs. For some people love and sex are distinctly separate phenomena that occasionally can be combined. Such folks can be truly in love with one person and enjoy sex with someone else. For others the concept that love and sexual pleasure are not inextricably entwined is heresy. If you have made an agreement with your partner and/or with yourself that sex outside your relationship is permissible, then there is no problem. Since you feel you "cheated," either your beliefs require reappraisal or your behavior requires alteration. If you can't manage that alone, a good psychotherapist can help.

Q I pick up one of the swingers' papers periodically and have noticed that mixed-gender couples looking for a third party want a woman nearly 95% of the time. Why? Since I've been noticing this for over 10 years, I don't see fear of AIDS as the reason. Most of the ads note that "wife is bi curious." Aren't men? The few ads requesting a male third party seem to want male thirds, fourths, fifths and more and "hubby will videotape." Any comments? Guesses? Facts, even? (By the way, I thoroughly enjoy your column and learn something quite often. I also enjoy the fact that I still have questions at 45. I was afraid I'd know it all and be bored!)

A I discussed your question with several knowledgeable others and we came up with several comments, guesses, and potential facts. I'll leave it to you to choose among them: Many of these scenarios are at the man's instigation, and reflect fantasies of his which the woman is willing to go along with but not willing to recruit her friends for. Voyeuristic men who get a charge out of seeing their woman being done by other men is a relatively common turn-on, while the opposite is not. Finding a man to cooperate in a sexual adventure is a lot easier than finding a woman to do so, so that seekers of women are forced to look further afield and place ads. While many men may indeed be bi curious, our society gives little permission to explore that curiosity. (It's not heterosexual women who use "cocksucker" as the basest of insults.)

Q I believe in love but I also believe that mature adults should be able to regard sex as recreation. I believe women are coming more and more to the attitude that many men have had, wanting short-term exploratory sex. But how can I read a woman's signals? Where would I meet such a woman? How could I ask her?

A There are far more men than women interested in no-strings-attached sex, which is why places that foster it, like commercial swing-party houses, usually insist that people arrive in male-female couples. Look for organizations, groups, and classes that deal with sex or nudity or nontraditional values (communes, open marriages, etc.). Women there, while not necessarily interested in casual sex, will at least be more likely to be willing to discuss the subject. As for reading signals, human females (fortunately or not, depending on your point of view) do not offer unequivocal rutting signs, like the baboon's blue bottom. When in doubt, ask — politely — and be willing to hear "no."

Q A couple with whom I've been friendly for many years have been getting closer and closer to me. I love and adore them both, but I keep feeling pinched and whacked out by the implicit demands of being connected to two people and more. I believe this has some-thing to do with my parents having labored to connect to us two children as if they were not a couple. I have become openly abusive toward my friends and, worse, toward their friends, and now they no longer return my calls. Please help me to figure out how to keep going forward with this lifestyle in which I profoundly believe. It grants every childhood wish and more. The straight life in no way compares. Maybe my longtime friends are not for me, though I hope I can eventually get back with them.

A Relating intimately with a couple really requires three separate relationships, any one of which could be problematic. Juggling all three requires enormous effort and talent. Try sorting out each on its own merits: your relationship with each of these two individuals and yours with the couple as a unit. If, as I infer, the relationship(s) have a sexual content, that needs to be sorted out and negotiated, along with other areas that may cause problems in any duo or triad — time, money, the inclusion or exclusion of others.

If your friends won't return your phone calls, write them a letter of explanation. Once you are a grownup, how you were raised is no longer a valid excuse for unacceptable behavior as far as I'm concerned. If your momma failed to teach you something you now need to know, or taught you erroneously, you are now capable of learning on your own what you perceive is needed. If you behaved badly because you were jealous, for example, don't blame it on childhood trauma. That's a weasel. Simply apologize for your behavior and explain, if you want their understanding, that you were feeling jealous. If jealously comes too easily into your life, for example, or bad temper, or abusive language or whatever (regardless of whether the cause is your family of origin or other faulty learnings), that's the province of a good psychotherapist. If it is your intent to seek other relationships with couples, it is particularly important that you master good communication skills, starting with how you talk to yourself.

Q If one person in a relationship wants complete monogamy and the other one does not, do you really think it's possible to negotiate some sort of an agreement without someone feeling either cheated or cheated on?

A Yes! The first step is that each partner must trust that the other is negotiating in good faith; if it is agreed upon to first discuss any outside connections, then each must do exactly that and trust that the partner will, too. Each must believe in the other's good faith, as well — that each partner wants this relationship to work and will put time and energy into making that happen.

After that, it's a point-by-point clarification of the needs behind the concepts — how does each feel about seeing old friends, making new ones, being sensual vs. being sexual and the definitions of each. Does the agreement exclude same- or opposite-sex liaisons? Does the partner want to know/tell beforehand, afterward, at all? Step by step, with the idea that whatever is worked out is for the moment, each begins to trust the process and can return to it as needed throughout the life of the relationship.

Q A long-time female friend of my girlfriend's recently stayed with us. The last night she was here, I woke up with an erection. Leaving my girlfriend asleep in our bed, I went to the friend's room and touched her in her sleep. She awoke and we had sex. Later that day when we were alone for a few moments, the friend told me that she felt guilty, though flattered. We both agreed it wouldn't happen again. After the friend left (she lives far away), my girlfriend confronted me with her suspicions and I admitted what happened. I told her, truthfully, that I do not know why I did it. I wasn't particularly attracted to the woman.

I am shocked that I took the doubled risk of unprotected sex and of losing my girlfriend. I must have been temporarily insane! Was it male ego, conquest, power? I wasn't fully aware of how much I love my girlfriend until I realized I nearly blew the whole relationship, and I don't even understand why! Do I need professional help? An adjunctive problem is that my girlfriend now hates this woman and says she is no longer a friend since a "friend" wouldn't have let me do it. She gets angry if I try to defend the woman's vulnerable state. I feel even worse to have wrecked what was a close friendship. I am intensely grateful that she has forgiven me, but since it was my doing, how can I get her to see that her friend is no less her friend?

A You have lost respect for yourself. Your girlfriend has lost respect for you and for her friend. And I sense that you have lost respect for her in the way she refuses to allow you your share of culpability. In any case, several relationships have been dramatically altered and I wonder whether that might have been your intention.

First, let's tackle your relationship with you: Since all behavior has its own logic, part of you was sending some message to another part of you by your actions. If you really have no inkling of what was going on (establishing your independence, testing limits, sheer shit-disturbing), a trained therapist would be very helpful in figuring it out. That way, you could deal more effectively in the future with whatever needs prompted your midnight foray. Your girlfriend's relationship to her girlfriend is not really your concern (beyond your judgments about her attitude and actions). You've done what you can. Deal with your feelings, allow her hers.

Q With each passing year I feel more like an oddity. Time was when a person who wanted to explore non-traditional sexual relationships (read: nonexclusive) could find others of like mind, especially in the San Francisco Bay Area. It seems of late, however, that like in the realm of politics, there has been a swing to the right. I have no intentions of ever having a traditional relationship, and would like your advice on how to survive and prosper during what seems to be increasingly conservative times.

A If your taste always had and still did run toward young women with long straight hair bedecked with flowers, wearing patchouli oil, and sporting dirty bare feet, I'd bet you'd experience the same thing — that's it's harder to find them now than it used to be 20 years ago. So you have a choice of looking harder for those few who still do exist (in your case by joining organizations that support non-traditional relationships), or else finding a compatible woman who is willing to accommodate your preference (read: agree to conduct the kind of arrangement you want regardless of what Society is currently touting).

I am in what might be called a love "V" (as opposed to a triangle) — I love two men and they both love me. That sounds terrific except that the past year indicated we all get hurt feelings when I try to be in a relationship with both of them, so I recently had to make a decision. Both men are loving, dedicated, and sincere. "Max" is playful and sexy but erratic, and his life is unstable. "Seymour" is kind, stable, and secure. Our sexual chemistry is okay, but not great. I decided on Seymour because I felt we had a better basis for a long-term (possibly lifelong) relationship.

My problem is that I still love Max and am very drawn to him physically. It deeply saddens me that I will have to exclude him from my intimate life (sexual and otherwise) and that I will be excluded from his. My question is: How do I handle my feelings for Max? I'm looking for creative ways to keep him in my life without tension. Am I being insincere, dishonest, or unfair to Seymour to attempt this?

A Our popular culture historically abounds with such dilemmas as yours, and my professional and personal experience has been that whatever the choice and however it's made — whether by head, heart, or groin — the chooser generally winds up longing for the road not taken. (I recently watched an old stinkeroo movie from the

'60s, "V.I.P.," with a great cast, in which every one of the mini-dramas played out in the fog-bound airport lounge revolved upon a similar dilemma: the dull husband or capricious lover, the exciting mistress or the loyal secretary.)

I personally feel that the best decision is not an either/or, but both: "I want you both in my life; that's my decision!" I don't have a creative solution for you on how this can be accomplished, but I'm sure that if you want this strongly enough, you'll find your own. As for being unfair to one man for attempting to do so, you'd be unfair to yourself if you did not.

You had a letter about a love "V" which is similar to my problem. When I am with one woman, I worry about the other. They both want a monogamous committed relationship. They are distinctly different otherwise, and I have often wished I could roll into a ball the aspects of each I like. A friend suggests that I should discontinue both relationships. To avoid confusion all around, I'm not sleeping with either one, but I would sure like more than coffee and conversation. Is there any way — such as a book or thought process — for me to figure out definitely if I'm overly critical, afraid of commitment, afraid I'll never meet another woman, whatever?

A The possibilities you list are just arbitrary labels, like the spate of pop psych books about those who never grow up, love too much, came from less than ideal families, etc. Essentially, all of us do what we want to do, and then try to explain it with a theory. One thing at a time and stay in the moment, treating each relationship as a separate entity rather than one half of a two-pronged problem. Do you want to pursue a love affair? Then pursue that without promising exclusivity. If she won't play on your terms, see what you can negotiate. If nothing is satisfactory, one of you will undoubtedly break it off. Eventually you will either find a woman with whom you are willing to be exclusive, or one who's requirements don't strike you as confining.

Q I am sweetly, happily, and inconveniently involved with a woman who currently happens to live 3000 miles away. We've had ups and downs for the last one and a half years, the time we've been geographically separated, but manage to see each other every month or two. Last year we decided to have an open relationship, allowing for flings while at opposite ends of the country. I agreed unwillingly and never thought I would be interested, but now I am. I don't believe that it is really okay, that she wouldn't get jealous, as she claims, and that it wouldn't mess everything up. I also don't think I could not tell her and lie. We will live together starting this summer and I will no longer have the chance to play that I now theoretically do. What do you think? (Did you think I'm male? I'm female.)

A You already know that love's a gamble. The odds get worse when it's a long-distance relationship, when it's a same-sex relationship, when it's an open relationship, and so on, but people do beat the odds all the time. The best you can do to hedge your bets is to clarify as much as you can ahead of time, and take it from there.

Was part of your agreement to open the relationship that you would disclose other liaisons — beforehand or at all? Why not check whether she would want to know? You seem to feel you would have to tell by your own nature. Could you keep dirty details to yourself, if your partner said she had no wish to hear about them? Suppose she does get jealous, which she may, even if she doesn't think she will. What would she have you do in that case? Can you reiterate the primacy of your relationship, and give her the power to ask you to end any others? Would you want that or are you likely to feel resentful? "I would like some clarification on the nature of our open relationship agreement. How do you think it might be if..." is a good place to begin.

Q I recently moved to this area, right into the home of my girlfriend. We have fun together much of the time, and our relationship has come a long way in the past two months. A few weeks ago I met one of her good friends, let's call her Sally, who I thought was a knock-out, and we started seeing each other on a friendly basis. I started feeling more for Sally. I don't want to spoil anything I could have with Sally (friends is okay) and I don't want to lose my relationship with my girlfriend. Stay? Leave and see what happens with Sally? Leave the area entirely and head on my way? (I know I love this city!)

A Why either/or? Fie on the way our society defines relationships: "Friends are not sexually attracted to each other," "You can't have warm feelings for more than one person at a time," all sorts of erroneous dicta that only serve to confuse when feelings tell you otherwise. You have two relationships. One with the woman whom you call your girlfriend, one with Sally. Sit down with each of them and assess her wants and expectations in regard to you, yours in regard to her. Once you have a clearer picture of where you stand in each situation, you might be more ready to come to some conclusion. When you have a difficult choice on a restaurant menu, do you get up and leave hungry? Then why would you see leaving the area as a solution to this? Even if you wind up alienating both women, you will still have this lovely city to explore on your own.

Q A few years ago, my then-fiancé John and I moved put of our home to live separately, and some months later we broke up entirely, though remaining good friends. Not long afterward, he started going out with — and then moved in with — my best friend Gertie. Since then *she* has broken off her relationship with me entirely and has jealous fits if he mentions my name. John keeps encouraging me to remain friends with her. I've done my best to restore our friendship but am continually rejected. Consequently, John wants us to remain friends surreptitiously, behind her back. Other mutual friends agree, even my current sweetheart.

I dearly treasure John's friendship but I don't want to be dishonest — partly from my own sense of integrity, but also because I think their relationship is too important to risk through deceit. He thinks I'm moralizing. I think it seems less risky in the long run for him to stand up to Gertie now and continue our friendship, than to pretend I have disappeared but see me anyway. I'm deeply disturbed about this. What should I do?

A What do you *want* to do? Sometimes putting the question to yourself in that way clarifies the situation. If the answer is impossible, such as "I want to see him and I want that to be all right with her," keep on phrasing the options that do exist in terms of what you want, rather than what you *ought*. Focus your concern not on your opinion of what is best between the two of them, but what is best for you, your relationship with yourself first and then your relationship with John, since you have none with Gertie. Shakespeare said it better than I have here: "To thine own self be true...thou canst not then be false to any man."

Q I am an English Lit major doing my first year of work toward an M.A. I've been thinking about writing a book about swing houses and party life, keeping it clean enough to be sold everywhere. I know that people are generally curious about this lifestyle. I thought of doing it as an M.A. thesis, but the academic crowd is still too prudish or might get some wrong ideas. Are there any books on swinging/party houses, and is there a market for one?

A I can't tell you whether or not there is a market for your proposal but a reputable literary agent would be willing to make an educated guess. That's their job. I've read many articles on the topic, even a thesis or two (while researching my own, which was on the agreements couples make about sex outside their relationship). You might consider writing an article about swinging first and see if you can place it. That ought to give you some firsthand input about whether the idea is worth pursuing in either thesis or book format.

Q Have I died and gone to heaven? In a heterosexual male fantasy come true, I've twice found myself in bed with two straight women friends (different ones each time). Each time the lovely cuddly energy turned sexual with one of the two women, while the other (in both cases a former lover of mine) was left out or had her sleep disturbed. What's the proper etiquette for two of the three taking psychic leave for a while? Is it only my couple conditioning that makes it awkward? Any tips on how sexuality can flower from a bedded threesome? Any question I've forgotten? Are we having fun yet?

A What you have described is not a threesome except in the most technical of senses. A threesome involves three people being sensual/sexual *together*, not one sleeping through it all, or pretending to. After all, many good experiences are possible with six hands, three mouths, three genitals, and acres of sensitive flesh. What you have described is a genuine etiquette problem...which I'd love to see Miss Manners handle! Should you "find yourself" again in bed with two women ("Oh my, how *did* I get here?") and no one seems inclined to share and share alike, in my opinion good manners dictate that the active participants take physical, as well as psychic, leave and remove their bounding energy to another room.

♀◀♂◀♀▲♂▼♀▲♂▶♀▼♂

The Nature
of Relationships

♀◀♂◀♀▲♂▼♀▲♂▶♀▼♂

Q How can he love me and not want to be with me always? I am 29 and have been seeing a very nice man for the past 18 months. I love him and he tells me he loves me. We have great sex. He is very busy and I'm tired of seeing him only on weekends. I have tried so hard to convince him to live with me or/and marry me. I am getting paranoid about being almost 30 and would like to really get involved; he doesn't want to. Talking to him is out of the question. He does not like to talk about our relationship. He feels everything is fine with it and I am being difficult. Do I stick around not knowing where the relationship is going or do I get my act together and move on to a new and hopefully better mate? What would you do if you were me? Keep in mind, leaving him is the last thing I want to do.

A I know how hard it is for someone to contemplate the possibility that her or his reality is not *the* reality, but that's what's going on here. For you, obviously loving someone means wanting to be with them more than two nights a week. For him, the relationship *is* fine and your wanting to change it *is* being difficult. Neither reality is wrong. Is it possible for you to find some middle ground between hanging in there and loving him while your clock ticks away toward 30, and leaving him entirely? How about resetting your goal to age 32, for instance, or announcing to him that while you want to continue your relationship, you are also going to start exploring possibilities with other men as well. Telling him, not as a threat, but as a practical alternative to your situation of wanting more than he is willing to give.

Q You meet someone who is attractive, charming, and says all the right things...yet that little inner voice tells you, "Don't trust this person." Should we always listen to our intuition?

A Yes. But if the person is all that charming, you needn't turn away immediately. Just proceed with more than usual caution.

Q I have a wonderful relationship with my boyfriend and have no reason to feel insecure, but I find myself feeling jealous of the women in his past. They've remained friends, so I've met several of them. The thought of him in bed with them makes me irrationally angry, yet it is an incredible turn-on for me. I imagine their lovemaking in great detail. However much sexual fantasy pleasure I get from these mental images, they really upset me and make me anxious. Can you give me any advice on how to understand and help myself?

A Albert Ellis has written a book called *How To Stubbornly Refuse To Make Yourself Miserable About Anything* which covers it all better than I can. Briefly, however, you can either ask for reassurance from your lover when you are bedeviled, or you can mentally change the channel from thoughts of him with other women to thoughts of the two of you, thereby reassuring yourself. Try both and anything else you can think of to remind yourself that, while they are still in his life, it is you who are now in his bed.

Q A little over a month ago my boyfriend spent the night with another woman. I'm a virgin and so was he before he slept with that woman. I'm very hurt and angry. Sex was something we wanted to explore together. What I'd like to know is whether there are any excuses for infidelity and can a relationship survive it? I guess I'd like to know how other people feel and how they deal with it.

A The question here is whether there is any "excuse" *you* can accept that will allow you to re-establish a loving relationship with your boyfriend. He told you about his betrayal. Was it to hurt you, or to seek forgiveness and repair trust? Many relationships survive broken agreements, and some may emerge even stronger for it. *The Monogamy Myth: A New Understanding of Affairs and How To Survive Them* (1989, Newmarket Press) might offer different perspectives, or you might consider a couples' group that would encourage discussion about how others handle instances of broken promises.

Q Do you think it's true that there's no such thing as sexual incompatibility, that if you're incompatible it always indicates other problems in the relationship? Can't two people who love each other just really be incompatible?

A We will both agree that natural *compatibility* exists — two people who like to spend approximately the same amount of time pursuing the same activity (e.g., "We're both bird watchers," or "We both enjoy oral sex on Saturday mornings."). So then, of course, there is a natural incompatibility (e.g., "I like to lie in bed having sex on Saturday mornings and my partner likes to be up and out early to bird watch."). I wouldn't be so Pollyanna-ish to say that Love always finds a way, but I would hope that two people who do love each other could find something sexual to do together that feels good to both of them, even if what they do discover would not be the first choice of titillation for either of them.

Q I'm 25, single, healthy, love being intimate, and enjoy sex as a meditation. I've been in love many times but never found anyone to inspire me to be intimate or present during sex. I just go animal when someone touches me just right. My brain shuts off. I can begin feeling verbal or connected afterward, usually when my lover just wants to sleep. So, is this normal? I get the sense that there's a difference between sex and making love and I'm missing out on the latter. Will the right person be the difference or is it me?

A Lovemaking, being present, implies consciousness: "I am aware of you, of us; I am taking pleasure in your pleasure." The emotions that accompany this are a product of what you are telling yourself about the experience. You can talk out loud or keep it in your head. Animal, as you call it, is a feeling state rather than a thinking one. I believe the simultaneous experience of intense states of thinking and feeling is probably impossible, no matter what your sentiments for your partner — earthy, spiritual, or a wonderful combination thereof. You want to chat and come at the same time? Some people can't even walk and chew gum!

Q Every man I've ever been seriously involved with has gotten married to his next girlfriend. This has happened five times now! The latest was a man who always said he was incapable of having a relationship. Two boyfriends I left, two left me, one was fairly mutual. None of my girlfriends have experienced this. Is this a common phenomenon? I'm starting to feel paranoid about having another relationship.

A For every nonvirgin man who gets married, someone had to be his previous girlfriend, right? Therefore, what's been happening to you has happened at least once to many, many women. How come you have gotten such a disproportionate share? Bad luck, bad karma, bad choice, bad timing, maybe some of each. It might help to try some fact-finding by talking to those men who might still be in your life, and asking for input from your girlfriends about your choices and your behavior. If you can't find any explanations that satisfy you, perhaps you could comfort yourself with the possibility of all those men thinking, "I guess I've had the best there is, so I'd better settle down and quit searching for anything better."

For the first time in many years I must disagree with you. I am referring to your response to the correspondent who complained that five of her former male friends ended up marrying the woman they met right after her. Over the years I had several similar experiences: Women I had been seeing got into a new marriage, committed relationship, or motherhood soon after they got out of my life. What I came to conclude is that I served as a catalyst for these women and that our encounters awakened some emotional process dormant till then. Rather than subscribing to your correspondent's feeling of paranoia, I would like to encourage her to take pride in whatever she ignited in the heart of her five ex-partners. Maybe she and I should organize a support group for frustrated catalysts, or start a sour grape tasting club?

Q Perhaps I'm superimposing my own difficulties on all queerdom, but I don't think so. Why does it seem on the surface that lesbians are able to sustain long-term relationships, whereas gay men (myself included) are always searching for it but so rarely find someone to nest with?

A In my own acquaintance, two out of three of the happiest long-term couples I know are male-male, and one of the unhappiest couplings is female-female. Clearly, then, this is not a case of "Men always...Women never..." I don't want to get into that age-old argument about causes here: nature (the biological urge toward many partners for male animals in order to insure the continuation of the species) vs. culture (virile men are supposed to "tomcat" around. Women who behave that way are called nasty names). Whatever the cause(s), the average male has a harder time staying contentedly coupled than the average female; two men in one couple raises the likelihood of discontent. Like heterosexual females, you will just have to look harder for a fellow nester than a person who seeks a female partner. Having found a likely candidate, be sure to learn the necessary skills for a happy long-term coupling, primary among them being good communication.

Q A two-pronged question, if you will. First of all, my girlfriend recently consented to anal intercourse and now says she prefers it to vaginal intercourse. She nearly always comes that way, albeit with manual stimulation of the clitoris. The other night during a domestic fight (one that had nothing to do with sex, by the way), she laid it to me, claiming any man who "goes anal" is definitely a latent homosexual. This worries me. Is there any psychological evidence to support this thesis? She also gets off by watching me masturbate. When I comply, she laughs at me afterward. When I complain, she says to "quit whining," that the laughter is just part of "the trip." Is it OK for me to feel awkward jerking off in front of this gal? Does my embarrassment point to some deep-seated insecurity?

A Do you know what I'd worry about if I were you? Not whether you aren't a latent homosexual (because everyone is, who is not a blatant homosexual, and they are latent heteros), not whether it's okay to feel embarrassed when you know you're going to be laughed at — my wonder is that you can get it up at all under the circumstances — but why you don't recognize the cruelty and rudeness of your bitchy girlfriend for what it is. *That's* your evidence of deep-seated insecurity. I suggest you look this woman in the eye and tell her you will not accept her no-win double binds any longer (the damned-if-you do and damned-if-you-don't set-ups she constructs) and then, if you still want to, agree on sexual acts which you both can enjoy without guilt or shame.

Q Recently I broke up with another boyfriend and am soul-searching. It's scary to realize I attract the same characteristics in a man time after time. I seem to attract men who want an open relationship or ménage à trois experiences. I feel insecure when I am with this type of man. Am I alone or do other women have this experience? Sometimes I think women can change this fickleness in men by not tolerating this behavior, but I can only start with myself. I would like to know what percentage of heterosexual men between ages 25 and 35 in San Francisco practice commitment-oriented relationships. Have you ever tried a survey?

A I see you struggling with forming realistic expectations and I applaud your objective. However, statistics, even if there were some way to give you valid ones on this, are really of no use. If I stated that 1 man out of 3 or only 1 man out of 37 had or did what you prefer, you'd still be looking for that.

Commitment, giving primacy to you, being reliable, is not the same as monogamy. You can have one without the other. Some men give lip service to an exclusive relationship but cheat, others have good intentions but fail, others maintain their standards...until they don't, still others would not make such an agreement in the first place but behave monogamously nonetheless.

There are more men than women who would prefer a sexually open relationship and I don't know whether that's nature or culture, and a ménage à trois is a common fantasy. Any woman can ask for sexual exclusivity. If she's lucky, she may attract a man who desires the same or is willing to agree to it in order to have a relationship with her. You can also examine other possibilities in light of a particular man and a particular relationship. There may be one (man or relationship) good enough for you yourself to also accommodate.

Q If some woman wants to save herself for her one true love, God bless her. If other women take a more casual attitude, that's cool too. What I don't understand are these modern gals with a string of lovers in their pasts for whom sex is suddenly sacred. Commitment? I mean...everybody else gets away with it, but I'm expected to pay with my life. Am I supposed to feel special?

A My dear man, I cannot explain women, even that small segment called "modern gals," within the confines of this column, but here are some truisms to ponder: Some people's needs change over the course of their lifetime. Some people learn from their experience and stop doing what no longer works for them. Many people lump all sorts of vague wants and needs such as protection from disease, a wish to feel valued, a need for some sense of certainty in an uncertain world, a hope for a future, and so on into that fuzzy ball of wax (ugh, what a metaphor!) called Commitment. Anyone who requests it may rightfully be asked to explain her/his terms. Lastly, if you view sharing sexual pleasure as "getting away with something" at a woman's expense, I'm afraid I'm casting pearls before...well, let's just say I don't have much hope you'll get what I'm saying.

Q I love my husband dearly and I love my new baby. I'm pleased with the job I will be returning to shortly and I feel I have many good social friends, a nice place to live, and a good life. I wouldn't change any of it, but something has got to go. I already feel stretched to the breaking point and I don't have one minute to myself. How do other people manage?

A By setting priorities. In any couple, there is time together as lovers and time together as domestic partners; time as a social unit, perhaps time together as a family unit. If the couple fails to build into this some time as playmates, too, spending time the way they spent it when they were courting, everything else starts coming apart at the seams. They're not as interested in sex, they're short-tempered with other family members, they're not as much fun for their friends. It's even more true for individuals. Unless you take some time to refresh and replenish yourself, to actually hold private Q & A sessions with yourself, you will not be as effective a wife, mother, worker, friend, etc. So if you can't justify an hour or so a day, an evening or more a week, an afternoon or so a weekend, just for your own sake, do it for the benefit of all those others in your life who will receive more from a woman who can also give to herself.

Q I am a black gay man and my lover is white. Although we've only been together for a short period of time, we are in love and plan to wed. Before meeting my lover, I was about 70% passive in the bedroom. My lover believed he was active, but we have since realized that he, too, prefers being passive. During our lovemaking I am expected to always take the active role, which does very little to stimulate me. I love this man with all my heart and I believe that we could be very happy together, but am I supposed to just let go of my needs and cater to his? He has told me that I can see other men if I want as long as I don't tell him about it, yet I love him too much ever to be unfaithful. Is it wrong of me to enter into a permanent relationship knowing he may never satisfy my sexual needs?

A Not wrong, but foolhardy, don't you think? Hang the labels. Black or white, active or passive; if neither of you finds it exciting to do something sexual to the other, and both of you lie there wanting to be "done," I think you're in for some grief. Negotiating an open relationship, as your lover suggests, is one way out of the dilemma. Take whatever good stuff is available within your relationship and supplement the rest elsewhere. If both of you agree to that arrangement, it's not being unfaithful, it's being practical.

Perhaps you could work out some sort of "scoring system" so that each of you will satisfy the other about 50% of the time and take his own satisfaction vicariously the other 50%. Other than intercourse, could you occasionally settle for using dildos, mutual mouth or hand stimulation, side-by-side self-pleasuring?

If you can't negotiate a workable agreement about sex, then the two of you better sit down and do some honest assessing. How likely are you to continue to "love with all your heart" someone who engenders such frustration?

Q A recent question in your column had to do with the dilemma of responding to either sleepiness or horniness. I seek your advice for my related problem. My long-term lover who is very sexual under certain circumstances gets up at 5:30 AM to race-walk. By the time she hits the sack at 10:30 or 11 PM after dinner and/or a movie or TV she almost always conks out even though I'm feeling amorous. (And I do let her know.) On rare occasions I seduce her in her sleep, but most of the time she hates to be awakened. So, one partner is almost always sleepy or very quick to fall asleep (her), while the other, me, is almost always horny.

Whether rational or not, this pattern during the week makes me feel as though she never wants me since she doesn't allow time in her busy schedule, and it's nice and exciting to be wanted. Saturday morning, an occasional Saturday night, or Sunday morning as the only times we can really enjoy a sex life together isn't enough for me, and one or the other of us may simply not feel like it at those designated times. Any ideas?

A Yes. Consider sex before dinner, instead of a movie or TV, after she comes in from race-walking, right after work...anytime other than when retiring or waking. Both of you need not be "ready and willing" for sex at those times, but a suggestion of a lie-down and a cuddle may lead to something hotter. If not, at least you will feel more connected to each other and less low-priority.

Q Admittedly an age-old question: How do I get him fired up again? Being open, responsive and inviting with no result only seems to emphasize the fact that apparently I have no clue, after 11 years of knowing him, about what will provoke desire in him sufficiently for him to act on it. He used to appear at the door of my work room on relaxed Sunday afternoons and ask in an endearing and rakish fashion if I wanted to fuck. Now he often practices with his band on Sundays and doesn't schedule relaxation for himself. I respect and support what he's doing in his work and musical pursuits, but I think we ought to be able to manage more sex than once a year. Asking him to relax is pointless. Asking him to set aside time is also pointless. He has very exciting things demanding his time. I feel helpless. I like sex.

A The implication I get here is that you are not one of the "exciting things demanding his time," in your eyes or in his. I would also guess that this is a situation gone way beyond cooking his favorite dish or greeting him at the door in lingerie. Therefore, the operative word is not "exciting," unless you can get him to tell you what that would be for him, but "demand." You can't demand someone be turned on, more's the pity, but you can insist on his paying attention to you long enough to let him know of your unhappiness and your proposed solutions — requiring him to set aside a weekend morning or an evening a week to just hang out with you, seeing a relationship counselor together, opening the relationship to other partners for you, whatever.

   Whether wife or lover, you have every right to want *and insist upon* more than you're now getting. If you are so low on his priority list that he won't come through for you once he's made aware of your needs, I would seriously reevaluate this relationship.

Q I met this wonderful person not quite a month ago. We've seen each other every night since the day we met, and now we're talking about moving in together in October. Sometimes I'm afraid this is all going so fast that I don't have time to give it the proper thoughtful attention. Are whirlwind romances ever successful in the long run?

A Some are. Yours is put in jeopardy, though, if you're feeling rushed and out of control. You're not a passenger on an express train, but at the very least the co-conductor. Tell this wonderful person your feelings and see how they are honored or dealt with. Say you need some time off to be by yourself and then take it — an evening to yourself per week, a weekend retreat, an occasional time out to be with your friends and seek their input. If your lover fusses, look closely at that. What's her/his hurry and why the pressure? Don't move in together until you feel perfectly ready, willing, and able to do that comfortably. Real estate contracts are often more difficult to get out of than love affairs.

Q What happens when someone is sexually attracted to you, but you aren't sexually attracted to him? He's trying to get you in bed, you keep saying "Let's just be friends." Even subtle pressure can build up resentment. I feel guilty when I have to drop someone, but what is the alternative? Chemistry is immediate or not at all, right?

A Wrong, at least for many. Ask around. Most people end up marrying someone they have worked with, lived near, known for a while. Some chemistry is slow-acting and takes a while to sizzle or explode. As to what happens when you resent someone's behavior — be it pressure to be sexual after you have said no, or public nose picking — after you have told that person to please knock it off because you are uncomfortable with what he does, and he keeps on doing it anyway, you can say goodbye without guilt.

Q I would really appreciate it if you would take the time to answer this young, confused, 17-year-old man's problems. About three weeks ago I started becoming real good friends with this girl I have liked for a year. Talk about a dream coming true! We've become so close, open, and honest with each other. There is a major problem in that she has a boyfriend. They have been going together for a year. She says she loves him and vice-versa.

She told me that she likes me very much and is even starting to fall in love with me. I can't say I'm falling in love with her, but I like her so much and I've never felt like this about any friend before. We have even kissed and we just called it an innocent one. I feel bad about it and she does too. It didn't feel innocent. What should I do? Should I just stay as her friend, or what? It's hard to hide my feelings for her but I don't want to be stringed along either.

A Relationships do not come clearly labeled from day one — "This is a friendship," "This may be a romance." Every time you meet someone for whom and/or from whom there seems to be some warm feelings, all us must bumble our way along, experimenting, taking risks, and with great good luck — enjoying the process. Each of us must define ambiguous words like "friendship," "in love" and "innocent" for ourselves and compare what we come up with to the definitions offered by the other person. Try to become clear in your own mind. Do you want to do some more kissing? Do you want to put things on hold until she no longer has a boyfriend? What specifically do you want and what do you not want? Share your feelings and listen to hers. See if you can sort out together what you both want from each other and what you feel comfortable doing about it. Then, whatever you come up with, you can call it your special relationship.

Q My friend and I seem to have the same problem. We are each sexually enthralled with our respective boyfriend/fiancé. While they are obliging to our sexual needs, they do not initiate sex nearly enough. When they do, it's more of a signal for us to go ahead and jump them, rather than a true romantic or sexual initiative. We have also both noticed decreased likelihood of receiving oral sex. When questioned about this unseemly lack of sexual fervor, these men deny the problem, tell us to stop tallying sexual activities, or say we are exaggerating or are oversexed. Has our aggressive behavior made our men lazy, or might there be more to this? Are men threatened by our seemingly insatiable desire for sex? We just love it, and love it with them in particular, and we will do anything (and do so), so it can't be boredom, can it? We wish they would throw us on the floor as soon as we step in the door, rip off our clothing, and get on with it. We have developed fears that each sexual encounter might be our last. Help!

A Sounds like what we have here is a fairly typical pattern of one partner doing all the initiating and the other all the responding...in duplicate. That the old myth of "Men insist, women resist" is no longer always valid does not make a one-sided arrangement any more palatable for someone who wants it otherwise.

Rather than lumping your situation and your friend's into one problem, or worse, making a bigger lump with assumptions about "threatened men" in general, there is a need for one-on-one conversation — not between the two women wailing "Woe is us," but within each couple. You say, "Honey" (or a reasonable facsimile), "I would like you to be more aggressive sexually. What would it take to have that happen?" If there is something you can do, or refrain from doing, you will be more likely to learn it in an atmosphere of mutual problem solving, than in one of mutual blame.

Q I am in love with a man I've been involved with for three months. About six weeks into our very intense relationship, an ex of his surfaced and wanted to try again. They ended up in bed one night. The next day he told me he'd been unfaithful and begged me to take him back. I decided to see the value in his honesty and courage in telling me everything, and the value in our relationship, which up to that point had been wonderful. I haven't said the words "I forgive you," but we have become closer. I really feel he's done more than most would to repent and suffer for his sins, he regrets it so much.

In the past, I have "forgiven," and yet held it as a weapon, seeking revenge when the man in question was vulnerable. I'm afraid I'll do that again and I don't want to. Lately I've been a walking maelstrom of mistrust — his phone rings, and I think it's her, or "a" her. The last thing I want to do is reveal my insecurity, my weak hurt side, and have it backfire. He is already insecure about my ability to stay with him forever. If I'm honest, he might think I expect him to mess up again and therefore he will, or take my suspicion and turn it into confidence-bolstering masculine power. Should I be strong and silent, assuming it will dissipate with time? If not, how do I word it so that I retain my strength, my power, my confidence?

A Why do I picture you clad in black leather, cracking a whip? Maybe it's all that repentance and power, sin and forgiveness. Look, you are two fallible human beings trying to make a go of it together. He has imperfections, you have imperfections. The more each of you allows the other to see who is really there, the more and the deeper intimacy is possible. Since you already know how to "decide to feel" one way or another, look at this man, your relationship, your history, and make the decision to feel whatever way is likely to promote a healthy positive choice for you first, and the relationship second. Vindictiveness is not a healthy choice. If and when you feel it, wrestle it into submission. Acknowledging a feeling and acting on it are not at all the same thing.

Q I recently became sexually involved with a man I've known casually for two months. It's my pattern to become involved very shortly after I meet a man, have an intense sexual affair, and then it's over. I always end up feeling bad about myself and I want to change this pattern. I like this new man very much, but I feel I started sex with him before I was emotionally ready for it. My new idea is to put the sex on hold for a few months and to try to get to know each other in a different way. Do you think this plan sounds crazy? Is it possible to be nonsexual friends after you've been sexual? If he doesn't want to do it, does it mean I should drop him or that he was with me just for the sex? Am I unrealistic?

A Any arrangement about sexual conduct (or anything else) is possible if the parties involved agree to it. He may be shocked, outraged, annoyed, amused, or relieved about your proposal, all of the above, or none of them. There's always risk in asking for what you want — the risk that you might not get it, and the risk that you might. Both alternatives will undoubtedly have their down side. Rather than ask for something you don't sound all that sure is possible to attain, discuss your feelings with him and hear his. You can then make a decision about how you want to proceed with this relationship based on what appears to be possible. Framing any decision you both come to as "For now, we will..." helps to keep it all open to further negotiations.

♀◀♂◀♀▲♂▼♀▲♂►♀▼♂

Communication
Is the Best
Lubrication

♀◀♂◀♀▲♂▼♀▲♂►♀▼♂

Q Enclosed is a letter I'm tempted to send to a man I have known a little over two months and with whom I have enjoyed sex four or five times. Now he says he wants "an uncomplicated platonic relationship." He said to me, "I can see in your eyes that you want something more." A nonsexual friendship with him would be enormously complicated for me. I wouldn't be able to survive the sexual tension. Should I send the letter? Is it likely to confuse him even more?

A He doesn't sound confused to me. He seems to have stated his wishes quite clearly. There is never a real answer to why one loves or does not, in any case. There's no blame, no shame. Think of it as an incongruent fit between your present needs and wants and his. If you cannot negotiate a workable arrangement with this guy (face to face, not in an accusatory "why won't you love me" letter), then sigh, square your shoulders, and go forth to find someone who wants from you the same kind of relationship you want from him.

Q How do I talk lovingly and sensitively to my new love of eight months about his difficulty having erections? He takes great pains to please me orally and always does, but I feel badly when, more than half the time, he is unable to get or maintain an erection. He is very shy about talking about sex. Is there a delicate way I can bring it up (no pun intended) that will express my pain at his frustration and my desire to help without sounding patronizing?

A You can be sure that he too is aware of his difficulty, and no doubt imagines all sorts of ways you might be feeling about it, none of them positive. Since he's shy, think of your broaching this subject as a kindness, which it is. Reassure him that you are always satisfied but you are worried that he might not be, therefore could the two of you talk about what you could do to please him. Hearing from you, even more than once, that you do not think him less of a man because of his erratic erections is the most loving and sensitive thing you could do for him.

Q My sister still lives with my family in a relatively small town in Missouri. She wants to come out — in both senses. She'd like to tell our parents that she's gay and she wants to come out here where I live. She's asking for my help in both of these things. I don't know what to tell her. Do you?

A You could certainly offer an opinion on family dynamics, such as whether to tell Mother or Father first, together, or separately. Is there a religious counselor or valued family friend who could be brought in to ease the way for your sister? I gather you're not willing to do it for her or with her, which may have been what she was asking for indirectly. Do some soul-searching and life-examining of your own, and let your sister know what you are willing to offer in the way of help for both issues. Can she stay with you briefly if she moves out here? As long as she wants? Not at all? Spell it out so she can assess her resources.

Whatever the degree of your involvement, let her know about the educational booklets put out by PFLAG (Parents and Friends of Lesbians and Gays): "Read This Before Coming Out to Your Parents," "Can We Understand?," "A Guide for Parents," and "Why Is My Child Gay?" which are available for $1 each from PFLAG, P.O. Box 20308, Denver, CO 80220. She might also find out about the closest chapter of this supportive organization. A concerned and willing stranger close to home might be more help at this time than a reluctant and distant sibling.

Q My husband of less than two years has turned out to be sexually addicted to materials (books, mags, videos), places (strip joints, massage parlors), and people (women). When confronted, half the time he admitted and confessed his behavior and half the time defended it. I gave him the ultimatum of therapy or out, and he left. I find myself pregnant and he wants in again. I maintained my position of "therapy first," and poured my heart out in a seven-page letter: ("I love you but I must love myself," "Deal with your problems in therapy first then call me in on it.") His one-line response: "Do you want to go to dinner?" Is he toying or asking forgiveness? What do you think?

A I think your original position of "therapy first" is absolutely appropriate. Sure, hear what he has to say over dinner, but as to reconciliation — therapy first — whether his alone, yours as a couple, or yours alone. For starters, you might call the free support groups for family of those with addictions. The National Self-Help referral source is 1-800-222-5465.

Q I'm a 28-year-old male. I was in a car accident in junior high and lost a limb. I was socially isolated for many years. I finally got tired of feeling sorry for myself, finished college, and now have a good job. I started dating a year ago and am presently dating two women, both about my age. I am getting hints that each is thinking a lot about marriage in general. I agree that 28 is a "marrying age" and I do believe in marriage. However, I don't feel that I'm ready to get married or even to live with a woman after dating for only a year. I want to meet and be friends with more women first. How do I convey to women that I'm not really a marriage/roommate candidate yet — not because I want to be a playboy, but because I don't feel completely developed?

A A person needs no reason for marrying or not, other than preference. Congratulations for taking charge of your life, now just hold onto the reins. If you're worried about leading someone on with false expectations, state your case. I can't see that you will have very much trouble expressing yourself. You did it quite wonderfully in your letter. The next time a woman begins to "hint" about your prospects or intentions, tell her what you've told me.

Q After my negative HIV test — which I took because I had more than one partner in the last couple of years — my new partner and I have slowly and conservatively moved into a sexual relationship. I find her very exciting, but I miss certain things. She only does one position — missionary. She does not enjoy oral sex on herself; says she is too sensitive. She has an orgasm quickly and that is usually enough for her. I miss multiple positions, performing oral sex, sexual aides. I would like the commitment she desires, but I'm not sure I can be completely satisfied in the sexual arena. She is pretty set in her ways. Do you have any suggestions on how I can tell her I need more excitement?

A You know this woman; I don't. How, if ever, have you been able to lead her into agreement on other matters? Logical argument, demands, wooing, patience? You might suggest a sexual enhancement book or class as a basis of discussion, maybe start slower with books on massage rather than overt sexuality. Exchange histories. What was she taught about sex as child? ("Nice girls don't?") Pay her lots of compliments for any deviation from her set piece. You might also put in plain words what you'd like, what you perceive that she likes that is different from that, then see if the two of you can problem-solve together. Sex doesn't have to be "your way, my way, or no way."

Q I have had sex with prostitutes on a few occasions, always using condoms. I would like not to mislead my partners on the likelihood of an HIV infection and yet avoid embarrassment as much as possible. All I can think of saying is that the likelihood is very small, but not zero, and ask them to understand that I do not want to discuss the specific risk factors. Any suggestions?

A If your greatest risk factor is, indeed, intercourse with prostitutes using condoms, you could simply say that while you have had several (a few, many) sexual partners, you are aware of and always use safer sex practices. This is presuming you follow the same guidelines with noncommercial partners too. You could, of course, also be tested periodically for HIV infection, which would let your partners assess health risks with greater assurance.

Q I am in a bind. I made an arrangement to live with my boyfriend on a temporary basis to see what could become of us. He does not love me and has told me so. He often dates other women, but has promised not to have sex with them. Our roommate has made it clear that he is falling in love with me and wants a relationship. We have been growing closer and closer. The men have been friends since high school and I do not want to break up the friendship. I don't know what to do. Can you suggest a plan?

A Surprise, surprise! What I suggest is some good clear communication, one relationship at a time. Clean things up with your boyfriend about where you two stand — fears, wants, expectations. Ask how he feels about your moving forward with his friend. If he doesn't want you to and you still do, you win because it's your life. Next, have a good talk with Man #2 about your hopes, fears, etc. Allow the two men to work out between them the issues between them. A three-way "Let's all let it all hang out" discussion may be great for clearing the air in one fell swoop, but it's risky business. If even one of you three can be expected to shout, throw things, or otherwise act up or act out, I'd get my drama fix from the movies.

Q Can you tell me how even to discuss with a 71-year-old spouse already insecure about her desirability, the *need* of an older husband for his reading of sexually explicit material (pornography to some) to enhance his flagging libido? I should like not to have to "bootleg" reading, but I find it an important adjunct even to extended foreplay.

A I'm reminded of an old cartoon I have always found more sad than funny. The drawing is of an aging couple lying side-by-side in bed, both staring mournfully at the ceiling. The caption reads, "What's the matter? Can't you think of anyone else either?" Obviously, fantasy plays an important part of many people's married sex, but I think most of us would like to feel that our simple presence is enough to drive our mate wild with desire. Any evidence to the contrary destroys that particular fantasy.

For the sake of kindness to the woman you love, you may need to keep on "bootlegging." If you place a higher value on honesty (a difficult dilemma, I grant you) have a talk with her outside of bed, tell her all the many things about her that please you, inform her of the facts of sexual arousal for you, and ask her how she wishes you to handle this situation. She may prefer you without an erection rather than with reading material in hand. In that case, you might save your erotica for private times and take mental rather than physical pictures into the marital bed.

Q I would like to ask if there is any subconscious or other meaning when women brag about the size of their bowel movements. I have intimately known three very different women who occasionally commented about the length and width of their bowel movements. One of these women enjoyed anal sex very much, one moderately, and the other said she would never want to try it, refuting my theory that this was somehow connected to a woman's desire for anal sex, that commenting on the size of her bowel movement implied that she was "loose enough" to enjoy it. I have asked several sex information sources to no avail and am still deeply puzzled. Is it possible that this has something to do with the obsolete theory of penis envy? Please set me straight on this.

A I can't. There isn't *an* answer to the meaning of a particular topic to all people. Trying to give one would be as factual as those dream books that tell you that dreaming of a white horse means a fear of feather pillows or some such. Coming across three woman who have introduced this topic in the first place seems peculiar enough, to have their intent be identical would be very odd indeed. Should it happen again, I'd ask "Does your mentioning this mean..." and test your next hypothesis.

Q I've been having a relationship with a woman for more than two years. Our overnight and weekend encounters have been kept secret from her father and other relatives. I asked her to marry me, but she said she didn't want marriage and was not sure of herself. Then she revealed to me that she's planning on bringing her three daughters, who I thought were her nieces, here from her mother country and setting up a household with them and her father who she helps support.

I don't want to be her boyfriend for the rest of my life. I want a wife and I want children. She's 41 and it wouldn't be fair to ask her to have another child with me. I love her but she will not commit to me other than to say she wants me around forever. I'm very frustrated with this situation. When I say I want to break up with her and find someone else, she cries and we continue for a few more weeks. It's endless. I feel both cruel and impatient and as if I'm wasting my time. Am I being a schmuck or are my feelings valid? Please tell me.

A Your feelings of frustration are valid. It doesn't look like you're going to get what you want — a wife and children — if she won't marry you or have a child with you. Can the two of you devise some comfortable place for you to be in her extended family? Can you settle for being important in her children's life, rather than begetting your own? It looks like you both need to do some honest soul-searching singley, and then some problem-solving together. With all the secret-keeping that's been going on, a realistic appraisal of your chances of satisfaction with her may not be easy.

Q I would like your opinion on something. I just returned from a "romantic holiday" with a man I've been dating for about two months. Essentially, it was a sexually based relationship, but I believe we both were hoping it would develop into "the real thing." Okay, the holiday: About the fourth night, I woke up about 3 AM and he wasn't in bed. He was taping one of the porn videos we had watched together, which was, in fact, such a turn-off sexually that he couldn't make love the night we watched it. So, anyway, here we are, just the two of us in this romantic setting and I wake up with my lover watching a porn flick which is guaranteed to not even get him excited! So I got pissed. What's the point of bringing a lover with me who would rather watch porn than make love to me? He replies something to the effect that one can't make love on demand and that I am insatiable.

So, what I want to know is, who blew it? Was it so unforgivable to get angry at finding my "lover" enthralled with a porn show instead of in bed wanting me? Was I too controlling? Uptight? Was I not giving him his own space? Or was he being insensitive and immature?

A When a person is attacked and blamed, the logical response is to go on the defensive and/or counterattack. Had you said what was true for you, an "I statement" such as "I feel hurt that you're watching other people have sex instead of coming in here and being with me," he might have said what he was feeling (perhaps under pressure to perform sexually), rather than to react by calling you names. There is no winner here, only two disappointed, defensive, uncoupled people. Consider learning more productive communication skills for the next time around.

Q My boyfriend is always looking at nude photos of his old girlfriends when I'm not home. An old girlfriend of his recently confessed she and he have been secretly contacting each other through phone calls and letters. I know he doesn't really care about this old flame, but I hate the secrecy. I came upon three letters she wrote to him hiding at the bottom of his drawer. Am I crazy taking offense at his behavior? He thinks porno mags and photos of old girlfriends nude have nothing to do with me and if I were more secure it wouldn't bother me.

A What I hear you asking me is "Who is right?" so that one of you can then hurl an "Isadora says so" at the other. Instead of a "You're a pervert" vs. "Well, you're insecure" battle of insults and accusations, how about some straight-talking "I" messages: "I feel jealous (or threatened or upset or whatever is true) when you (look at porn, reminisce about old loves, hide the fact that you've been talking to what's-her-name)." If he responds with his feelings about your behavior in a similar way, "I feel insulted (or manipulated or spied upon) when you (monitor my reading material, check my drawers, etc.)," then maybe the two of you can come to some trade-offs about offending behavior, rather than continue in a power struggle where someone has to lose not only the contest of wills, but her/his dignity, too.

Q I am a healthy 23-year-old gay woman. My lover of 5 months is 32. This is my first real relationship with a woman and we have only recently begun sleeping together. My problem is that her breasts are very hairy and she insists upon braiding her hairs. They are at this point three inches long. I find this not to my liking. She insists that lots of women have hairy breasts. This is news to me. I like this woman very much and would not want to jeopardize our relationship. Is there any way I can tell her that this is not attractive to me and to shave?

A My guess is that whatever comment you made to which she responded by telling you that lots of women have hairy breasts already contained the message that you find them unattractive. Maybe not. Maybe you were wonderfully discrete and she was not being defensive, only educational. Most women have varying amounts of hair on their breasts, although quantity and length enough to braid is more than slightly unusual. You can say something nice (and true) about the weight or shape of your lover's breasts and then, perhaps, that you would like to see or feel them smooth, would she consider depilitating them. I would also guess that someone who paid that much attention to hairs that they were braided would not take kindly to a suggestion to get rid of them. So if you get a negative response, you alone must decide whether it's worth pursuing into the inevitable power struggle over who will get her way.

Q I am a 24-year-old male and have had four boyfriends in the past six years. The problem is I usually lose sexual interest two to three weeks after our first sexual encounter. My boyfriends have been understanding. I was still physically attracted to them, but unable to perform sexually. I have had lots of one-night stands and rarely have performance problems in those brief encounters. In the past, because of my young age, I dismissed it as a phase I was going through. Recently I met this guy I really like and I'm worried he might not be so understanding. Help!

A Most people who care about a man will be understanding about an occasional lapse in his "get up and go." I don't see a whole lot of people feeling all that understanding of someone they are interested in telling them with his body "Now that I've gotten to know you I'm no longer excited by you." So if that is what is happening for you — that as affection and familiarity increase, excitation decreases — and it is not just a case of your being unwilling to ask for what would sexually turn you on, then I see only two choices for you: Resign yourself to a continuing separation of your sex partners and your affectional partners, or find a good therapist to assist you in perfecting the consolidation of the two. You might indeed outgrow it, but how many boyfriends are you willing to go through while you hope you do?

Q Our six-year-old, who at four was obsessed with the subject of death, is now equally fascinated with sex. I have tried to give honest, minimal answers to all of her questions, but she is not the kind of child to whom you can say "the egg meets the sperm" and expect her to take that at face value. Her interest seems very premature. Last week she and a girlfriend were playing in bed, lying side by side giggling, and pretending to have sex. I suggested they play another game, which they did, and I tried to be calm and detached so as not to damage their psyches.

I've explained that sex is an adult activity, her body is her own, etc., and have also told her I'm more than happy to answer any questions, but that sex is not really a topic for general conversation at school. (I am waiting to be called by the parents of her Seventh Day Adventist friends, outraged because we've explained conception to out daughter.) Perhaps you might have some guidelines for raising a sexually healthy, well-informed person who will have sex by choice when she is ready, and will know how to do so safely and perhaps sanely.

A I'm a parent, too. Don't I wish I had such a formula! Educator Sol Gordon has written several books for children and parents on sex; one written with his wife Judith seems tailored to your question: *Raising a Child Conservatively in a Sexually Permissive World* ($8.95). For ordering information on this and other books on "self-esteem education," whose role in healthy personality development he stresses, write Ed-U Press, 7174 Mott Rd., Fayetteville, NY 13066. Another great source of "sex stuff for kids 7 to 17" is The Sexuality Library (938 Howard St., San Francisco, CA 94103) which carries Joani Blank's *A Kid's First Book About Sex* ($5.50) and *The Playbook for Kids About Sex* ($5.50) and other books in that category. Six years old, by the way, is just about on time for interest in the subject.

♂ ▲ ♀ ◀ ♂ ◀ ♀ ▲ ♂ ▼ ♀ ▲ ♂ ► ♀ ▼ ♂ ▲ ♀

This is No Fun:
The Somber Side
of Sex

♂ ▲ ♀ ◀ ♂ ◀ ♀ ▲ ♂ ▼ ♀ ▲ ♂ ► ♀ ▼ ♂ ▲ ♀

Q Is it possible for a man or a woman to survive early (age 5 to 7) incest by an aunt or an uncle, have only positive memories, and escape unharmed emotionally and psychically?

A I believe it is possible for a child to perceive interfamilial and/or intergenerational sex experiences as positive rather than traumatic. However, given the prevalent beliefs of our society, I think it is extremely difficult for that person to maintain that perspective when everyone insists it be called a molestation and abuse and therefore must be psychologically damaged (which *is* far more often the case).

Q After long hours of contemplating my sexual history, I fear that I suffer a sort of "performance anxiety." Could you fill me in on the details of this wretched miserable phenomenon? Why is it picking on me and how do I get it to go home?

A You're the bully and only you can play David to your own Goliath. Performance anxiety of any sort — sexual, social, professional — is the result of what you tell yourself. If you set it up so that you *have* to adhere to a particular standard of perfection or your lover will leave you, your friends laugh at you and your family disown you, of course your anxiety level will rise. Tension interferes with smooth performance of any sort, resulting in a less-than-optimal outcome, a self-fulfilling prophecy, which is then added to your bag full of torture implements for next time — e.g., "You failed last time, Bozo, so you will continue to fail in the future." Psychologist Albert Ellis calls this "the tyranny of *mus*turbation."

Learn to restructure events when you talk to yourself. ("It would be lovely if I excelled here but the real point is to have a good time and I'm going to bend my efforts in that direction," rather than, "If I don't do perfectly my life is ruined forever.") Should you feel yourself begin to get tense, take a few deep breaths, remember that anticipation feels much like anxiety, and rename what you're feeling so it works for you, rather than against you.

Q In the year we've been together, the man I love has shown an apparent disinclination toward monogamy. From time-to-time he says he wants a committed one-to-one relationship, as I do, but he can't seem to resist pursuing other women. We broke up and reconciled about four times this past year. Each time he leaves, he tells me I'm not right for him, he doesn't love me, and he wants to be free to date others. He comes back, usually after a couple of dates, professing to want a serious monogamous relationship with me but also saying that he is a "sexaholic" and sees nothing wrong with being (safely) nonmonogamous. Despite the stress and pain from this on and off, I love the person he is and I'm willing to try with him. Do men with a compulsion for promiscuity ever change? I have suggested counseling for us, but he's vehemently prejudiced against it and I'm not sure we can afford it anyway. Do you think we can work something out on our own?

A Nothing is impossible, but I wouldn't be overly optimistic unless somebody changes something. Since he isn't willing, looks like it's up to you. At the risk of sounding judgmental (gawd forbid), it sounds like your behavior in insisting on sticking with him and hoping he'll change is just as compulsive as his running around is. If you cannot afford private counseling — and you find this out by phoning therapists and clinics and discussing fees and practices with them — consider joining a therapy group or investigating a free 12-Step Program such as CODA.

Q I am a young woman in love with a wonderful man who takes the time to fulfill my needs in bed. The problem is that I get nauseated when I have to deal with come. Every time I see it or have to clean it up off me after sex, I try my hardest not to be ill. That's a problem because I want very much to perform oral sex on him. I was raped many years ago and went through years of counseling. I am as over it as possible. While talking this over with a girlfriend, she said that the rape might have something to do with my problem. I disagree. Can you help?

A It's possible that your extreme aversion stems from your horrible experience, but it is not necessary to decide for sure in order to make some changes. You can attack this two ways — by altering the stimulus or altering the response. You can keep exposure to the barest minimum by having your man wear condoms. Yes, even for oral sex. That way you can do what you like and never have to touch, look at, or come into contact with his ejaculate. You might also visit a behavioral therapist who deals with phobias and, through desensitizing techniques, bring about changes in your reaction.

Q I have been in a 12-step program for four years and am dealing with issues about being intimate with men. My intimate feelings are on again/off again, the same feelings I had for my own father. When it comes to a guy I'm interested in being intimate with, this dysfunctional attitude has made it easier for me to dismiss my uncomfortable feelings and resort to promiscuous sex rather than deal with the guy, tell him my needs, and be honest with my feelings. The last sexually intimate relationship I had was three years ago when I was 19. My own opinion is that I am afraid of being hurt and abandoned. I feel like I'm walking on a fence, swaying from side to side, when it comes to getting "real." What is your opinion?

A That you are distressingly normal. Every human being on earth has had or will have ambivalent feelings about becoming intimate with another person. Becoming intimate is a step-by-step series of risk-takings. Like peeling an onion, each person reveals another less public and more tender layer, leaving herself more vulnerable to being hurt or abandoned. Naked and revealed, a few more onion layers get put back on. Open, closed, open, closed, the process is ongoing in varying degrees with each new person and within an existing relationship as well. Of course, your ambivalence is mirrored by the other person approaching intimacy who has his own history and expectations. How this affects the process of establishing an intimate relationship is wonderfully illustrated in Mc Cann and Shannon's *The Two Step: The Dance Toward Intimacy* (Grove Press, 1985, $9.95). In your case, be aware of the process as it unfolds, share your concerns, and resolve to move forward at your own comfortable pace, reminding yourself that the rewards of intimacy are worth the scary parts of getting there.

Q The first time I had sex I was an insecure little girl with romantic ideals of mutual respect and love and a sinking feeling that it was impossible. I also thought I'd better get it over with for fear no one else would be desperate enough to want me. What's more, I hated myself for suppressing my fears and ignoring how shallow the experience was. I've held onto the images and sensations of that first experience and been celibate ever since. If a man now expresses feelings of attraction, I have nightmarish flashbacks of that first man's face and hands. I feel like I have to work this out alone because it is too much to ask any present friend or potential friend and lover to be as patient as I need him to be. How can I begin to exorcise my personal ghosts and let someone into my life? P.S. I can't shell out a dollar a minute for 20 years of therapy.

A If it were true that all psychological help took forever to create change (which it should not) and *did* cost $1 a minute or even more (which it often does), I'd still ask how in your position, you could afford not to avail yourself of it. Just a few points of clarification here, since I can offer no quick fixes to such a complicated set-up.

Your self-esteem was abysmally low before you had sex; your disappointing first and only experience only added weight to the stick with which you're beating yourself. Try presuming that present or potential friends are adult, so they could — on their own — give or withhold consent about whether they might be willing and/or able to help you along on your road to recovery. Some people love to be saviors, so by not asking for help you may be depriving them of the opportunity to do what they do best.

Some mental health clinics and psychology graduate school programs offer low and sliding-scale fee supervised counseling where you get the benefit of input from trainee and trainer. Cognitive therapies, which I especially like, are relatively short term, usually a matter of weeks or months rather than years. No-cost support groups such as Overeaters Anonymous or Adult Children of Alcoholics abound in every community. See if you even remotely fit the profile of others there and take what growth tools they freely offer.

If you still feel you must do this absolutely alone, browse in your library for the many excellent self-help books on raising self-esteem. Whatever your means, please take the next step out of the place you are. You signed your letter "Fear Incarnate," which sounds like an awful place to stay stuck.

Q How can a woman from an extremely dysfunctional background get her sexual needs met while she's not at all able to play her part in a healthy loving relationship? I have been celibate for most of my 20s. I am hungry and tired of sublimating, but I don't want sex to be just a fucking fix either. Right now, sexual frustration feels stronger than whatever "recovery" I'm after.

A You seem to have worded yourself right into a corner — not able to be in a sexual relationship and not willing to have sex outside a relationship. Sublimation need not mean doing without and thinking of other things. For example, play Fill in the Blanks: "I use sex to provide..." Some common answers are touching, orgasms, validation as a woman, exercise. You can get more touch in your life by taking up ballroom dancing, getting massages, and hugging your friends. You can provide your own orgasms by broadening your masturbation patterns as to method or locale. You can do volunteer work in order to feel validated, or flirt more in safe settings. See how that works?

I would also rethink your original absolutes. You might not be ready for the sustained intimacy you eventually hope to achieve, but you might be able to arrange some sort of relationship to provide you with sex within an ongoing framework. There are many men who are looking for just that kind of casual and friendly "Bounce Buddy" arrangement. Once you move from the "This Is the Way It Has To Be" mindset, all sorts of possibilities present themselves.

I am writing to express my frustration at your approach to counseling. A woman wrote you about wanting more sex and getting into a relationship. You didn't say anything specific, just "flirt more" and "change your mindset." How does that help?! I have the same problem. No girlfriends or dates and I'm very sexually frustrated.

A What I do here is offer suggestions, resources, and potential avenues of exploration, not counseling, which is a two-way exchange of much greater depth. I do hear your sexual frustration and I heard hers, but there is no easy answer. One can't *get* sex, like measles or candy bars, unless we're talking about commercial sex, which, while it is an option, isn't a legal one except in Nevada. A relationship with another person that includes a mutual exchange of sexual pleasure (or even nonmutual, for that matter, if for some reason the other person is willing to simply fork it over in return for marriage or back rubs or companionship at the movies) takes time and energy to develop. Flirting and changing one's mindset not only increase the likelihood of beginning a relationship leading to sex, they can also offer some intrinsic satisfaction which can lighten the load of being without it.

Q After being celibate for 8 years, I sought counseling about my fear of trusting and being vulnerable. When I was on vacation in New York, I met someone. We made love. I think I was able to discard my inhibitions because I was taken out of my ordinary routine into a whirlwind of extremes. Without losing the uniqueness of the experience, I would like to feel that it is also a symbolic turning point, to build on it and use what I learned in the next situation, but I don't know how or if this is possible.

A I have in my office a poster by Virginia Anne Church based on the teachings of Maxie Maultsby Jr., M.D., a Rational Emotive therapist, listing five steps to take in order to change a belief:

1. You recognize what the belief is. In your case it might be "No man is trustworthy" or "Being vulnerable in sex is always dangerous" — and that you can change it.
2. You stop acting or thinking on the basis of that old belief (which you have already done once).
3. You substitute a new, rational, and more personally meaningful belief for the old one (such as "My experience in NY was a turning point for me; I am obviously learning how to make appropriate choices of who and how to trust.").
4. You act in light of the new belief.
5. You continue to behave in this rational new way *even though it feels phony* to act this new way. Eventually the new belief will become real and a part of your "natural" behavior if you persist.

   It all comes down to this: The way to reenforce a new decision about beliefs or behavior is to act "as if," and to continue to do so until "it is." In other words fake it until you make it.

Q Do you have any advice on how to recover from not only a lost love, but a lost euphoric wonderland? I seem to be living for the past fantasy and the possible reclaiming of that fantasy in the future.

A I am reminded of a sign with an all-too-poignant motto on it: "Someday *these* will be the good old days." A dozen philosophies offer the answer to your problem, which is to be aware of the present moment and enjoy it to its fullest. Of course enjoy your memories, and exercise your fantasies for the future, but what is real is what is now. Carpe diem! One of my clients hoping to counteract the same tendencies sets the little buzzing reminder on his watch for seven or eight random times throughout the day. When it goes off he stops whatever he's doing and takes a 60-second "awareness break": "What am I feeling? What's going on in my body? What around me is pleasant or exciting to my senses? What do I hear that I like? What do I smell?" He says it's amazing to him just how often the buzzer interrupts a memory or a fantasy rather than a moment of conscious living in the present.

Q I used to be a healthy horny lesbian, then I got cancer and had my breasts removed. My lover couldn't stand the heat so she took off with a bubblehead beauty queen eight years ago. In the interim I flipped out, spent some time on an analyst's couch, and took pills for depression. The thing is, I have no sex drive, I hate my body, and am generally all-around miserable. Is there such a thing as a sex therapist for lesbians? Life without sex is a drag.

A I don't care how long you were "on the couch," more (or different) is needed. There are sex therapists who work with lesbians, and there are some who are lesbians themselves. I don't think you necessarily need a sex therapist, though, just a good generalist who can assist you with your self-esteem and socializing skills. If you can't get a referral from a friend, look at the therapists' ads in the gay newspapers. I agree that living a life without sex when you're missing it is certainly life at less than its fullest, but life spent living in a body you can neither change nor make peace with is a hell of a lot worse. Please do find yourself a sympathetic counselor and get to work.

Q For me, this was a year of heartbreak. One relationship ended when I moved from my home town. Later, a new boyfriend went back to Australia. The thought of spending the rest of my life meeting people, getting to know and care about them, then being separated and having to start all over again, makes me want to cry. It hurts. I want to crawl into bed and never come out. I would be much happier if I didn't want companionship. Is there an easy way to learn to be content with a lifetime of solitude? Is there any way I can learn to not need companionship?

A Many people live a life of casual relationships, taking pleasure in the camaraderie of co-workers, club members, neighbors, and brief sexual affairs, which can supply companionship without intimacy. Therefore, it's not necessary to become a hermit. Instead, you can just not let yourself care deeply or become attached to any one individual. You might also choose to live in a small town where people tend to do a lot less coming and going than they do in your metropolitan area. I think a more productive solution for you would be to learn to handle the inevitable pain accompanying separation from someone dear in such a way that you are not devastated. Most people find that the joys of intimate relationships are worth the inevitable accompanying sorrows.

Q Recently something happened to me that left me asking some disturbing questions about myself. I know I'm not a masochist and I've never had those rape fantasies that a lot of women supposedly have. But a few months ago I was raped, and during the rape I had an orgasm. Is there something wrong with me or is this something that sometimes happens with women who get raped? I know I didn't "secretly want it" or any of that garbage, but I don't understand how my body can react that way to something my mind is disgusted by.

A Your response is not at all unusual to woman *or* to men who have been raped or sexually traumatized. Our bodies are "designed," if you will, to respond to certain stimulation and often do, with or without our "permission." Sexual Trauma Centers and rape hot lines have counseling and support groups available to anyone involved in a recent rape. Please do avail yourself of their services so that you might the sooner come to peace with yourself and what happened to you.

The woman who was disturbed because she had an orgasm during rape should have been told some specific examples of anomalous orgasms. A friend of mine happened on the scene of a horrible accident, saw a severed human limb lying on the ground, and he ejaculated. Since the letter writer seemed to think sexual arousal was the only implication that could be drawn from her experience, this type of story puts things in perspective.

Q I have to take Imipramine, a medication used to control panic attacks and severe depression. It works very well, but as a side effect I have been getting less horny. I notice I can still get off using mental images, but even that seems less effective than before. Is there any way of getting back to my horny old self without totally dropping the meds?

A The point of a tranquilizer is to dull feelings such as terror or grief that you find too painful to experience at their fullest. Such medication makes no distinction between "good" and "bad" emotions, so you will also dampen joy or desire. You and your physician must experiment with adjusting the dosage, being aware that the more of anything you allow yourself to feel, the more you will feel of everything. Only you can judge where an acceptable, if never an ideal, compromise lies.

Q Sometimes during intercourse I get sharp pains deep inside. I feel my uterus getting pushed around. I'm wet enough to port a flotilla and I've had all the STD tests, so I figure it's either mental or the man is too big. Are there any exercises I can use to relax, or to strengthen the ligaments of my uterus? Please don't suggest I give up everything but penises that never hurt. I'd starve on three inches.

A I don't know of any spot exercises that are that specific. If you have had the cervix (the mouth of the uterus) checked for any condition that would contribute to its hypersensitivity, I'd experiment with different positions for intercourse. For instance, vaginal entry from the rear seems to create a shorter vaginal barrel than missionary style.

I just read the question from the woman who experiences sharp pains deep inside. I went through the same thing for nearly two years while my doctor did pelvics and "found nothing." I told myself it was "mental" too, tried to "relax," experimented with different positions, made changes in my diet, etc., *finally* got an ultrasound, and ended up with a laparoscopy in which a large endometrial cyst and great quantities of adhesions were removed. Endometriosis should always be suspected in painful intercourse. You could save this poor woman months or years of futile experimentation by saying so. At least she could try and rule it out. I was fortunate in that surgery gave me considerable relief. I'd never suspected endometriosis because my periods were a breeze, but endo has many symptoms besides painful periods. The National Endometriosis Association (1-800-992-ENDO) is a great resource. My local chapter saved me from the hysterectomy recommended by the first ob/gyn I consulted.

A Leprosy is one possibility when one's skin itches, too, but I'd first rule out a bug bite. A change of sexual position is the easiest thing to start with. If that doesn't work, there are, as you so luckily discovered, other avenues of exploration.

The woman who complained that sometimes she "feels her uterus getting pushed around" during intercourse may be experiencing this only during the several days of the month when the cervix is lower than usual. I thought of this because of a fertility awareness class I took which I really think is a great idea for women with or without partners. It's an astonishing education and can really improve your life — not only from freeing you occasionally from birth control, but by making miscellaneous weird bodily changes become normal and friendly.

A I love the way you put that. Such classes are often given by hospitals, women's clinics, and Planned Parenthood centers.

Q Sometimes after ejaculating I get an aching pain in the area between my scrotum and anus. It goes away after a while. What causes it and what can I do to prevent it from happening?

A A pain in the perineum is most likely to be a normal event after a strong spasm of ejaculation. There are many delicate internal structures near that area that could be saying their anthropomorphic version of "Wow! What a workout!" However, I've said it before and I'll say it again, pain is your body's message of "Pay attention here!" So were it my pain, I'd have the part in question checked out by a specialist in that area, in this case a urologist. And if you got a physician's pronouncement that all is normal but the pain you experience persists to the degree that it interferes with your sexual pleasure, I'd seek other opinions.

Q Being 25 and single and thinking I would never be one of those who ended up without that perfect person to start a family with, I am getting worried. I know you'll say I'm young, but I want a large family and want to know the person a few years before I take that gamble. Time ticks away. I seem unable to form and maintain long-term relationships. I am a great guy whom, once women know, grow to love. I've been asked to marry several times, but I just seem to run away and pursue someone who will hurt me. I think this is a reflection of some sort of masochism. Do you know a good book/ therapist for men who initiate and pursue relationships with women who aren't interested?

A Two good, basic how-to-have-a-good-relationship books I like are *Intimate Connections* by Burns and *Pairing* by Bach and Deutsch. Other authors who write informatively on understanding what makes a relationship work are Tina Tessina, Susan Campbell, and Margaret and Jordan Paul. I'm wondering if you are misinterpreting the normal investigative process — "Will this person make the kind of partner I want?" — as a problem when encountering blind alleys. Rejections from either party or aborted beginnings are to be expected most of the time when the two people don't know each other from birth. If, however, you really are sabotaging potential good relationships, either by your choice of partners or by your behavior once you are in a relationship, the place to explore that is in therapy. Chose a therapist by recommendation or reputation, and by your intuitive level of connection (if that person feels, appears, sounds, or smells right).

Q My companion and I have been together for about 10 years. Since our son was born more than six years ago, I have gradually lost interest in sex with his father, to the point that now I just push him away every night. I care about him, and I'm miserable with this situation and wish to be sexual again, but I feel blocked. Do you have any suggestions as far as reviving my sexual interest?

A Lack of sexual desire for a partner one still has good feelings for is so common these days that it even has its own nickname — ISD, inhibited sexual desire. In general, I usually recommend counseling for anyone who is feeling miserable in a situation where she sees no solution. Good counselors are option explorers and co-problem solvers, interested in your better future often more than in your bitter past. In my own counseling practice, my first step with couples experiencing ISD is to urge scheduled time alone for each of them and time alone together, at least once a week. The time *must* be used to just be who you are (or discover who you are), rather than be in your accustomed roles as parents, spouses or householders. If you begin again to think and feel as the woman or man you once were and to do things together as two grownup friends, you may well rediscover and rekindle the desire which brought you together as lovers in the first place.

Q I wrote you once and it helped a lot, so maybe you can help me again...and maybe it'll just help to unload. I have been married since last spring to a man my age (25) who is a big-time grouch. I mean, this guy can complain about everything. He has anger oozing out of every pore. He is capable of being sweet, but anger is his first reaction to almost every situation. I care about him, and sometimes I still love him, but he makes me nuts. I, on the other hand, am predominantly cheerful. I love sex and I've been to bed with seven men since we've been married, but sex with him just repulses me. I'm so terrified of confronting him with this, but shouldn't I end this marriage?

A Something's got to change, that's for sure. Were I you, I'd hustle my buns into therapy. Go alone if you want to figure out why you married him in the first place and what to do about either changing or ending this relationship. Go with him if you feel there's any chance of renegotiating an honest, affectionate marriage despite your differences. If you already know you made a mistake and want out but are afraid of his angry, or violent reaction when you tell him that, arrange to break the news in a way that maximizes your safety — with others nearby, or by letter after you've left.

Q I am a 25-year-old female graduate student and I have a crush on my thesis advisor. I have been using the sexual excitement I feel when I'm with him to fuel my dedication to my research. Recently he made it clear to me that he wanted to have an affair with me. Having such an affair would certainly ruin my career. In an effort to get him to back off, I have been pointing out his shortcoming as a scientist and as an advisor to him and to myself. That he is less than perfect doesn't change my feelings for him (which he does not know), but he now feels hurt and is even vengeful toward me.

It's not feasible for me to change advisors now since I'm less than two years from finishing my Ph.D. What I really want is to continue with my obsession for him without his knowing about it, and without him ever thinking of me as anything more than a very bright and successful student. Please advise me on the best way to proceed.

A You seem to be handling your own feelings and are clear on what you want and what you don't. Good. However, wanting him to feel any particular way is useless; you cannot control someone else's feelings. You might, though, affect his behavior by your own (as you already have done by becoming overtly critical). Could you confess that your comments were aimed at achieving a comfortable distance between you since his personal attentions were inappropriate?

Once spurned, whether he could then maintain the desired professional distance sounds doubtful from what you tell me. I'd strongly consider switching advisors. Even one year of discomfort and unsureness about what motivates any of his responses to you seems too much. Working with a new advisor, while not as provocative, would allow you to reevaluate whether you want to do anything about this other mutual attraction.

✍ Thank you so much for printing the question from the female graduate student and her thesis advisor. During the two years I have been in my graduate program, I have been subjected to propositions from faculty members, often during class time and in front of the entire class. Innuendo, overtly suggestive body language, and grossly sexual language have occurred. When I say I find this kind of conduct by professors revolting and that I don't wish to have anything to do with professors who behave this way, I am always told I am imagining the conduct or that it isn't objectionable because so many people respond to it. It is deeply satisfying to know that it is okay for a female graduate student to refuse to have sex with her male professors for personal or career reasons, even if she has an interest in him.

Thank you also for indicating that spurned male faculty do engage in angry and vindictive conduct, that it is difficult to have a normal student/teacher relationship and that the discomfort resulting from such situations is real and hard to deal with. When I say so, I am told my response to men is abnormal.

A Sexual harassment, using a position of power to impose unwanted verbal or physical attentions on another, does not just occur from male professors to female students. A study of 1300+ random students reported upon at a recent Society for the Scientific Study of Sex conference stated that more males than females reported instructor-student sexual contacts, with attitudes about such contacts ranging from negative to positive. "Although 75% of attempted or completed sexual contacts began during the educational relationship, the majority of participants reported no feelings of coercion." (E.L. Algeier) But even if everyone were doing it and everyone else liked it but you, you have a right to refuse unwanted attentions, and to report such attentions to the powers that be if they persist.

Q My girlfriend and I enjoy an active sex life. However, she recently told me she was sexually abused as a child by a relative. As a result of this trauma, she cannot have an orgasm while with another person. She can when she masturbates, but she has to think of abusive thoughts. I understand that healing from child sexual abuse takes patience and special attention from both of us. She has a counselor, but is there anything I can do to help her heal sexually? Her not being able to have an orgasm with me is very frustrating for both of us. She feels incomplete, I feel incompetent.

A As you said, for your girlfriend to come to terms with her trauma may take time. Meanwhile, if she is willing, you might encourage her to masturbate to orgasm while you hold her or lie quietly nearby as a bridge between solitary and partnered orgasms. Perhaps she would allow you to join her in a few sessions with her therapist where you can address what is happening to you as a couple. If not, perhaps her therapist might recommend someone who is experienced in sexual matters and in couple counseling. There may not be any immediate changes in your girlfriend's behavior from a few brief couple counseling sessions, but they might work wonders regarding changes in your unhappy feelings.

Q I have been working at this office for a little over three years. For the most part, my current work situation is good. I am generally happy and get along well with my co-workers. Two and a half years ago, we were invited to a Christmas dinner at a restaurant by my boss. At the end of the meal my boss offered to pay for my cab fare home. I had only been working for him for a short time and was impressed with his warmth. I showed my appreciation (and greeted him Merry Christmas) by giving him a peck on the cheek. He used that opportunity to fondle my breasts. I broke away from him and left. Later on I called him at home and told him how upset I was with his behavior. He apologized and no other incidents have occurred since then.

I continue to keep my distance from my boss, and avoid socializing with the office staff when I know he will be around. I still feel angry about it. In every other way my job is too good to leave. Is there anything I can do to make me feel more comfortable socializing with my boss?

A Yes, acknowledge that he made an error in judgment responding to signals he thought you were sending (a kiss on the cheek in a cab near your door could mean "Let's get personal"), and that you made an error in judgment by sending a signal which could be confused. (I don't think kisses of any sort have any place in business relationships.) Since there have been no more incidents, forgive him and yourself for those errors and feel free to socialize with office personnel if and when you want to.

Keep in mind that when lines between business and social relationships get blurred, particularly when alcohol is involved, anything is likely to happen. That's no excuse for inappropriate or rude behavior, but it is often seized upon as such. Why do you think office parties got their reputation?

Comment: In a previous column, I responded to a letter from a women whose boss nonconsentually fondled her breast after she kissed him on the cheek. I hope that we are all in agreement that touching another person in personal areas of the body, (that is a touch other than a formal handshake or a sympathetic touch of back or arm) without expressed consent is at best rude (an "affectionate" poke in the belly, rub on the head, or pat on the bottom) and at worst, in cases where sexual behavior is not agreed upon, criminal and insupportable. I wish with all my heart that we lived in a world where each of us could go about our lives free from fear of personal intrusion and physical assault. Since that is not the case, cautioning someone, male or female, to use good judgment about whom he/she kisses or whom she/he gets into a car with, is just that, an urging of commonsense self-protective measures and not, as current rhetoric has it, "blaming the victim."

Q I've been married to this woman since 1983. For the first three years, every time she gave me head, she would manage to "accidentally" jab her thumb nail into the glans of my penis. I was patient and civil as possible. I told her it was terribly painful and a real turn-off, but she persisted. After three years I told her she absolutely must stop or I would strike her, though I refrained from hitting her for another year or two. When I did she finally stopped. Now what she does is go down on me until I get good and aroused, then she seemingly loses interest, leans against my erect penis, stretching the skin and tearing it, while she picks blackheads out of my pubic area, which is just as painful. Before you ask me what I am doing with this woman for seven years, please tell me if in your opinion any psycho/sexual therapy will help.

A My first question would not be what you are doing with this woman after seven years (unless you hired her simply as a fellatrice), but why she still agrees to do oral sex with you after being bullied, bitched at, and battered. Yes, therapy would help, with its aim being to get this covert battle out in the open where you both can learn to express your anger cleanly and fight fairly. At the very least, it will be easier on your pubes.

Q People don't like to talk about mothers who molest their children, especially daughters. Maybe they don't think it exists. I was about seven. She said it was a medical treatment. But even I knew that something was wrong, so I got up and walked away. She never referred to it again. I "forgot" all about it until I was almost 30. When I began to remember this and other things, I began to understand why I've feared and hated her so. I never told my father because I thought it would hurt him.

Now I can't because he's dead. Part of me wants to confront her, but she'd probably deny it, and I would have sacrificed all semblance of a normal life for nothing. I can't just forget it. This is ruining my life. I have never told anyone before. I can't trust a therapist. Is there a book or support group or other help for people like me?

A Adults Molested as Children United (408/453-7616) will give you the name of the nearest support group of people with a similar concern. Farmer's *Adult Children of Abusive Parents*, and Gil's *Outgrowing the Pain*, are two of many good books on the topic. Perhaps as you explore resources, you might reconsider your distrust of therapy and make the effort to find a compassionate guide on the path toward healing and resolution.

Q My problem is that I am a man in a profession working with kids and in the past couple of years I have become attracted to some of the children, which has left me feeling guilty and confused. I never have and never will let myself act on these feelings, but they are a terrible burden and I would like help in understanding them and doing whatever I need to do to make sure they do not control my life. I have tried bringing this problem to a therapist twice, but have felt threatened by both therapists' reactions. One told me to pack my bags, quit my job, and head for the hills. The other, though not quite so obvious, changed his entire demeanor in such a way that I felt I had made a terrible mistake in confiding in him. I am no monster. I want help confronting this problem. How do I find a nonjudgmental therapist to help me?

A I'm sorry you had such distressing responses from previous therapists who are, of course, humans with hot buttons, and blind spots too. In general, the way to at least increase the probability of making a good client-therapist match is to phone a likely candidate (in your case, someone who specializes in sexual issues) and, with no need to identify yourself fully, ask about professional expertise in this area, comfort with this subject, and anything else you can think of which might assure you of competent care. If you can be as direct with them as you have been with me, most therapists will be equally forthright.

I address this to the person who was troubled by feelings of attraction to children and had difficulty finding a sympathetic therapist. Having feelings of attraction toward a child doesn't make you a child molester, any more than one who imagines the death of another is a murderer. Not long ago I lived, for the first time since being a child, in a group situation with three small children. I found myself attracted to two of them and I am sure that the feelings were reciprocated. I did not act on these feelings beyond the expression of my affection; no sexual connection occurred. But at first the satisfying sense of loving and being loved seemed tainted by sexual speculation on my part, and I struggled to deny those feelings. Knowing that I had never been and never would be a child molester, how could I have the stirrings of one?

I eventually realized that the feelings themselves were true and natural and forgivable, that the difference between me and a molester was more a case of activity than mind. It is very hard to help what you think, but when in a position of responsibility toward others, particularly those who are smaller, weaker, or dependent, it is reprehensible not to help what you *do*. The sin of an adult who molests a child is the same as that of a therapist who sleeps with a client, or the teacher who becomes involved with a student. It is an active betrayal of trust by a person in an authoritative position.

When I was in therapy, I was attracted to my therapist and believe that he was attracted to me; when I was a teacher I was attracted to some of my students; when I was married I was attracted to other people; when I lived with children I was attracted to them. My therapist, my students, my young friends, my husband, and I were all able to maintain the status quo of our relations. I know myself to be a responsible, trustworthy, and conscientious person, sensitive to the needs of others, yet I reserve the right to have what thoughts I will.

My relationship with the children whose home I shared was enhanced when I came to a fuller understanding of my protective role in our relationship, when I knew that I would keep them safe from myself as well as others, when I knew that wherever my thoughts and feelings might range, I need not and would not seek to betray them. I hope that the person who wrote you can begin to accept him/herself more. We supposedly do not live in an age of Thoughtcrime. This person has been very unfortunate to encounter therapists who practice as though we did.

Comment: Beyond Survival, a network/newsletter-magazine for and about survivors of physical, sexual, and emotional abuse and neglect, is $20 for one year's subscription to 1278 Glenneyre St., #3, Laguna Beach, CA 92651. Because of the sensitive nature of its topic, a subscriber can request the mailing label be addressed without the subscriber's name on it.

Index

For a free catalog of
The Crossing Press books
Call toll-free
800-777-1048